The Thi

Nigel West is a military hist

and security issues. He is the author of over a doz

most recently *The Secret War for the Falklands*, *The Crown Jewels: The British Secrets at the Heart of the KGB Archives* and *VENONA: The Greatest Secret of the Cold War*. He has also edited *The Faber Book of Espionage* and *The Faber Book of Treachery*. In 1989 he was voted 'The Experts' Expert' by a panel of spy writers selected by the *Observer*. He is currently European editor of the Washington DC-based *Journal of Intelligence and Counterintelligence*.

Also by Nigel West

Spy! (*with Richard Deacon*)
MI5: British Security Service Operations 1909–45
MI6: British Secret Intelligence Service Operations 1909–45
A Matter of Trust: MI5 1945–72
Unreliable Witness: Espionage Myths of World War II
The Branch: A History of the Metropolitan Police Special Branch
GARBO (*with Juan Pujol*)
GCHQ: The Secret Wireless War
The Friends: Britain's Postwar Secret Intelligence Operations
Molehunt
Games of Intelligence
Seven Spies Who Changed the World
Secret War: The Story of SOE
The Faber Book of Espionage
The Illegals
The Faber Book of Treachery
The Secret War for the Falklands
Counterfeit Spies
The Crown Jewels:
The British Secrets Exposed by the KGB Archives (*with Oleg Tsarev*)
VENONA: The Greatest Secret of the Cold War

Fiction

The Blue List
Cuban Bluff
Murder in the Commons
Murder in the Lords

The Third Secret

The CIA, Solidarity and the KGB's Plot to Kill the Pope

Nigel West

HarperCollins*Publishers*

HarperCollins*Publishers*
77–85 Fulham Palace Road,
Hammersmith, London W6 8JB

www.**fire**and**water**.com

Published by HarperCollins*Publishers* 2001
1 3 5 7 9 8 6 4 2

First published in Great Britain by
HarperCollins*Publishers* 2000

Copyright © Westintel Research Ltd 2000
The Author asserts the moral right to
be identified as the author of this work

ISBN 0 00 653180 6

Set in Bembo by
Rowland Phototypesetting Limited,
Bury St Edmunds, Suffolk

Printed in Great Britain by
Omnia Books Limited, Glasgow

All rights reserved. No part of this publication may be reproduced, stored in a retrieval system, or transmitted, in any form or by any means, electronic, mechanical, photocopying, recording or otherwise, without the prior permission of the publishers.

This book is sold subject to the condition that it shall not, by way of trade or otherwise, be lent, re-sold, hired out or otherwise circulated without the publisher's prior consent in any form of binding or cover other than that in which it is published and without a similar condition including this condition being imposed on the subsequent purchaser.

Contents

‘The papal assassination attempt would dog the CIA for years.’

Robert M. Gates
Director of Central Intelligence

‘The situation in Poland and the danger that is emanating from Poland are not simply Polish matters. They affect us all.’

Leonid Brezhnev,
General Secretary, CPSU

‘We had to have plausible deniability. Of course the Russians knew we were involved. But they didn’t know how far.’

Edward Juchniewicz
CIA Deputy Director for Operations

Illustrations

Acknowledgements

My thanks are due to the many intelligence professionals who made this book possible. I owe particular gratitude to those who assisted my research in Rome, Warsaw, Paris, Sofia and Washington DC. I was privileged to know Bill Casey, who kindly invited me to the DCI's office in Langley on 31 August 1981, Geoffrey M.T. Jones of the Veterans of OSS, and the late John Shaheen. Others who have helped me include Michael Nelson, David Ensor, Bob Gates, Ben Weiser, Dr Caes Webes, Ben Fischer, Hayden Peake, Rafal Brzeski, Admiral Fulvio Martini, Ambassador Hugh Montgomery and many others, too numerous to mention by name.

I also gratefully acknowledge the generous help of Dr William McClintock, SACLANT's official historian at Norfolk, Virginia.

My admiration goes to General Dick Walters, truly a living legend, who recalled that when a Pole had been asked whom he would shoot first if Poland was invaded, an East German or a Russian, he replied without hesitation: 'The East German.' 'Why?' The answer: 'Business before pleasure.'

ABBREVIATIONS

ADDO Assistant Deputy Director of Operations
AFL-CIO American Federation of Labor – Congress of Industrial Organization
ASIO Australian Security Intelligence Organization
AVH Hungarian Intelligence Service
BfV Security Service, West Germany
BND German Federal Intelligence Service
BRIXMIS British Military Mission into the Soviet Sector
CIA Central Intelligence Agency
DCI Director of Central Intelligence
DDCI Deputy Director of Central Intelligence
DDO Deputy Director of CIA Operations
DGSE French Intelligence Agency
DI CIA Directorate of Intelligence
DIA Defense Intelligence Agency, USA
DIE Romanian Intelligence Service
DIGOS Italian Anti-Terrorist Police
DO CIA Directorate of Operations
DS Bulgarian Intelligence Service
DST French Security Service
FBI American Federal Bureau of Investigation
FCD KGB First Chief Directorate
GCR Groupement de Controlles Radio-electrique
GRU Soviet Military Intelligence Service
HPSCI House Permanent Select Committee on Intelligence
HVA East German Intelligence Service
ICBM Inter-continental Ballistic Missile
ISI Pakistani Inter-Services Intelligence

IUL Italian Social Labour Federation
KBP Cabinet Committee for Public Security, Poland
KBW Internal Security, Poland
KGB Soviet Intelligence Service
KHAD Afghan Security Service
KOK Homeland Defence Committee, Poland
KOR Committee to Defend the Workers, Poland
KPPRM Economic Planning Committee of the Polish Council of Ministers
KWR Dutch Signals Intelligence Agency
MGB-MVD Soviet Intelligence Service
MI5 British Security Service
MI6 British Secret Intelligence Service
MIT National Intelligence Organization, Turkey
MO Polish Citizens Militia
MSW Ministry of Internal Affairs, Poland
NE Near East Division of the CIA
NFIB National Foreign Intelligence Board
NID National Intelligence Daily
NIE National Intelligence Estimate
NIO National Intelligence Officer, CIA
NKVD Soviet Intelligence Service
NSA National Security Agency, USA
NSDD National Security Decision Directive
NSPCG National Security Planning and Coordinating Group, USA
NSPG National Security Planning Group, USA
NTS Union of Ukranian Nationalists
OGI CIA Office of Global Issues
OMON Ministry of the Interior Special Forces
ORMO Citizens' Militia Voluntary Reserve, Poland
OSS Office of Strategic Services
OUN Ukranian Nationalist Resistance
PFLP Patriotic Front for the Liberation of Palestine
PGU Soviet Intelligence Service
PLO Palestine Liberation Organization
PNG *Persona non grata*
PRC People's Republic of China
PUWP CC Polish Communist Party Central Committee

PZPR Communist Party of Poland
RCMP Royal Canadian Mounted Police
RFE Radio Free Europe
RPG Rocket-propelled grenade
RUMNO Military Intelligence, Bulgaria
SACEUR Supreme Allied Command, Europe
SACLANT Supreme Allied Command, Atlantic
SAPO Swedish Security Police
SB Polish Security Service
StB Czech Intelligence Service
SCC Special Coordinating Committee of the US National Security Council
SDECE Intelligence Service, France
SE Soviet / Eastern Europe Division, CIA
SEAL US Marines Special Forces
SID Servizio Informazioni Difesa
SIFAR Servizio Informazioni Forze Armate
SIPO Swedish Security Service
SIS British Secret Intelligence Service
SISMI Military Intelligence Service
SKS Student Solidarity Committee, Poland
SOE Special Operations Executive, UK
SOVA CIA Office of Soviet Affairs
SP Industry Guards, Poland
SRI Serviciul Roman de Informatii
SSCI Senate Select Committee on Intelligence
SW Prison Guards, Poland
TIR Transport International Routier
TKK Provisional Coordinating Committee Solidarity, Poland
UB Security Office, Poland
VPK Soviet Military Industrial Commission
WOP Frontier Guards, Poland
WRON Polish Military Council of National Salvation
WSW Polish Military counter-intelligence
ZOMO Polish Riot Police

Introduction

Many devout Roman Catholics believe that on Sunday, 13 May 1917, on a barren hillside of the Serra de Aire, just outside the tiny Portuguese village of Fatima, north of Lisbon and in the almost geographical centre of Portugal, the Virgin Mary appeared in the first of a series of six apparitions to three young shepherd children. Two of them, Jacinta and Francisco Marto, aged ten and eleven, were to die as children, but the third, their ten-year-old cousin Lucia de Jesus Santos, was to become a Carmelite nun, burdened with a vision of hell and three secrets that had been entrusted to her by Our Lady of Fatima on 13 July 1917, the day of her last appearance which occurred at Valinhos, a remote spot, closer to the village of Aljustrel.

The first secret, imparted at a place known as Cova da Iria, was a glimpse of hell, and a prediction of the imminent death of her two cousins; Francisco died the following April, and Jacinta succumbed to pleurisy after an abdominal operation in February 1920. The second secret included the assertion that if Russia was reconverted to Christianity, many years of war and persecution could be avoided. Lucia, by this time Sister Maria Lucia of the Sacred Heart, revealed this second secret to the Vatican in July 1941, immediately following the Nazi invasion of the Soviet Union. She kept silent about the third secret, however, until June 1943 when, apparently in poor health and living in a community of the Dorothean Sisters at Tuy in Spain, she was asked by Bishop da Costa of Leiria, in whose diocese Fatima was located, to write it down for Pope Pius XII. Stricken by mental and physical anguish, she was unable to do so until January the following year when she wrote it on a single sheet of paper and placed it in an envelope sealed with wax. On 17 June

1944 she entrusted it to the Bishop of Gurza who hand-delivered it later the same day to the Bishop of Leiria.

Apparently da Costa offered the envelope to the Vatican's Holy Office, which declined to accept it, so in December 1945 he placed it in a second envelope addressed to Cardinal Cerejeira, the Patriarch of Lisbon, to be delivered upon his death. Realizing that the message had not reached the Vatican, Sister Lucia now demanded that it be made public upon her death, or at the latest in 1960.

It was not until mid-March 1957 that Pope Pius XII asked for the document, prompting its delivery to the Vatican by Monsignor Cento, the Apostolic Nuncio to Lisbon. Surprisingly, it was not read by Pius XII, who placed it in the Secret Archives of the Holy Office on 4 April 1957 and who died on 9 October 1958, but by his successor John XXIII who, according to his secretary Monsignor Capovilla, broke the envelope's seal for the first time on 17 August 1959 at Castelgandolfo, the Pope's summer residence. John XXIII had the text translated by Monsignor Paulo Jose Tavares, the Secretariat of State's Portuguese translator, and then by Cardinal Ottaviani, the Prefect of the Holy Office. Having finally read it in Italian, the Pope decided not to divulge the contents and on 8 February 1960 the Vatican announced that the third secret of Fatima would not be published. This policy was followed by Paul VI who was elected on 21 June 1963 and recovered Sister Maria Lucia's manuscript from the Holy Office on 27 March 1965. Although he certainly read it, he made no public comment. The only official word came on 25 July 1966 in the form of a pastoral letter from the Bishop of Leiria, asserting that Fatima did not 'concord with auguries of universal catastrophes. Fatima cannot be reduced to sensational prophecies of terrible wars. Much less can her message, essentially pacific, be directed against any country in particular.' On 11 February 1967, as the fiftieth anniversary of the apparition approached, Cardinal Ottaviani confirmed that the third secret would not be published.

The same policy was applied by John Paul I who, as Cardinal Luciani, had been sufficiently impressed to have made a pilgrimage to the Cova da Iria in July 1977, and to have met Sister Maria Lucia at the Carmel of Coimbra to talk to her about the third secret.

During his first pastoral visit to Germany in November 1980, Pope John Paul II broke with convention and intimated in a private audience that the third secret of Fatima was an apocalyptic prediction of an avoidable, probably thermonuclear, holocaust that would kill millions. He gave no further details, and when word leaked of the disclosure those present acknowledged that the Holy Father, now known for his interest in the supernatural, appeared to attach considerable weight to the gravity of what he had revealed.

The following year, on 13 May 1981, on the anniversary of the first apparition at Fatima, Pope John Paul II was hit by three bullets fired at almost point-blank range by a gunman in St Peter's Square, Rome. One of the bullets passed within a few millimetres of his central aorta, and it remains his fervent belief that his life was saved by the Madonna of Fatima, saying that 'in the designs of Providence there are no mere coincidences'. Indeed, precisely a year later, His Holiness, still weak from his ordeal, ordered a new translation of the original text, which he had read on 18 July 1981, to improve the sense of 'certain expressions in the Secret proper to the Portuguese language' and then travelled to Fatima to place the bullet that had been removed from his chest on the altar at the centre of the shrine. Early in 1984, following his long recovery from his wounds, he arranged for the three-and-a-half-foot statue, which had dominated the cave-like shrine, to be moved to the Vatican, where he celebrated a special rededication on 24 March. As he later said: 'One hand fired, and another guided the bullet.'

On 13 May 1991 John Paul II went back to Fatima to meet Sister Maria Lucia, then eighty-four years old, and to share a public celebration of his miraculous escape from death a decade earlier, and to give thanks to the Virgin Mary for the liberation of Europe from Communism. He remained unshakeable in his belief that his deliverance had had one purpose that he was duty-bound to accomplish.

The full text of the third secret remained unpublished for 83 years, although Cardinal Ratzinger disclosed in October 1984 and again in June 1985 that he too had read it. He also told an Italian journalist, Vittorio Messori, that the secret concerned 'the dangers threatening the faith and life of Christians'. Over the years, numerous journalists and scholars have speculated about the precise details of the secret, including a Father Alonso who amassed a private, fourteen-volume study of the subject, having been appointed to investigate it by Bishop Venancio in 1966.

The second secret predicted the end of the First World War and the outbreak of another 'during the Pontificate of Pius XI', and warned that 'when you see a night illuminated by an unknown light, know that this is the great sign given you by God that He is about to punish the world for its crimes, by means of war, famine and persecutions of the Church and of the Holy Father'. Academics concluded that the night illumination was most likely the unusually spectacular *Aurora Borealis* (Northern Lights) which occurred on 25/26 January 1938. The second secret also offered a remedy for the disasters:

> To prevent this, I shall come to ask for the consecration of Russia to my Immaculate Heart, and the Communion of Reparation on the First Saturdays. If my requests are heeded, Russia will be converted and there will be peace; if not, she will spread her errors throughout the world, causing wars and persecutions of the Church. The good will be martyred, the Holy Father will have much to suffer, various nations will be annihilated. In the end my Immaculate Heart will triumph; the Holy Father will consecrate Russia to me and she will be converted, and a period of peace will be given to the world.

John Paul II undertook this solemn consecration on 25 March 1984, urging the world's bishops to participate from their respective dioceses.

Sister Maria Lucia gave her most comprehensive account of the third secret to a priest, Father Fuentes, in December 1957: 'The Blessed Virgin has told us that many nations will disappear from the face of the earth, that Russia will be the instrument of chastisement of the world if we do not obtain beforehand the conversion of that poor nation.' Apart from Father Fuentes – and Father Alonso who died in 1981 without releasing the conclusions of his decade of study – the only other person known to have discussed the third secret with Sister Maria Lucia is Cosme do Amaral, who became Bishop of Leiria and who was apparently authorized to make the following comment during a question and answer session held at Vienna's University of Technology on 10 September 1984:

> The Secret of Fatima speaks not about atomic bombs, nor about nuclear warheads, nor about SS-20 missiles. Its content concerns but our faith. To identify the Secret with catastrophic announcements or

> with a nuclear holocaust is to distort the meaning of the message. The loss of faith of a continent is worse than the annihilation of a nation; and it is true that Faith is continually diminishing in Europe.

Nothing further was divulged until John Paul II's visit to Fatima on 13 May 2000, where he again met with Sister Lucia and announced his intention to publish the full texts of the three secrets, and to simultaneously release a commentary and modern translations. Sensationally, he revealed that his own assassination had been foretold in the Third Secret, which was finally made public by Cardinal Ratzinger on 26 June on the Vatican's internet site. The vital passage was interpreted by the Pontiff as a glimpse of a world beset by destruction:

> After the two parts which I have already explained, at the left of Our Lady and a little above, we saw an Angel with a flaming sword in his left hand; flashing, it gave out flames that looked as though they would set the world on fire; but they died out in contact with the splendour that Our Lady radiated towards him from her right hand: pointing to the earth with his right hand, the Angel cried out in a loud voice: *'Penance, Penance, Penance!'*. And we saw in an immense light that is God: 'something similar to how people appear in a mirror when they pass in front of it' a Bishop dressed in White 'we had the impression that it was the Holy Father'. Other Bishops, Priests, men and women Religious going up a steep mountain, at the top of which there was a big Cross of rough-hewn trunks as of a cork-tree with the bark; before reaching there the Holy Father passed through a big city half in ruins and half trembling with halting step, afflicted with pain and sorrow, he prayed for the souls of the corpses he met on his way; having reached the top of the mountain, on his knees at the foot of the big Cross he was killed by a group of soldiers who fired bullets and arrows at him, and in the same way there died one after another the other Bishops, Priests, men and women Religious, and various lay people of different ranks and positions. Beneath the two arms of the Cross there were two Angels each with a crystal aspersorium in his hand, in which they gathered up the blood of the Martyrs and with it sprinkled the souls that were making their way to God.

On 27 April the Holy Father had sent Archbishop Tarcisio Bertone, Secretary of the Congregation for the Doctrine of the Faith, and Bishop Serafim de Sousa Ferreira e Silva, Bishop of Leiria-Fatima, to see Sister Lucia at the Carmel of Saint Teresa in Coimbra to obtain her interpretation of this passage. They presented her with the envelope containing the secret. Recognizing her handwriting, she said, 'This is my letter.' Sister Lucia agreed that the third part of the secret was a prophetic vision, similar to the first two. She repeated her conviction that the vision of Fatima concerns the struggle of atheistic Communism against Christians and the Church, and describes the terrible sufferings of the victims of the faith in the twentieth century.

Asked whether the principal figure in the vision was the Pope, Sister Lucia replied at once that it was. 'We did not know the name of the Pope; Our Lady did not tell us the name of the Pope; we did not know whether it was Benedict XV or Pius XII or Paul VI or John Paul II; but it was the Pope who was suffering and that made us suffer too.'

Turning to the passage about the Bishop dressed in white, Sister Lucia was in full agreement with the John Paul's claim that 'it was a mother's hand that guided the bullet's path and in his throes the Pope halted at the threshold of death'.

The chapters that follow have little to do with religious faith, Catholic dogma or the supernatural, but rather they recount the extraordinary story of one man's dedication to the task of freeing the people of the Soviet bloc from communist totalitarianism, the zeal with which the CIA under the leadership of Bill Casey assisted him, and the KGB's ruthless determination to stop them. A unique tale of espionage, subversion, plots and counter-plots, with the CIA and the KGB engaged in what few perceived at the time to be the final manoeuvres of the Cold War, the story that emerges is of a complex conflict waged between ideologically-motivated zealots who were determined to exploit the first signs of an escalating economic collapse in the Soviet bloc, and a monolithic, obsolescent regime that took increasingly desperate measures to save itself. Dominating the scene is the first Slavic Pontiff, one of the most truly extraordinary figures of the century, a man of mystical beliefs who played a hitherto undisclosed role in a series of events which was to lead to the collapse of Communism in Europe.

Chapter I

St Peter's Square, 13 May 1981

As the tourists and pilgrims pressed forward on a sunny Wednesday afternoon to catch a glimpse of Pope John Paul II on his weekly tour of the Vatican, standing in his specially adapted *campagnola*, the vehicle later known as the popemobile, three shots rang out and panic gripped the crowd. The Pope, nearing the completion of his second and final circuit of the square and heading back to the San Damaso courtyard, slumped to the floor, blood from his abdomen rapidly staining his white silk cassock. He had been hit by three bullets. One entered just below his stomach, another his right hand, and the third his right arm. His long-serving Polish secretary (and confessor), Father Stanislaw Dziwisz, having been seated immediately behind the Pontiff, cradled the wounded man in his arms and muttered a prayer. Meanwhile the terrified spectators, more than seventy thousand in total, reacted in different ways: some ran for cover in panic, fleeing the gunfire; others were frozen to spot, dazed by the enormity of what they had just witnessed. Two women fell to the ground: twenty-one-year-old Rose Hall, on a pilgrimage from Jamaica, was hit in her left arm, and Ann Odre, an elderly American from New York, suffered a chest wound. Security staff from the Vatican's Central Office of Vigilance, uniformed carabinieri, plainclothed DIGOS anti-terrorist officers and City of Rome detectives searching for pickpockets pressed forward through the crowd to what they thought was the source of the gunfire. Sister Letizia simply grabbed the young man dressed in a grey suit standing beside her, tenaciously gripping the wrist that held a heavy Browning semi-automatic. The more the would-be assassin struggled, the tighter the small but sturdy nun held on, until she was joined, moments later, by two carabinieri who seized the weapon and swiftly snapped a pair of handcuffs on his wrists.

The popemobile's driver, urged on by shouts from Father Dziwisz, made a dash for the Arch of Bells where an ambulance was waiting with its engine running. The Pope was taken on an eight-minute journey to the Policlinico Gemelli where a special intensive care and operating suite on the ninth floor was maintained on permanent stand-by. Since the unexpected death of his predecessor, John Paul I, of a heart attack in his bed in the Vatican, which had followed the unfortunate and probably avoidable demise of *his* predecessor, Giovanni Montini, Paul VI, at Castel Gandolfo, the authorities were determined never to allow a pope to be without the very best modern medical attention. In keeping with this aim, the hospital's bloodbank maintained an extra-large stock of John Paul II's relatively rare blood group, 'A' rhesus negative. Fully conscious until given a general anaesthetic before surgery, but with his blood pressure falling dangerously, the Pope whispered a last word to his private secretary crouched beside him: 'Madonna.'

One of the Gemelli's three principal surgeons, Dr Francesco Crucitti, who had driven himself across Rome to the hospital, operated on John Paul to staunch the blood loss, repair damage to the colon and small intestine, and perform a temporary colostomy. During the following five hours Crucitti cut away twenty-two inches of perforated intestine and supervised a major transfusion of five pints of blood, thus taking the Pope out of immediate danger. One of the bullets had missed his main abdominal artery by a fraction of an inch, and had come close to severing his spinal column.

As the news flashed around the world that the Holy Father was undergoing emergency surgery for gunshot wounds, the Italian police embarked on one of the most remarkable investigations ever undertaken, one that would have ramifications that only the most seasoned conspiracy theorist could ever guess at.

By 1981 the Italian public had endured more than a decade of terrorism and political assassinations. The previous August, right-wing extremists had detonated a bomb at the Bologna railway station killing eighty-five bystanders and wounding more than two hundred. In March 1978 the leader of the ruling Christian Democrats, Aldo Moro, had been abducted in a hail of automatic fire that had left his five bodyguards dead while in a motorcade through busy streets on his way to the parliament building. Two months later his body was recovered from the boot of a car, dead from a single shot to the head. He had been murdered by the Red Brigades, a sophisticated group of leftist urban guerrillas dedicated to 'direct action'.

In the weeks that followed Moro's assassination, Italy underwent one political crisis after another, culminating in the P2 scandal which led to the imprisonment in the United States of Michele Sindona, one of the country's best-connected bankers, on fraud charges linked to the collapse of the Franklin National Bank. Sentenced in March 1980 to twenty-five years' imprisonment on sixty-eight counts of fraud, misappropriation of bank funds and perjury, Sindona unsuccessfully attempted suicide. He then guided investigators on a trail that implicated the highest in the land. Even the most hardened political commentators were shocked when they discovered the scale of the corruption that had been centred on the Masonic lodge known as 'Propaganda 2'. When the list of P2's 962 members was published in May 1981, dozens of intelligence officers, carabinieri, judges and bankers were implicated in a clandestine organization that had exercised unsuspected power in successive Christian Democrat administrations. Italy was plunged once again into political turmoil, with numerous overlapping security agencies pursuing several different lines of inquiry with varying degrees of efficiency and enthusiasm.

Responsibility for investigating the assassination attempt on the Pope was divided between several separate branches of government, and more became involved as the preliminary interrogation of the suspect developed in its complexity; these included the carabinieri, the Servizio Informazioni Difesa (SID), the anti-terrorist police (DIGOS), the military intelligence service (SISMI), and the Servizio Informazioni Forze Armate (SIFAR). Initially, the putative assassin, a twenty-three-year-old Turk, carrying a Turkish passport, number 136635, issued the previous August in the name of Faruk Ozgun, was questioned at the Questura police headquarters in Rome. During seventy-five hours of continuous interrogation the first part of his story emerged. He made no attempt to deny to the examining magistrate, Judge Luciano Infelisi, that he was the gunman, and offered regret only for having wounded the two tourists.

The day after the suspect's arrest, the DIGOS chief commissioner, Lidano Marchionne, received a dossier hand-delivered by two representatives from MIT (the Turkish National Intelligence Organization whose headquarters were on Ataturk Boulevard, Ankara) which contained detailed background. The suspect's name was not Ozgun, although a legitimate passport had been issued in the provincial town of Nevsehir to a local resident, a twenty-eight-year-old textile worker, using an application form bearing photos of someone else. That person was Mehmet Ali Agca, a notorious murderer convicted of shooting Abdi Ipekci, the respected editor of the moderately leftist *Milliyet* daily newspaper on 1 February 1979. He had been arrested on 25 June 1979, but five months later had made a daring escape from the top security Kartal-Maltepe military fortress. His first attempt to escape, during a psychiatric examination in which he had acquired a gun and taken several staff hostage in the prison hospital, failed, but the second succeeded. He had simply bribed a soldier, changed into military uniform, and strolled past eight gates and security checks to freedom. In the inquiry that followed, a junior soldier was sentenced to fifteen years' imprisonment for accepting a bribe to facilitate the escape. The day after his breakout, Agca had written to *Milliyet* threatening to kill the Pope if he did not cancel his scheduled visit to Istanbul. The short letter gave the impression of having been written by an Islamic fanatic preoccupied with an Israeli–American conspiracy against Mecca, but there was nothing in Agca's background to show any previous religious commitment; he was not a regular attender at the mosque, and he was known to drink alcohol.

Mehmet Ali Agca had been born into a Sunni Muslim peasant family in Hekimham, in the east of the country, his father being an uneducated farm labourer, and had later moved to the nearby city of Malatya. He had attended the local high school, had a reasonably distinguished academic record, and in 1976 had enrolled at Ankara University to read history and geography. Two years later he switched to an economics course at Istanbul University, and it was here that, according to his own confession, he seems to have encountered terrorism and, accompanied by two Turkish friends, had attended a forty-day course at a training camp south of Beirut run by the Palestine Liberation Organization (PLO).

Sentenced to death *in absentia*, Agca had been on the run until his arrest in St Peter's Square. Although the Turkish authorities had issued several international arrest warrants, no trace of him had been found until that day. There were reports of several sightings in Germany, which resulted in official requests from the Turkish embassy in Bonn for information on 3 October 1980 (following a tip from Frankfurt), 6 November and 11 December in Berlin, and 29 December at Bad Wurzach, but Agca was never found.

Attention was focused on what had brought Agca to Rome and the most immediate clues were the Browning 9mm semi-automatic, a shoulder-bag, 300,000 lire and three scraps of paper in his pockets bearing scribbled notes. One was a schedule of the Pope's public appearances marked in Turkish, 'May 13th Wednesday, appearance in the Square; May 17, Sunday, maybe appearance on the balcony; May 20, Wednesday, Square without fail'; another was a list of local telephone numbers. A search of his hotel room, number 31 on the third floor of the Pensione Isa, on the via Cicerone close to the railway station, revealed only a bottle of hair dye, some torn up postcards of St Peter's Square in the wastepaper bin, and a written statement, presumably intended to be found, in which Agca claimed that he had shot the Pope in the interests of freedom in Afghanistan and El Salvador.

The research into the Browning was to prove intriguing, for the serial number, 76C23953, showed it to have been manufactured at the Fabrique Nationale plant at Herstal in Belgium, and supplied via a dealer in Liège to another in Zurich, Wilhelm Glaser, who had sold it to an elderly purchaser in Muhldorf, near Salzburg, named Otto Tinter, bearing a licence issued in Vienna in July 1980 to Horst Grillmaier, a local dealer. Further inquiries established that Grillmaier, who was arrested and questioned in May 1981, had sold the weapon to a Turk, Oral Celik, who had then given it to a Turkish butcher, Omer Bagci, on 2 April, and he had carried it back through Switzerland to Milan, handing it to Agca on 9 May, four days before the assassination attempt. Celik, coincidentally, also came from Malatya, and was rumoured to have been a key figure in the right-wing political terrorist group known as the Grey Wolves. As for Grillmaier, he was well-known as an intermediary in the arms trade, with good connections in Eastern Europe and Turkey, and was reputed to have had a Nazi past. In January 1983 he was implicated as the consignee of a lorryload of 700 Soviet weapons, including seven Dragunov sniper rifles, and 15,000 rounds of ammunition, seized by Austrian customs on the Czech frontier at Kleinhaugsdorf, which served only to emphasize his continuing business interests rather than his politics. Under interrogation Grillmaier identified his client as Paul Saalbach of Munich, whom the federal German authorities acknowledged as a BND officer.[1]

None of this proved very much except to demonstrate that Agca had not acted alone, and to show how easily a 'legitimate' weapon can disappear and fall into the wrong hands. As for the two Turkish intermediaries, Celik disappeared, apparently to Bulgaria, but Bagci was arrested in Olten, Switzerland, in June 1982 and extradited to Italy to face charges of smuggling and supplying the gun. Under cross-examination, Bagci, who had a clean police record, confessed to receiving the gun from Celik and delivering it to Agca in Milan.

The first task of the DIGOS inquiry was to establish Agca's movements between Christmas 1979 and his arrest eighteen months later. Although the results were far from conclusive, because Agca often contradicted himself during his lengthy interrogations in Rome's Rebibbia prison, collateral evidence was gathered to reconstruct a schedule of his travels. There was, however, no confirmation of his own somewhat vague version of what happened immediately after he had escaped from prison in Turkey. He said he had been sheltered by a network of friends, and then had slipped over the border to Iran in April carrying 40,000 Deutschmarks supplied by supporters. According to the Turkish police, he was strongly suspected of having killed Haydar Serangah, the police informant who had denounced him for the killing of Abdi Ipekci, and who had been found murdered at the end of December 1979.

The first part of Agca's story was impossible to substantiate, but it was possible to show that by early July 1980 he had travelled to the Bulgarian capital Sofia and checked into the Vitosha, a popular and expensive hotel. It was during the fifty days he spent in Bulgaria that Agca had acquired an authentic passport, bearing his photograph, but issued in the name of Faruk Ozgun. Thereafter he had used the passport to visit Yugoslavia, France, England, Belgium, Switzerland, Denmark, Austria, Hungary, Tunisia, Spain and finally Italy, arriving in Rome on 15 December to stay at the Pensione Hiberia.

According to Agca, the passport had been bought for 60,000 Turkish lire from another Turk, and the transaction had taken place in the Hotel Vitosha in August 1980. The passport revealed much about the holder's movements, for it contained a currency stamp for DM 540 issued by the Osmanli Bank in Istanbul on 27 August, a Turkish frontier stamp marked Kapikule, the frontier post outside Edirne, on 30 August; a Bulgarian entry stamp for the next day at Kapitan Andreev; and a Bulgarian exit visa stamped three days later at Kalotina, suggesting that Agca had left Sofia for Yugoslavia immediately he had taken delivery of the passport on 31 August. Significantly, anyone taking the document at face value would be bound to accept that the holder had transited through Bulgaria to Yugoslavia from Edirne in a single day; they would certainly not conclude that the person concerned had spent almost two months in Sofia. The obvious interpretation was that this amounted to a well-planned attempt to conceal Agca's true movements, and obliterate almost all of his visit to Bulgaria.

Subsequent inquiries at the passport office in Nevsehir revealed that the next passport issued in sequence to Agca's, number 116635, and on the same day, also went to a local resident, one Galip Yilmaz. However, when traced to the University of Frankfurt where he was registered as a student, it was clear that Yilmaz was not the person to whom the passport had been issued, for the current holder was an officially accepted political refugee, a teacher named Omer Ay who had been granted provisional asylum on 27 May, having been smuggled out of Turkey in a sealed truck six weeks earlier. Acting on an official Turkish request, Ay was arrested in February 1982, in Hamburg's red-light district on the pretext of a minor motoring charge, and challenged about the passport in the false name. Having denied any connection with Agca, Ay admitted the bogus passport application in the name of Yilmaz, whose identity card he had borrowed, and eventually was extradited to Turkey in October after a lengthy court battle. Based on his own version of events, Ay had simply used a common subterfuge to obtain false travel documents, and had moved with his wife to Hamburg where they had drawn welfare benefits. According to his police dossier, he was suspected to have been active in émigré politics. However, there was no evidence to link him to Agca or to any plot to assassinate the Pope. As the Turks investigated the paper trail of forged documents in Nevsehir they arrested a local teacher, whom Faruk Ozgun had allowed to use his identity, and a corrupt policeman, but neither was implicated in anything more serious than passport fraud. Thus far the evidence revealed nothing more than a well-established trade in false Turkish documents, a familiar story of benefits fraud in Germany, and an inexplicable attempt to cover up a lengthy sojourn in Bulgaria.

Upon analysis, Agca's pattern of continuous, seemingly purposeless travel appeared to have changed after his arrival in Rome, where he stayed at the YMCA and in various cheap pensiones for a total of thirty-four days. During the next five months he was to visit Milan twice, Palermo, Naples, Perugia and Genoa. In between, he made short trips to Budapest, Vienna, Zurich and Lucerne, and took a fortnight's package holiday to Palma de Majorca. During four days in Perugia, in April 1981, he registered at the university, paid $210 as a foreign student for a language course, obtained a three-month student visa, but turned up for only one lesson, on 10 April.

Naturally, Agca's peregrinations raised the question of money, for there was no evidence that he had undertaken any work on his travels, and he could not have supported himself on the DM40,000 he claimed to have had when he left Turkey. Although the trail was barely warm, the DIGOS team set about reconstructing what was known of Agca's movements, a task replete with unexplained gaps that was to take eighteen months. They began with the certainty of his departure from Bulgaria on 31 August. He seemed to have entered Yugoslavia by bus. The next confirmed sighting of him was in Zurich where he had stayed at the Hotel Ruetli between 9 and 12 September. This was followed by a stay at the Hotel Kronein Lucerne, from 27 to 31 October, but where had he been in the meantime? The dates on the Turkish arrest and extradition requests suggest he had visited West Germany.

Agca next showed up in Italy, taking a flight to Tunis on 28 November to stay first at the Hotel du Lac before moving two days later to the Mediterranean resort of Hammamet. Two weeks later, on 13 December, Agca took the ferry to Sicily and stayed overnight at the Hotel Liguria in Palermo, but was in Milan two days later for a meeting (with Musa Celebi, see Chapter II). However, Agca checked into the Pensione Hiberia in Rome on 15 December and stayed until 19 December, being seen again at the Hotel Archimede in Rome between 26 December and 17 January. On 18 January 1981 Agca moved into the Pensione Isa for a single night, and was there again from 28 to 30 January. On 4 February he was spotted in a café in Milan, and on 6 February spent a night at the Hotel Anker in Aarau, Switzerland. On 3 March he held a meeting with Musa Celebi in Zurich, and disappeared for a month, re-emerging on 3 April to enter Switzerland from Austria at Diepoldsau. By 5 April Agca was back in Rome at the Hotel Archimede, leaving on 8 April by train for Perugia where he stayed for four days at the Hotel Posta before returning to the Hotel Torino in Rome. Again Agca dropped from sight, but was in Milan again on 19 April to buy a package holiday from the Condor Travel Agency for the Hotel Flamboyan in Majorca, where he flew the following week, on 25 April. On the night of 19 April, having made his purchase at the travel agency, he reportedly spent the night with a prostitute in Genoa.[2]

Little is known about what Agca did in Majorca during the next fortnight, although he made several long-distance calls, one of which was to Musa Celebi, the subject of a routine telephone intercept by the police in Frankfurt. However, Agca was back in Milan on 8 May, where he met Omer Bagci, before registering at the YMCA in Rome for a single night on 9/10 May, and switching to the Pensione Isa where a room had been reserved for him, and where he remained until his arrest, having paid for three nights in advance.

Agca's itinerary demonstrates no obvious shortage of cash and the Italian investigating magistrate, Ilario Martello, whose final report was to cover 1,243 pages, concentrated on the paper trail associated with the money and Agca's gun. In December 1982 he issued a series of arrest warrants, including one for Oral Celik, the Turk from Malatya who, according to the MIT, had been working as a tourist guide in Erzurum when he was last known to have seen Agca. Despite the many hours of research put in by investigators across Europe, the conundrums remained. What had been the purpose of Agca's constant travels? Where had his money come from? What had motivated him to stalk the Pope? Although these questions could not be answered in the initial stages of the Italian inquiry, some troubling conclusions could be reached quite quickly. First, Agca did not conform to the personality profile of the reclusive, unstable, religious obsessive so familiar to forensic psychologists looking into the backgrounds of other putative assassins. Nor did he conform to the conventional profile of low self-esteem, low IQ, poor academic performance, demeaning employment, dysfunctional background with strong hints of chaotic behaviour. There was none of the characteristic, stereotypical brooding self-analysis, complex family relationships, lapses into unprovoked violence or sociopathic behaviour. On the contrary, Agca's mental agility and self-control, combined with the degree of calculation indicated by his travels, his sophisticated contacts, his clandestine meetings and his skilful evasion of border controls revealed a pattern of behaviour far more familiar to counter-intelligence personnel who recognized the hallmarks of a fellow professional who either displayed a surprising aptitude for covert activity or had studied the tradecraft. In short, Agca seemed more likely to be an accomplished hitman than a homicidal maniac.

As for Oral Celik, his disappearance was short-lived. His movements across Europe were monitored by a dozen separate intelligence agencies, and he was eventually arrested and imprisoned in Switzerland for ten years on drug-smuggling charges. He now lives in some considerable style in a villa on Turkey's Aegean coast, ready to denounce the papal assassination plot as a Western conspiracy, a line curiously reminiscent of the one peddled by the KGB.

Agca's trial in July 1981, presided over by Judge Severino Santiapichi and heard by a jury of six, lasted just two days because Agca dismissed his lawyer and refused to recognize the court's jurisdiction over the episode which, he argued, had occurred on Vatican territory. Santiapichi rejected Agca's defence, citing the 1929 Lateran Treaty. Thereafter Agca declined to participate in the proceedings, and he was sentenced to life imprisonment. In his subsequent judgment, issued on 25 September, Santiapichi reviewed the case and concluded that Agca had executed 'a task entrusted to him by others in a plot obscured by hatred', but noted that 'the evidence . . . has not permitted us to uncover the identity or the motives of the conspirators'.

CHAPTER II

The Bulgarian Connection

Initially there were just two reasons for linking Ali Agca to Bulgaria. The first was the period of nearly two months he had spent in Sofia in the summer of 1980, after which his movements had been relatively easy to document based on the Ozgun passport, supported by inquiries conducted elsewhere. The second was one of the scraps of paper found in his possession at the time of his arrest.

This extraordinary item of evidence listed five local Rome telephone numbers: two were for the chancellery of the Bulgarian embassy, one was for the Bulgarian consulate, another was for the Balkanair airline office, and the last turned out to be an unlisted number for a Bulgarian diplomat, Todor Aivazov. Under cross-examination, after a year in custody, Agca described having met three Bulgarian contacts in Rome, having visited the homes of two, and recalled the unlisted home number of the third. When confronted with a collection of surveillance photographs, Agca identified the three men: 'Kolev' was Todor Aivazov, a cashier at the embassy; 'Petrov' was Major Zelio Vasilev, an assistant military attaché; and 'Bayramic' was Sergei Antonov, deputy head of the local Balkanair office since 1977. To support his claims, Agca recalled visiting Antonov's apartment at 29 via Pola, and Aivazov's at 36 via Galiani, and gave a detailed account of the interiors of both. On 10 May, for instance, all four had met at Antonov's apartment and Agca remembered that they had been served tea by 'Bayramic's' wife, accompanied by her ten-year-old daughter. In addition, Agca asserted that on the two afternoons prior to the day of the attempt on the Pope's life he had been driven to the Vatican by Antonov in his Lada 124 for dress rehearsals, and on the day itself he had been collected by Aivazov and Antonov in a rented blue Alfetta from an agreed rendezvous in the Piazza della Reppublica, and had been taken to Aivazov's home to fetch a bag containing two guns and a stun-grenade. The trio had then driven to the Vatican, parked in the via della Conciliazione outside the Canadian embassy to the Holy See, and walked into St Peter's Square. There the three had split up, allegedly having agreed an exfiltration plan involving the use of the stun-grenade to cause panic and a diversion, and having the Alfetta close by for use in the getaway.

Not surprisingly, all three Bulgarians were known to SISMI which suspected Antonov to be a Darzhavna Sigurnost (DS) officer. As he was not protected by diplomatic immunity, he was arrested as he left his home on the way to work on 25 November 1982 and was charged as Agca's accomplice. To the outside world this development was entirely unexpected, for hitherto the Italian authorities had made no mention of any possible Bulgarian connection. He was the last of the trio identified by Agca, for Aivazov had flown home a fortnight earlier on 12 November, and Vasilev had been withdrawn to Sofia much earlier, on 24 August.

Under interrogation, Antonov claimed that he had spent 13 May at his office at Balkanair, an alibi supported by his staff, and that his wife Rosica had picked him up around 7 p.m. The fundamental flaw in his account was that it conflicted with an official Bulgarian statement, apparently issued to counter Agca's memory of the final planning conference held on 10 May, which insisted that Rosica had left Rome by car on 8 May and had driven with friends through Yugoslavia, arriving in Sofia on 10 May to see her daughter Ana, so neither could have been in Antonov's apartment as claimed by Agca. However, if Rosica had been out of the country on 13 May, she could not have been in Rome to supply her husband with the one part of his alibi that could be double-checked.

Although Agca never attempted to conceal his part in the shooting in St Peter's Square, for almost twelve months he consistently refused to give his interrogators at Rebibbia prison any detailed assistance, and it was not until May 1982 that he suddenly began to cooperate. Quite what prompted this unexpected change is unclear, although he may have been influenced by the realization that he was not going to be rescued in the same way as he had been assisted to escape from his imprisonment in Turkey. Alternatively, he seems to have feared an attempt on his own life, a contingency that his prison guards had always planned for. Agca had been sentenced to life imprisonment on 22 July 1981 and, to the surprise of his lawyers, he had declined to exercise his right of appeal, perhaps indicating that he expected to be released imminently.

In his new testimony, amounting to a hundred pages dictated during the first week of May, Agca filled in many of the gaps missing from his original statements, and described how his escape route from the Vatican had involved being smuggled out of the country in a Bulgarian embassy truck covered by diplomatic immunity. When DIGOS checked this particular claim, it was confirmed that the only heavy transport negotiated by the embassy in the entire year had been scheduled to leave Rome on 13 May. Agca also named the man who had supplied him with the gun at the Milan railway station, Omer Bagci. When arrested in Switzerland, Bagci admitted his part in the plot. Agca also made two further astonishing admissions that were to prove much more difficult to substantiate.

Agca's first claim was that he had met his three Bulgarian contacts in Sofia, where he had been hired by a Turk named Bekir Celenk to assassinate the Pope for a fee of DM3 million. Celenk, ostensibly a tobacco trader involved in purchasing huge quantities of cigarettes from the Bulgarian state monopoly and smuggling them into Turkey, ran a business in London, the Oscar Maritime Shipping Company, and spent his vacations cruising the Mediterranean on his Panamanian-registered motor-yacht. He also lived in a luxury villa in Bulgaria and maintained a suite in the Hotel Vitosha; Agca said he had stayed there in room 911. After their initial encounter the two men supposedly had held further meetings in Switzerland, Austria and Italy, and had spoken on the telephone during Agca's final holiday at the Hotel Flamboyan in Palma de Majorca. Celenk had kept Agca in funds, and had employed a subordinate, Musa Serdar Celebi, to make regular payments, including one in Zurich on 3 March 1981.

Although Agca's identification of Celenk sounded authentic, it was too late to have him arrested. Having been seen in Munich, he drove to Zurich and Vienna in his Swiss-registered car, and then went to ground in Sofia, refusing any comment whatever, his reputation as a major Turkish gangster, tolerated if not sponsored by the DS, enhanced. Celebi was not so lucky, and the twenty-eight-year-old Istanbul University law graduate was arrested on 3 November in Frankfurt where he was employed ostensibly by the Turkish Federation, a non-political welfare organization representing the interests of Turkish expatriates. In fact, Celebi was very active in Turkish politics on behalf of the right-wing National Action Party and in 1981 had founded a Turkish-language newspaper, *Yeni Hedef*, in Germany. Having initially denied knowing Agca, Celebi was extradited to Rome and admitted under interrogation that he had met Agca, without realizing who he was, once in Milan. This confirmed Agca's statement in which he said that Celebi had come to Milan on 15 December 1980 to hand over a further wad of DM1,000 as part of an assassination plot. Articulate and sophisticated, Celebi was far from the usual Turkish henchmen that Celenk tended to surround himself with in Sofia. Instead, Celebi came from a middle-class background, was well qualified, and upon his graduation had been recruited into the Turkish customs service in 1976.

Celebi was also confronted with a German police transcript of a telephone conversation he had conducted with an unknown person calling from Majorca at the end of April 1980 which included the statement, 'I have received the money. I will now go to Rome and finish the job.' The German BfV security service had routinely tapped Celebi's telephone in Frankfurt, but had not realized the significance of the call which had been made from Agca's hotel at the precise time Agca had said.

Agca's assertion, linking Celebi to Celenk, looked plausible and explained for the first time the source of Agca's financial support, but his second allegation sounded even more extraordinary. Soon after his arrival in Rome in early January 1981, he attended a meeting at the Hotel Archimede with Antonov, Vasilev and Aivazov to discuss the assassination of Lech Walesa who was scheduled to have an audience with the Pope a fortnight later, on 18 January.

Agca claimed that his discussion with the three Bulgarians centred on the possibility of blowing up the Solidarity leader's car in Rome, but apparently Agca had demurred, pleading insufficient experience. The question was, could Agca really be believed? If so, it would add credibility to his charges against the Bulgarians; if not, the proposition of a Bulgarian connection might be undermined. Confirmation was to come partly from Agca himself, but also from a completely unexpected source, unrelated to the plot against the Pope.

Arriving on 15 January, Walesa had spent five days in Rome, staying at the Hotel Victoria. Strangely, Agca proved that he had been well-briefed about Walesa's busy itinerary, and even knew that some rooms in the Victoria had been refurbished just before his arrival. But how could the Bulgarians have had access to such information? From the SISMI surveillance photographs Agca identified the key figure in his discussions as a fourth Bulgarian, hitherto unmentioned, who turned out to be Ivan T. Dontchev, long suspected of being the DS *rezident* in Rome. Agca said that Dontchev, whom he had visited at his home, had relied on a source within the Italian trade union movement for access to details of Walesa's schedule, and this turned out to be true.

Dontchev had left Rome for Sofia in October 1982, thereby escaping an arrest warrant eventually issued in July 1983, but his principal agent, Luigi Scricciolo, who was then head of the foreign department of the Social Labour Federation (IUL), was not so lucky, and was denounced by his wife Paola and cousin Loris for his involvement in an abduction carried out by the Red Brigades in Verona on 17 December 1981. A senior US army officer attached to NATO, General James L. Dozier, had been seized from his home by the urban terrorists, but had been rescued forty-two days later in a dramatic joint US and Italian raid on the apartment in Padua where he had been held. Among those arrested was the organizer, Antonio Savasta, a twenty-seven-year-old Marxist revolutionary who had joined the Red Brigades in 1976 and had led the kidnapping and murder of Giuseppe Taliercio, director of a chemical factory, earlier in 1981. Savasta had become a key *pentito*, providing damning testimony against his former comrades, compromising dozens of other Red Brigadists, and had implicated Scricciolo. Savasta knew most of the Red Brigade's leadership, all of whom came from much the same middle-class leftist background, and effectively dismissed rumours of direct foreign intelligence involvement in the terrorist movement, with just a few exceptions. Their weapons had been supplied by Libya and George Habash's Popular Front for the Liberation of Palestine (PFLP), presumably with tacit Soviet approval, and Mossad had attempted but failed to establish contact back in 1975, with offers of money, arms and even the identities of two alleged carabinieri informers. The triumvirate at the head of the Red Brigades – their founder Renato Curcio (imprisoned in April 1978, his wife Margarita Cagol having been killed in a shoot-out with the carabinieri in 1975 during a kidnap rescue), Alberto Francheschini and Mario Moretti – never allowed foreigners to share their secrets, and resisted such temptations, but they did maintain contact with numerous intermediaries, like Scricciolo, who had acted on instructions issued by KGB surrogates. However, Curcio and Francheschini were reported by the defector General Jan Sejna, formerly the Czech deputy foreign minister until his escape to Italy in 1968, to have undergone military training at a Czech StB facility in Karlovy Vary and at a GRU-run course at the Doupov parachute school outside the resort town. For his part, Savasta claimed that the DS had offered weapons to the Red Brigades in return for the opportunity to interrogate Dozier, a rendezvous had been arranged in a Rome cinema, but the Bulgarian representative had failed to turn up. This was apparently the limit of the DS's contact with the Red Brigades, or so the Moro Commission concluded, thereby confirming the terrorists' policy of independence from all intelligence agencies.[1]

In the aftermath of Aldo Moro's murder there was a long and sustained judicial investigation to establish the extent to which foreign intelligence agencies had supported, penetrated or directed the Red Brigades, and there were plenty of leads to pursue. Early in 1981 Maurizio Folini had been named by the *pentiti* as a link with the PLO and a key figure in an illicit arms procurement programme, but although the weapons clearly had Eastern European origins, nothing was discovered to substantiate Sejna's claim, later made in his autobiography *We Will Bury You*, that Red Brigade terrorists had undergone training in Czechoslovakia.[2] One of the earliest *pentiti*, Patrizio Peci from Turin, whose testimony resulted in hundreds of arrests (and the reprisal murder of his brother Roberto in 1981), described the delivery of guns through Austria and Hungary, but insisted that the terrorists had trained themselves, an opinion shared by Savasta and another turncoat witness, Marco Barbone. Peci had been a senior figure in the Red Brigades and in his confession described how he had sailed to Beirut twice in a yacht to pick up weapons, among them a consignment of Czech-made Skorpions of the kind that had been used to kill Aldo Moro. According to Peci, the Skorpions has been landed at Mestre and delivered to Mario Moretti of the Brigades' Rome column.

Peci's widely circulated confession helped to create the theory of a worldwide terrorist conspiracy orchestrated by the KGB; a proposition developed most convincingly by the Rome-based American journalist Claire Sterling in *The Terror Network*, her 1981 analysis of the purported links between the Red Brigades and Moscow.[3] Sterling's problem was the minimal evidence available to sustain the claim that the KGB had masterminded a terrorist offensive and coordinated the efforts of the Provisional IRA in Ulster, the Basque separatists ETA in Spain, the Red Army in Japan, Dev Cenc in Turkey, the Red Army Faction in Germany, Action Direct in France, the Belgian Communist Combatant Cells and various different Palestinian groups. Briefly, Sterling's central thesis was that Western intelligence agencies, in particular the CIA, had conspired to suppress this information for fear of undermining detente, which itself was a wholly bogus product of a sophisticated KGB campaign of deception. Denouncing the former director of central intelligence (DCI), William Colby, a former Chief of Station in Rome who, in August 1979, expressed scepticism about any external direction of Italy's wave of terrorism, Sterling asserted that Giangiacomo Feltrinelli, the millionaire publisher who was killed while assembling a bomb near Milan in March 1972, had visited Prague twenty-two times before his death, and that another senior figure in the Red Brigades, Fabrizio Pelli, had worked for Radio Prague's Italian-language programmes. Combined with the unsubstantiated claim, originally made in 1976 to Shin Beth (the Israeli security service) interrogators by Ludwina Janssen, a Dutch volunteer from Red Help, that forty Cuban instructors had trained Red Brigades volunteers at a *fedayeen* camp at Hauf in South Yemen, Sterling posited the view that the KGB was fomenting global revolution. Significantly, although the author sought to demonstrate Moscow's involvement through Colonel Gadaffi in every terrorist cell from the Polisario Front in Morocco, through Baader-Meinhof to the Basque and Kurdish separatists, she never once mentioned the Bulgarian DS.

Sterling's determination to link the Czechs to terrorism was not entirely novel. Semtex-H, the explosive most closely associated with terrorism, was manufactured by Sythesia Pardubice at Pardubice, 90 kilometres south-west of Prague, and very little effort, if any, had been made by the communist authorities to prevent an estimated thousand tons from being exported to such well-recognized terrorist sponsors as Libya and Syria. The Czechs were also responsible for creating and running the Seventeenth of November University in Prague, based on the Patrice Lumumba University in Moscow, which was intended to give political education to Third World students. Of the 4,500 students enrolled at the Seventeenth of November University, the StB defector Jozef Frolik estimated that about half came into contact with his organization. However, there was a considerable difference between developing the Marxist ideologues of the future and providing training in terrorist tradecraft. While the Doupov site was certainly used for live firing exercises to train Spetznaz special forces, there was nothing to suggest any terrorists had ever been there.

Despite the lack of any credible evidence to support her thesis, extracts from Sterling's book published in the *New York Times* Magazine in March 1981 were seized on by the incoming DCI, Bill Casey, who had been alerted to the story by ex-President Nixon. Casey became convinced that the author had found proof that Moscow was masterminding global terrorism, and on 4 March asked his new deputy (DDCI), Admiral Bobby Ray Inman, to undertake a study of international subversion, terrorism and espionage, paying 'special attention to the degree to which it may be organized, supported, directed and coordinated by forces hostile to us in the world'.

During the initial tour of Europe customarily undertaken by a new DCI to introduce himself to his overseas stations, Casey – accompanied by the chief of the CIA Directorate of Operation's European division, Alan Wolfe – had tackled Duane R. 'Dewey' Clarridge at a gathering hosted by the Paris station early in February. He found that the Chief of Station and his deputy, Don Healey, were far from persuaded that the Soviets were actively backing terrorists. Casey returned to the topic when he visited Rome on 27 April, having made a whistle-stop tour to Tangier, Tel Aviv, Cairo and Riyadh. Clarridge was an extremely experienced officer and had studied the Red Brigades since his arrival in Rome in August 1979, after a stint of six years at headquarters in Langley. He was unconvinced by *The Terror Network* and was appalled to see that Casey and the president's new secretary of state, General Alexander Haig, seemed entirely enamoured of the notion that the KGB was the common denominator in every terrorist group. Indeed, Haig had asked for a detailed analysis of current Soviet targets and principal operational techniques, and had demanded it be delivered by 1 June. (Haig, of course, had a personal motive for pursuing the terrorism issue. On 26 June 1979, a few days before his retirement as NATO commander, his car had been blown up by a remotely-detonated landmine laid in a highway culvert near Ouberg. Haig narrowly escaped with his life and immediately saw a Soviet hand in the assassination attempt, attributed by the police to the Red Army Faction, a view reinforced by Hans Josef Horchem, then director of the West German BfV, who stated: 'the KGB is engineering international terrorism. The facts can be proven, documented and are well known to the international Western intelligence community.')

Casey and Haig insisted that the Agency prepare a national intelligence estimate (NIE) to assess the scale of Soviet sponsorship of international terrorism. However, to their dismay, the draft NIE prepared by the CIA's Office of Soviet Analysis concluded that the KGB could not be fingered as the godfather of terrorism, documenting Soviet unwillingness to deal with Abu Nidal and stating firmly that the KGB did not support the Red Brigades or the Red Army Faction. This view was, however, in direct contradiction of a rival Defense Intelligence Agency report, written by Charles Davis, submitted by General Eugene Tighe which came to the opposite conclusion. Appalled by the lack of what he saw as a clear focus, Casey commissioned another analyst, Lincoln Gordon, to reassess the evidence, and his study, entitled *Soviet Support for International Terrorism*, reached an even more embarrassing conclusion based on work undertaken by Dick Kaufman, the DI's principle terrorism analyst, and Dick Holm, then the CIA's chief of counter-terrorism. A careful examination of Sterling's book showed that her core sources had not been from within the intelligence community, as Casey had assumed; instead, she had relied on newspaper cuttings, one of which was easily traceable to a CIA-inspired propaganda campaign run by Howard E. 'Rocky' Stone, Dewey Clarridge's predecessor but one at the CIA station in Rome, intended to create the impression that Italy's lapse into escalating urban and political violence was a direct consequence of growing Soviet influence. Thus a feature article that had been manufactured for local consumption had come full circle and, like a self-fulfilling prophecy, was threatening to influence the new administration's policy. In short, the station in Rome, and in particular the CIA officer Frederick D. 'Fricky' Vreeland, had been altogether too successful in planting a fake newspaper story. In reality, the true position was altogether different.

Although DIGOS strongly suspected that the Red Brigades liaised closely with Palestinian extremists, and believed that the latter had supplied logistic support to the group that had bombed and strafed Fiumicino airport on 27 December 1985, no proof was ever found that the Italian terrorists had taken any direction from either the KGB or the Bulgarian DS. This was also the view held by General Giuseppe Santovito, the director of SISMI, the Italian military intelligence service. Indeed, it was Luigi Scricciolo who was himself the main evidence of a link, tenuous though it was, between the Red Brigades and the DS.

Scricciolo, ostensibly a respected trade union official who had visited Poland to advise Solidarity and had hosted Walesa's visit to Rome in January 1981, was arrested on charges of complicity. During his interrogation he confessed to having worked for the DS since 1976, his wife Paola being recruited three years later. He identified his DS contact as Ivan Dontchev and, more remarkably, confirmed that he had supplied the Bulgarians with details of Walesa's itinerary in Rome because they intended to assassinate him. Faced with a detailed statement from his wife, Scricciolo confessed to having acted as a talent-spotter, recruiting Italian students destined to study at American universities, developing a covert link to the Red Brigades, through his cousin Loris who was a member of the Rome 'column', and reporting on what he knew about Solidarity in Poland. More significantly, he lent weight to three of Agca's charges: that the DS had plotted against Solidarity, that they had planned to kill Walesa, and that the whole scheme had been masterminded by Ivan Dontchev.

Agca's claims about an officially sponsored Bulgarian attempt on the Pope's life looked increasingly credible, although there was only circumstantial evidence to link it to Todor Zhivkov's regime. Agca said he had stayed in Sofia for six weeks, but the Bulgarian authorities issued a denial, observing that the only evidence, contained in the

Faruk Ozgun passport, suggested that the holder had merely transited the country to Yugoslavia in a single day. However, if Agca *had* stayed at the Hotel Vitosha for an extended period, that in itself would strongly suggest a degree of official approval. The Vitosha was widely believed to be a DS facility with many of the rooms wired for sound, then a common feature of Eastern bloc hotels frequented by foreigners, and it was inconceivable that anyone could stay there for long without attracting the attention of the DS. The same could be said for the other two Sofia hotels named by Agca: the Sofia Grand Hotel and the Novo Hotel Europa. He had been a fugitive at the time, certainly travelling on false papers, although he may not have used the forged Indian passport, in the name of Yoginder Singh, that he claimed to have acquired while in hiding in Iran. As an escaped convicted murderer, Agca was the subject of several Interpol circulars, and he was certainly a notorious figure within expatriate Turkish communities in Europe, his activities regularly appearing on the front page of *Milliyet.* To have slipped across the Iranian frontier and taken refuge in that country, itself then in the midst of civil upheaval, had the ring of truth and did not necessarily require any official collusion, whereas illicit entry across the heavily guarded Bulgarian frontier was an entirely different proposition, as was being able to live openly in a luxury hotel in the capital of a totalitarian police state in which individual freedom of movement was tightly regulated. In this context, attention was focused on Agca's passport. If he already possessed one in the name of Yoginder Singh, why replace it?

Agca's original statement had described in detail his acquisition of the Ozgun passport and, in verifying his version, DIGOS obtained the first confirmation that Agca had indeed been in Sofia in July 1980. Agca recalled that the intermediary who had supplied the Ozgun passport had been a Turk who had also given him two contact telephone numbers in Munich: 89–530489 and 89–531070. The German Bundeskriminalamt traced the numbers to 43 Bayerstrasse, a building occupied by the Vardar Import-Export Company which was managed by a Turk, Omer Mersan. He was arrested on 21 May 1981. Vardar traded with Sofia in electrical goods but was believed to be implicated in illicit activities, including the smuggling of arms and drugs. When Mersan was questioned about whom he had met at the Hotel Vitosha the previous July, he admitted having encountered Agca, whom he claimed had used the name Metin, but denied any knowledge of counterfeit passports. On the basis that there was no charge for Mersan to answer, and no evidence that he had sold a fake passport, he was released by the German police, and the matter was dropped. In retrospect, this interrogation provided the only collateral support for Agca's stay at the Vitosha. So, although Mersan had distanced himself from any trafficking in illegal Turkish passports, he had confirmed that Agca really had been in Sofia at the time he had maintained.

Quite apart from the suggestion that Agca's presence in Sofia had been tolerated, there was also the issue of his financial support. Who had paid the bribes that had enabled him to escape from Kartal-Maltepe prison? How had he paid his hotel bill at the Vitosha? Where had the money come from to pay for the Ozgun passport?

Working on the basis that Agca had been in Sofia for six weeks, had stayed at the hotels he had named, and did buy the Ozgun passport, the focus switches to the Bulgarians. What would have motivated the DS to put a fugitive killer like Agca on the payroll? The answer lies in the culture of totalitarianism that relied so heavily on a ubiquitous security apparatus charged with that most fundamental responsibility, the suppression of counter-revolutionaries. The Russian Revolution of October 1917 placed a heavy burden on the Chekists who were to act as the sword and shield of the proletariat, and few can doubt the willingness of the NKVD and its successors to eliminate perceived opponents of the regime. Sometimes the assassinations and abductions, which so characterized the extra-territorial Red and White conflict, were swift acts of retribution, while other plots took years to execute, the classic example being that of Trotsky's murder in Mexico after more than twenty years in exile. When his killer, Ramon Mercader, was finally released, in August 1960, he retired to Moscow where he received a hero's welcome, and is today buried in a cemetery near the Nova Divichi Convent, the graveyard reserved for the most exalted in the Soviet intelligence community, lying close to Konon Molody, alias Gordon Lonsdale.

The KGB was used as a model by all the postwar communist regimes, including Yugoslavia, Czechoslovakia, Albania, Romania, Hungary, Poland, East Germany, Cuba and Bulgaria, with each satellite taking on the role of surrogate, acting on instructions from Moscow. The overwhelming evidence for this relationship is contained in the testimony of dozens of defectors from all the relevant services who have described in detail the degree of control exercised from Dzershinsky Square. Indeed, on one occasion a Polish defector, Michael Goleniewski, revealed his dual responsibilities as a KGB source inside the Warsaw headquarters of the Sluzba Bezpiecznstwa (SB). While there can be little doubt of the tight orchestration maintained by the KGB over the other Warsaw Pact agencies, there remains a reluctance to acknowledge the extent to which the intelligence professionals were willing to conspire in cold-blooded murder. Equally, there was a resistance within the CIA's analytical arm, the Directorate of Intelligence, to accept that their Soviet counterparts still indulged in what they called 'wet affairs'.

The CIA's evident repugnance was not shared by other Western intelligence agencies, and the head of SDECE, the French intelligence service, Comte Alexander de Marenches, took the view that the Soviets 'take action, in the main, by means of a go-between'. De Marenches had actually warned the Vatican about an assassination attempt. He recalled in 1988: I took the decision to forewarn the Holy Father,

> and to send one of the general officers from my immediate staff, accompanied by a high-ranking and competent official, whom I shall refer to as MC. The Vatican was alerted to my colleagues' arrival by a senior French clergyman, a veteran of Free France, who acted as an intermediary. My vital piece of intelligence reached the Vatican in January 1980. The Holy Father replied that his life was in the hands of the Lord. I have a great deal of respect for his conviction, although I believe there are times when it would not be inappropriate to give the Lord some assistance.[4]

After Agca's attempt on the Pope's life, de Marenches was interviewed by Judge Martello in Paris, and even though he had by then retired, he refused to answer his 'thirty or so questions'. Nevertheless, he remained, until his death in June 1995, convinced that the KGB had orchestrated the entire affair, claiming that 'there were three important reasons for wanting the Pope dead'. John Paul II himself came from behind the Iron Curtain and therefore posed a threat as 'he understands all too well how these peoples' minds work. There is nothing the Communists hate more than someone who understands their methods.' He had also embarked on a historic mission 'to bring all sections of the Catholic Church back into the fold'. Third, the elimination of the Pope would mean the almost automatic election of an Italian replacement who would be more accommodating towards the Kremlin.

Twenty years later, when Vasili Mitrokhin defected, he brought with him new evidence to show the extent of the KGB's support for international terrorism. In July 1970 Brezhnev personally approved support for the PFLP, and the KGB arranged for an intelligence-gathering ship, the *Kursograf*, to sail from Vladivostock in an operation codenamed VOSTOCK with a large consignment of untraceable, foreign-manufactured weapons, for a night rendezvous with Dr Wadi Haddad off the coast of Aden. Two years later, in a similar operation codenamed SPLASH, the *Reduktor* dropped a cargo of guns and ammunition on to the Stanton banks, off the coast of Ulster, where they were retrieved later by the Irish Republican Army which had been pressing for them through the Irish Communist Party since the start of the 'Troubles' in November 1969. Both VOSTOCK and SPLASH were kept extremely secret, and remain the only best proof of what some had long suspected, that the KGB gave covert assistance to some of the most intransigent terrorist groups in the West.[5]

The DI's reluctance to link the KGB to murder and terrorism was matched elsewhere, including in the CIA's Rome station where Clarridge informed an influential visitor, Senator Alphonse D'Amato, that as yet there was nothing to support Claire Sterling's allegations of Soviet complicity in the assassination plot. This view, unwisely expressed directly to her at a Rome cocktail party by Vincent Cannistraro, one of Clarridge's staff, had elicited a furious response, and Casey got to hear of both incidents. When offered a meeting with Sterling by Herbert Meyer, his special assistant whom he had brought in from *Fortune* magazine, Casey seized the opportunity and, accompanied by the deputy director of operations (DDO) John McMahon, delivered a diatribe about how his staff were better at finding excuses for the Soviets than at digging for the real dirt. General Haig was equally dissatisfied and made two appointments to strengthen his hand: Woody Goldberg was given special responsibility on his staff to monitor Poland, and Hugh Montgomery, recently returned from the CIA's Rome station, where he had impressed the SACEUR (Supreme Allied Commander, Europe), was transferred from Langley to the State Department's Department of Intelligence.

For Bill Casey, the Reagan administration's newly installed DCI, the attempt on the Pope's life was an event of enormous significance, for he was convinced it implicated Todor Zhivkov and Leonid Brezhnev. The Bulgarian leader was considered so subservient to Moscow that a joke circulated about Brezhnev asking him whether or not he smoked. 'No,' replied Zhivkov. 'Should I?' The fact that an initial review of the CIA's evidence by the DO's terrorism expert Nancy Hooper, followed by another conducted by Fritz Ermarth the senior Soviet analyst, cut little ice with Casey. Indeed, there was a strong belief that, despite the DCI's enthusiasm, the Vatican was less than keen to perpetuate the investigation, and that this view had been expressed to the national security adviser, Judge William Clark, by his old friend Cardinal Casaroli.

As a devout Catholic, Casey was appalled by the prospect of the Pontiff's assassination, and it may have been the catalyst for the momentous meeting he convened at the F Street headquarters of the National Foreign Intelligence Board (NFIB) the following morning. Casey's chosen topic was the Soviet role in international terrorism, and Lincoln Gordon presented his twenty-page draft report. Although the NFIB recommended that further work should be undertaken by Gordon to see if any evidence of Soviet involvement had been overlooked, Casey, acutely aware that Ronald Reagan had only narrowly survived an assassin's bullet just two months into his presidency, thought he saw the KGB's hand in what had happened in Rome. Unfortunately, nobody else could.

Chapter III

Soviet Assassins

Intelligence professionals from both East and West are invariably reluctant to be drawn on the issue of their involvement in assassination because to acknowledge it would undermine their legitimacy and status; this is particularly true in the United States where protests of innocence from the CIA and FBI are widely disbelieved, and where the media have proved themselves more willing to give credence to conspiracy theorists than to experienced congressional researchers. The unpopular truth is that although the Pike and Church Committee inquiries set up to look into allegations of CIA misconduct revealed some embarrassing contingency plans, including evidence of the preparation of deadly shellfish toxins, not a single murder could be identified as having been carried out by CIA personnel. Despite exhaustive inquiries conducted into the deaths of Patrice Lumumba in the Congo, President Ngo Dinh Diem in Saigon and General Rene Schneider in Chile, none could be blamed on the CIA. Indeed, the CIA Chief of Station in Stanleyville, Larry Devlin, was a devout Catholic who defied his DCI's request, as relayed from President Eisenhower, to plot the death of the Congo's troublesome premier. His successor, David Doyle, was to give secret testimony to the Church Committee's counsel describing in detail how Lumumba had been beaten to death by members of his own cabinet, an event that had shocked and dismayed the local CIA station.[1]

The first reliable first-hand postwar testimony to be given about officially sponsored Soviet assassinations, sometimes referred to by the euphemism of *fizicheskoye ustraneniye* ('physical removal'), was supplied by Nikolai E. Khokhlov, who had switched sides in Frankfurt in February 1954, and by Bogdan Stashinsky who surrendered to the German authorities in Berlin in December 1961. Both were 'illegals', trained to operate undercover. They were despatched on missions into the Federal Republic to murder leading members of the emigré community, but neither completed his assignment.

'Liquidation', of course, had long been a feature of Soviet intelligence operations and the term was recognized by the Eastern bloc professionals as a transparent euphemism for cold-blooded, state-sanctioned murder. It had been an occupational hazard under Stalin and there had been numerous examples during the 1920s and '30s of assassination as a policy to silence the Kremlin's opponents. Among the more notorious examples in Paris had been the murder of the Ukrainian General Simon Petlura in May 1926, the seizure of the White Russian General Aleksandr P. Kutepov off a Paris street in January 1930 and the disappearance of General Eugene Miller in September 1937. Nor had the abductions and shootings been limited to exiled anti-Bolsheviks. In 1937 alone more than forty *rezidents* had been recalled to Moscow to disappear in the notorious cellars of the Lubyanka, and in subsequent years even Stalin's most ruthless henchmen, such as General Jan Berzin who had faithfully served the cause, suffered the same fate. What made Khokhlov's testimony so shocking was the fact that he had been trained exclusively for homicide.

Khokhlov had been a KGB killer since operating as a partisan behind German lines during the war and had played a key role in the assassination of Wilhelm Kube, the Nazi gauleiter of Minsk. He married Yania Timashkevits in 1952; coming from a Uniat Christian family, she secretly converted her husband to Orthodox Christianity. Accordingly, when assigned by his superior, Colonel Lev Studnikov, to kill Georgi S. Okolovich, the leader of the exiled Ukrainian nationalists headquartered in Frankfurt-am-Main, Khokhlov had called at his apartment on 18 February 1954 and had given himself up to his intended victim. Okolovich and his organization, financed jointly by the CIA and SIS, was an important target for the KGB because it distributed subversive literature across the Ukraine and supplied the CIA with volunteers willing to be dropped into their homeland as agents and guerrillas. Since Okolovich enjoyed close ties with all the Allied intelligence agencies, and was actually the director of the NTS's covert operations branch, he asked Khokhlov which service he wished to defect to. 'Not the British,' he had replied. 'My impression is that in the name of the British Empire they would cheat us or even betray us. As to the French, I don't know whether they could handle it.'

Having chosen the Americans, Okolovich had promptly put Khokhlov in the hands of the CIA station in Frankfurt and a debriefing session had been held at a safe house over the following weekend. Khokhlov described his mission to an astonished audience of two Russian-speaking CIA officers and a representative from the local SIS station. The defector identified himself as a captain in the Soviet intelligence service who had spent four years in Romania perfecting his illegal cover, and asked for resettlement in the West for himself and for his wife and young son Alushka. His story was so extraordinary that Leslie Humphreys, an SIS officer who was under consular cover and affected a bow tie, at first refused to believe that Khokhlov was anything more than an embittered émigré suffering from delusions, and became increasingly hostile to the Russian. However, as the defector described his background and demonstrated the depth of his knowledge about his target, the CIA officers gradually became convinced of his authenticity and transferred him to Camp King, the CIA's refugee screening centre located in the old Luftwaffe barracks 7 kilometres north of the city. Michael Burke, one of the CIA officers who was present at the time, recalled that the KGB officer 'had arrived in Germany . . . brilliantly briefed':

> Khokhlov was a slight, blond, scholarly-appearing young man of thirty-two. He wore rimless glasses and spoke gravely. He expressed himself well, answered questions adroitly, and pleaded that his wife Yania . . . be brought out of Moscow as quickly as possible. It was Yania, he said, who had convinced him to defect rather than to become an assassin. He claimed that he would have sealed his own death warrant had he refused the assignment. Now he begged the Americans to save Yania and the child.[2]

During a further interrogation conducted by specialists who flew in from Washington DC, Khokhlov established his credentials by identifying WOLF, the KGB's mole in the NTS organization who had supplied much of the data he held on Okolovich, such as a detailed schedule of his movements, the registration number of his Mercedes and a floor-plan of his apartment and of his office in Bad Homburg. This information was so accurate that it was obvious the NTS had suffered penetration at a high level. The mole denounced by Khokhlov, Nikita V. Khorunsky, had been an instructor at the main NTS training facility at Bad Homburg and was therefore well placed to compromise NTS agents and plans. A former captain in the Red Army, and married to a Russian, Khorunsky had fled to West Berlin in November 1948 because of his love for his mistress, Elizabeth Werner. Using the alias Georg Muller, he had been accepted into the NTS where he had become a lecturer, touring CIA schools at Bad Woerishofen and Kaufbeuren. He had established his political credentials by denouncing a Soviet deserter, Sergeant Vasili Graburov, as a probable Soviet spy, and thereby had gained access to the NTS unit which supplied the CIA with agents. Graburov, of course, had been a mere pawn discarded deliberately by the Soviets to further Khorunsky's penetration of the CIA, and the scheme had worked exactly as intended. However, the NTS and the CIA had begun to suspect the presence of a mole when four parachutists had been captured in the Ukraine in April 1953 within hours of landing. The émigré volunteers – Aleksandr N. Makov, Sergei I. Gorbunov, Danil N. Remiga and the leader, Aleksandr V. Lakhno – had been arrested so quickly that betrayal had been the most obvious explanation. According to *Pravda*, all four had been executed by firing squad within a month of their arrival. Khokhlov's identification of Khorunsky as the mole revealed the source of the leak.

Having accepted Khokhlov as genuine, it was decided by Tracy Barnes of the CIA that the defector should attempt to persuade his two Moscow-trained co-conspirators, Kurt Weber and Hans Kurkovich, to defect as well. According to Khokhlov, both were committed communists but they were disillusioned with recent events following the death of Stalin in March 1953 and the arrest of Lavrenti Beria. He said the chief of their department, Lieutenant-General Pavel A. Sudoplatov, had been 'sacrificed to the machine' and the Soviet intelligence apparatus was undergoing a debilitating purge which was sapping the morale of the illegals, the elite that expected better treatment.

> The majority of both legal and illegal residencies were recalled to Moscow for consultation. Temporarily, at least, there could be no question of the creation of new illegal residencies. The whole country was holding its breath and waiting. The strategy pursued by the post-Stalin government was to remove from itself the stigma of the dead dictator. The 'collective leadership' adopted ingratiating tactics towards people . . . A series of official statements 'exposed' the crimes of the former MGB-MVD leadership, and declared that such evils would not recur. A purge of the 'organs of state security' was instigated, and hundreds of dismissed employees began to wander through other institutions seeking work. No matter by what methods Stalin's heirs were trying to earn popularity for themselves, all were equally haunted by the fearful ghost of a people's revolution. They were astute enough to realize that this ghost could not be laid by promises of butter and consumer goods, nor by dressing the MVD wolf in sheep's clothing. At this same time, Soviet intelligence was being reorganized. In the new structure more emphasis was placed on the struggle against anti-Soviet organizations, both within the USSR and abroad.[3]

Whereas, Khokhlov explained, some months earlier it had been intended that 'Sudaplatov's service should create an illegal centre for co-ordinating the work of all combat groups in Western Europe. Organized in a neutral country, this centre should be isolated from all other intelligence networks.' The new management had abandoned the project. Once likely to have gained considerable status within the KGB, Khokhlov and his fellow illegals, who regarded themselves as rather more than mere thugs, had been sidelined.[4]

A veteran of the Spanish Civil War, Weber was a life-long communist who had joined the French Resistance and developed a talent for forgery and the procurement of weapons. He had even run an underground printing press for the Maquis. In contrast, Kurkovich was an adventurer who had specialized in the elimination of Nazi collaborators. He too had fought with the French and had once been rescued from the Gestapo by Weber who had made bogus papers requiring his release from a prison hospital. At the end of the war both had trekked home. Kurkovich had settled down with a young widow in Potsdam and Weber had found a job as a clerk in a police station in Kopenik. According to Khokhlov, they were skilled and dangerous illegals, but they were also a little disenchanted. Escorted by the CIA to the prearranged rendezvous in Augsburg, where they were to collect some special weapons for the murder from a cache hidden by an Austrian businessman, Khokhlov met Weber and Kurkovich and offered them political asylum in the West. Both men agreed, and all three were accommodated in the CIA's compound at Oberursel where they were interviewed by American, British and French intelligence personnel. Together they gave damning accounts of the training they had undergone at Kuchino prior to their deployment for 'wet affairs' in the West. When their stories were later made public, the CIA released photographs of the ingeniously lethal weaponry with which they had been equipped by the KGB, including a silenced pistol and a miniature gun capable of firing three potassium-cyanide-tipped dumdum bullets from inside a container disguised as an ordinary cigarette case.

Despite the defections, for the following fortnight the KGB continued to believe that the three illegals were still at liberty in the West and, under the CIA's supervision, an operation was mounted in Vienna to entrap Khokhlov's handler, Lieutenant-Colonel Oleg Okun. This scheme had been made possible because Nikita Khorunsky, the KGB's mole in the NTS, had defected to the French in January, so the KGB had not been surprised at his disappearance. A former prisoner of war held by the British, Khorunsky had infiltrated the NTS and had used his wife and brother-in-law to act as couriers and smuggle messages hidden in chocolate bars to the KGB in the Russian Zone. The fact that Khorunsky's original confession had been less than complete, and had omitted much of the detail subsequently supplied by Khokhlov, ensured him a five-year prison sentence in the Federal Republic before he was exchanged in a spy-swap with the East in 1959. However, for the time being the KGB evidently had failed to notice that Khokhlov and his two companions had suddenly dropped from view, and this had provided the CIA with the opportunity to make a pitch to his controller, Oleg Okun. The proposal was to corner Okun and break the news to him that his entire network had come under the CIA's control, and offer him and his family resettlement as an alternative to enduring the KGB's wrath at what it would regard as his criminal incompetence. As well as losing Khorunsky, Khokhlov, Weber and Kurkovich, he would also be told that his only other source inside the NTS, a Russian émigré named Shmelyov, had been compromised. The *coup de grâce* was to be delivered by the Austrian who had smuggled Khokhlov's exotic weapons into Germany concealed inside a car battery. Khokhlov had identified him to the CIA and assured his new handlers that the wealthy former communist was ripe for recruitment as a double agent. However, when the businessman was approached in April, soon after his return from a visit to Switzerland, he declined to cooperate and warned Okun who was promptly recalled to Moscow. Khokhlov was almost suicidal at the failure of the operation as he believed that the KGB would now be bound to realize that he had defected, but in fact Okun had attributed his betrayal to the coincidental defection in Vienna of his close colleague Piotr Deriabin. Having abandoned any chance of ever seeing his wife and child again, Khokhlov was persuaded to make a public statement at a press conference in Bonn on 22 April about his mission to kill the NTS leadership, in the vain hope that his notoriety might help save his family in Moscow. In June, when he learned that his wife and child had been arrested, Khokhlov abandoned his plan of resettlement in America sponsored by the CIA and took up residence under a new identity in Switzerland.

To the CIA's dismay, the subsequent investigation prompted by the various leads provided by Khokhlov had revealed his Austrian passport to be authentic, and to have been issued to 'Josef Hofbauer' at the request of the Soviet occupation authorities, a development that suggested other Soviet illegals might also be equipped with genuine documentation from the same source, thereby making the task of Western security agencies all the more difficult. The CIA was equally appalled to learn from Khokhlov that his mission, codenamed Operation RHINE, had been personally authorized by the new head of the KGB's First Chief Directorate, Aleksandr S. Panyushkin, who had been appointed in June 1953. The defector recounted how he had been introduced to Panyushkin, 'a tall, lean man in a grey suit'. His face

> was deeply lined beyond his age. Pale to the point of greyness, his expression spoke of extremely poor health. It was a complexion such

> as miners or workers in lead plants have. The impression of ill-health was also created by his stooped manner of walking, as though he had no strength to carry himself straight. When he spoke, his voice sounded soft and hoarse.[5]

Panyushkin, who between 1947 and 1952 had been the Soviet ambassador in Washington DC, and who had also served as a diplomat in China, allegedly had personally supervised the development at the KGB's Kuchino workshops of the project to perfect Khokhlov's assassination tools. Another of Khokhlov's unlikely assertions, that Panyushkin had even been the legal *rezident* in America in 1949 and 1950, while simultaneously fulfilling his ambassadorial duties, was also to be confirmed soon afterwards by no fewer than four other defectors who were to cross the lines in the coming weeks: the Petrovs in Australia, Piotr Deriabin in Vienna and Yuri A. Rastvorov in Tokyo. This evidence amounted to undeniable proof, if any was still needed, that assassination and the deployment of illegals were effectively official Soviet policies, endorsed at the very highest level in the Kremlin. Nor, as subsequent events demonstrated, was this some temporary aberration.

The defection of Bogdan Stashinsky seven years later was prompted not by revulsion at his murder of the Ukrainian politician Stefan Bandera, whom he killed with an ingenious cyanide gas-gun in October 1959, but by his love for Inge Pohl, a young German hairdresser whom he married and who later persuaded him to surrender to the federal authorities. Originally a KGB informer around Lvov where he had been brought up, Stashinsky had operated as a low-level penetration agent targeted against local nationalists, and in particular the OUN resistance movement. His cover had survived until early in 1952 when the murderers of the Ukrainian writer Yaroslav Galan had been arrested on his tip-off. Regarded as a traitor by the nationalists, Galan had been assassinated by members of the OUN cell Stashinsky had cultivated, which effectively terminated the latter's future in Lvov.

As a consequence of the Galan murder, Stashinsky had been sent first to Kiev to learn German, and subsequently to Karlshorst for training as an illegal. There he adopted the authentic identity of Josef Lehrmann, a German born in Lukowek, Poland. Until January 1956, when he was entrusted with minor tasks in the West such as mailing letters, he built up his legend as a metalworker in Zwickau. On his first assignment he travelled to Munich to service a KGB mole, an émigré journalist on the Ukrainian anti-communist paper *Ukrainski Samostinik*. He was to hold four further meetings with the agent, supplying him with money and messages from his wife who was still in the Ukraine, until the strain became too much for the agent and he was repatriated in the late autumn of 1956. Stashinsky replaced this source by recruiting another on the same newspaper, using a combination of bribery and blackmail, for the agent received cash for his information and was left in no doubt that his wife and family in the Ukraine were vulnerable to reprisals.

In the spring of 1957 Stashinsky was given a new identity, that of Siegfried Drager from Rehbrucke near Potsdam, and, armed with his authentic identity card, was sent to Munich to watch Lev Rebet, the exiled Ukrainian nationalist leader. Stashinsky kept his quarry under almost continuous surveillance from April until 12 October when, armed with a specially designed weapon, he encountered Rebet outside his apartment and sprayed prussic acid into his face. By the time Stashinsky had returned to Karlshorst, his victim's body had been found and the cause of death declared to be a heart attack.

While preparing for his second assassination, that of the OUN leader Stefan Bandera, and under the influence of his German fiancée, Stashinsky had begun to lose his commitment to the cause but nevertheless he fired a second, double-barrelled gas-gun directly into Bandera's face outside his home in Munich on 15 October 1959. Like Rebet, Bandera inhaled a lethal dose of prussic acid and died. Once again, Stashinsky returned by train and air to Karlshorst and reported the success of the operation to his KGB handler. The following month he was summoned to Moscow where he was decorated with the Order of the Red Banner by Aleksandr N. Shelepin, the chairman of the KGB. He was also granted permission to marry Inge Pohl, which he did in Berlin in April 1960. Their baby son was born a year later but died in August, prompting Inge and Bogdan to evade their KGB escort and, on the day before the wall was erected, to flee to West Berlin where they surrendered to the German authorities.[6]

At his subsequent trial at Karlsruhe in October 1962, Stashinsky confessed to the murders of Rebet and Bandera, and received a sentence of eight years' imprisonment, but he was to be released after less than four, and resettled in the United States. Prompted by the disclosures made by Khokhlov and Stashinsky, the US Senate's internal security sub-committee held a lengthy investigation of the KGB, conducting hearings between 21 September 1960 and March 1965. It concluded that since 1926 the Soviets had participated in fifty-one incidents of abduction and assassination. While some of the testimony was based on hearsay, there was also later evidence from some impressive sources, among them Frantisek August, the Czech StB deputy *rezident* in Beirut who defected in August 1969. He recalled that when he had been posted to London one of the targets had been a well-known émigré anti-communist journalist and campaigner, and 'pressure was brought on Czech Intelligence . . . to organize the liquidation of Mr Josef Josten'.

> The Soviet advisers to the StB – with their massive experience of such operations – suggested exchanging the milk bottles at Josten's front door with ones filled with milk impregnated with polio bacteria. Another suggestion for disposing of the troublesome journalist was that an easily broken ampoule of toxic gas should be put under the rubber mat in his car. When he got into the car he would tread on the mat and so the released gas would kill him instantly. The British department of the StB turned down these Soviet suggestions.[7]

For many years Khokhlov and Stashinsky represented the best evidence from inside the KGB's assassination branch, and although subsequent defectors described the reorganization that had occurred in 1961 following the embarrassing disclosures, none had any detailed knowledge of precisely what followed. However, the situation was to change when a joint MI5–SIS team exploited an affair conducted by a relatively junior Soviet diplomat, Oleg Lyalin, with a Russian secretary, Irina Teplyakova. When offered resettlement and the opportunity to meet his mistress in safety, the thirty-four-year-old Lyalin consented to his recruitment and was milked for everything he knew, until the end of August 1971 when he was arrested by the police in London on a routine drink driving charge. This unanticipated and inconvenient development forced Lyalin's hand and he accepted MI5's protection for himself and his girlfriend. With Lyalin in custody, 105 expulsions were announced and it was left to the KGB to draw the clear implication that Lyalin had fingered every one of his colleagues, as well as three low-echelon KGB spies recruited in London. In truth, of course, the operation, codenamed FOOT, had been planned for more than seven months, and the fact that news of it had not leaked was a cause of tremendous satisfaction to the two British agencies.

Lyalin's defection was especially embarrassing to the Soviets because he was a member, albeit a relatively junior one, of a First Chief Directorate (FCD) section known as Department V. Apparently this highly secret branch had been created in the aftermath of the defections of Khokhlov and Stashinsky, who had revealed the homicidal purpose of the Thirteenth Department of the FCD. The disclosure of the existence of a unit dedicated to assassination within the KGB, confirmed by two of its members, was intensely awkward, so during the KGB's reorganization in 1968/69 the Thirteenth Department had been abolished and its staff of around fifty officers transferred to Department V, a new section created with a broader role, encompassing sabotage, and placed within the illegals branch, designated Directorate S, under the personal authority of the chairman, Yuri V. Andropov. Its principal function was to plan disruption in target countries so that in the event of hostilities a fifth column of agents could be mobilized by radio to strike at the heart of government and create chaos.

Lyalin's own contingency plans for war seemed far-fetched, for he had been given responsibility, as the Department V representative in the London *rezidentura*, to draw up lists of leading figures for assassination, and to survey various sensitive military sites in England, including the early-warning radar installations at Fylingdales in North Yorkshire and nuclear bomber dispersal airfields, for sudden attack by Soviet *Spetsnaz* special forces. Lyalin's first-hand confirmation that the KGB still sponsored such activities was to cause acute political embarrassment in the Kremlin, and to prevent any further complications all Department V personnel were withdrawn from the field and Department V was abolished. Created in its place was the Eighth Department of Directorate S, which was henceforth restricted to a planning and training role, dispersing the officers with operational experience among the directorate's four geographical departments.

The expulsions announced in September 1971 hit the KGB hard. The *rezident*, Yuri Voronin, happened to be at home in Moscow at the time, but as his name was on the list he, like nine others, was banned from ever returning to London. Indeed, MI5's coup was so complete that Leonid A. Rogov, a minor official attached to the Soviet trade delegation, was the only person left in London to fulfil the role of acting *rezident*. The expulsions caught the KGB unprepared, and Lyalin's disclosures, although not on the same scale as those of Khokhlov and Stashinsky, led to a further reassessment of how the KGB could conduct deniable operations.

Curiously, it was Khokhlov who unwittingly reopened the debate within the KGB about 'wet affairs' when his new identity and address in San Bernardino, California, was discovered and reported to Yuri Andropov, accompanied by a request for permission to execute the death warrant issued by the Military Collegium of the Supreme Soviet. However, Andropov refused to sanction the murder, saying 'it was a long time ago . . . but bring me Lyalin or Nosenko and that's different'. Accordingly, Khokhlov's life was spared, although he was unaware of it. The precedent for Andropov's uncharacteristic clemency had been the interception of mail addressed to Evdokia Petrov's relations which had enabled the KGB to track her and her husband, Vladimir, in Australia. The Petrovs had defected in April 1954 and ASIO had given them the identity of Greek immigrants, but Evdokia's carelessness had allowed their cover to be compromised. For unknown reasons, the KGB had decided not to pursue them.

Andropov's preference for having Lyalin and Nosenko killed was understandable. Lyalin had inflicted catastrophic damage on the First Chief Directorate, and had wrecked the career of his *rezidentura*'s chief of counter-intelligence, Konstantin Zotov, who had known of his affair but had turned a blind eye to it. Zotov had been fired from the KGB and found a post in the passport bureau, but dozens of others in the British department had been compromised and their prospects handicapped. Similarly, Yuri Nosenko was an obvious target, not so much for the quality of information he had betrayed, but rather because he had been one of the privileged elite, his father having been minister of shipbuilding. His defection had been a huge embarrassment for his family and the *nomenklatura*, which explains Andropov's wrath.

What remains unexplained are two fundamental contradictions: if Andropov had drawn the line at authorizing the murder of Khokhlov, why would he have approved of the Pope's assassination (assuming for a moment that this is indeed what happened)? And second, if the DS was entirely subordinate to the KGB, could it have acted alone, without Andropov's knowledge?

On the first issue, we can detect an element of political expediency. Andropov was not opposed to the principle of assassination, but he drew the line at an operation that could be traced directly to Moscow. Only the KGB would have had the means and the motive to track down Khokhlov to his retirement home and kill him, and such an event would have precipitated a massive, predictable response from the FBI and CIA. He once had cancelled a plan, at a very late stage, to have the PLO's director of intelligence, Hani Hassan, abduct a CIA officer in Amman on the grounds that the Americans would quickly learn of the KGB's involvement. The target, who worked under diplomatic cover in the military attaché's office, never realized how close he had come to being seized off the street and interrogated at length. Similarly, it is now known that in May 1970 Andropov obtained Brezhnev's personal approval for a daring plan to abduct the CIA deputy station chief in Beirut, take him to Damascus and then have him flown to Moscow for interrogation. Codenamed VIR, the target was to be grabbed off the street by a team led by Dr Wadi Haddad, Dr George Habash's deputy in the PFLP. According to the defector Vasili Mitrokhin, Haddad was a KGB agent codenamed NATSIONALIST and the plan called for his men to ambush VIR while he was walking his dog close to his apartment. He would be drugged with a chemical prepared by the KGB's Department V and then driven into Syria where he would be handed over to KGB personnel at a rendezvous near Zabadani. The scheme's merit was that:

> Palestinian guerrilla organizations have recently stepped up their activities in Lebanon against American intelligence and its agents, [so] the Lebanese authorities and the Americans would suspect Palestinians of carrying out the above operation. The ultimate purpose of the operation would be known only to NATSIONALIST, on the foreign side, and to the KGB officers directly involved in planning the operation, and carrying it out, on the Soviet side.[8]

Andropov assured Brezhnev that, by using the PFLP as surrogates, the KGB would escape suspicion. According to Oleg Kalugin, the scheme was aborted the day before it was due to take place when Andropov developed cold feet and feared the CIA might retaliate, thus leading to a bloody conflict between the two espionage services.

On the other hand, Andropov had personally approved of the Bulgarian scheme to kill the dissident journalist Georgi Markov in London, although he had imposed a condition that the KGB's involvement should be limited to logistical help in constructing the weapon and training the required personnel. The argument on that occasion was that to refuse Todor Zhivkov's request for assistance in disposing of the troublesome and vocal dissident might be misinterpreted in Sofia as weakness. Quite what the excuse was for assisting in the attempt on Vladimir Kostov, who was probably completely unknown to Zhivkov, is uncertain. Formerly a well-known author, Kostov had been recruited by the DS in 1968 but while under journalistic cover in Paris, had defected in June 1977. On 26 August the following year he was shot with a poisoned pellet while riding a metro escalator, but survived the attack and gave his Western debriefers a compelling account of the relationship between the KGB and the two principal Bulgarian intelligence agencies, the DS and its military equivalent, RUMNO.

> Among leading members of the DS were a number of Soviet secret service officers of Bulgarian origin. Quite clearly, they applied in Bulgaria practices they had learnt during their service in the Soviet Union. In addition the DS included on its strength dozens of Soviet counsellors. In periods of tension or serious incident, reinforcements arrived immediately from Moscow and from the Soviet Embassy in Sofia. These counsellors kept a close watch on the activities of the DS at every level of decision. Soviet counsellors were at the elbow of every department head. Consequently the KGB knew in detail every file dealt with by the DS.[9]

Under lengthy interrogation, Kostov revealed that the DS had credited Yuri Andropov with the integration of the Soviet and Bulgarian services:

> The work, masterminded by Andropov, followed in two main directions: first, the establishment of a network of officers of double allegiance (one, official and open, in various sectors of the executive and administrative apparatus of the Communist Party; the other, unofficial and hidden, in the Secret Service); second, the extension of the policy of integration between the secret services of the USSR and those of the other socialist countries.[10]

Certainly, Andropov himself was entirely ruthless, as he had demonstrated when he was Soviet ambassador in Budapest in 1956, having taken a personal hand in the various deceptions involved to call in Soviet troops to suppress the Hungarian uprising. On the night of 3 November he had coolly assured Prime Minister Imre Nagy that the Red Army was being withdrawn, whereas in fact it was being reinforced from outside the country. Accompanying Andropov in Budapest at that time was Vladimir Kryuchkov, later the long-serving chief of the KGB's First Chief Directorate, and then Andropov's choice to head the entire organization. Andropov's ruthlessness in Budapest established his reputation. Nagy, for example, sought asylum in the Yugoslav embassy, and left three weeks later only after having received a guarantee of safe conduct. As soon as he emerged from the building he was seized by the KGB, and eighteen months later, on 15 June 1958, he was executed. Similarly, the commander of the Hungarian National Guard, Major-General Bela Kiraly, was invited by Andropov to bring his military leadership to a meeting at the Soviet base at Tokol on Csepel Island. Once the coup began, the KGB burst into the Hungarians' room and arrested the entire Hungarian delegation. The minister of defence, General Pal Maleter, was executed, but Budapest's police chief, Colonel Sandor Kopasci, was luckier. He too was summoned by Andropov and informed that Janos Kador had formed a new administration and wished to see Kopasci. The armoured car that was supposed to take Kopasci to Kador took him straight to prison, where he remained for the next seven years.

Kryuchkov had also played a key role in the Soviet invasion of Afghanistan, over Christmas 1979, during which the KGB, supported by GRU Spetsnaz troops, had surrounded the Duralamin Palace in Kabul and killed the American-educated President Hafizmullah

Amin. Once again, Andropov was heavily involved in the invasion, and, as documents released a decade later demonstrated, was one of the four members of the politburo who authorized it on 12 December, the others being Brezhnev himself, Foreign Minister Andrei Gromyko, and Defence Minister Dmitri Ustinov. As the elite 105th Guards Air Assault Division landed in Kabul and Bagram, and four motorized rifle divisions poured over the Oxus river, two battalions of paratroops fought their way into the palace complex and took control while, on 27 December, the KGB and Spetsnaz teams put Amin and his supporters up against a wall and shot them. The assassination plot, codenamed AGATE, was first disclosed by the KGB defector Vladimir Kuzichkin, himself an experienced Directorate S officer, who revealed that an Azerbaijani illegal, Mikhail Talybov, had been infiltrated into the palace as a chef with instructions to poison Amin's food, but the opportunity never arose. After Brezhnev had approved a full-scale invasion, the head of Directorate S, Vadim V. Kirpichenko, flew into Kabul to supervise the operation, together with the head of Department 8, Vladimir Krasovsky, and his deputy, Aleksandr Lazarenko. Unexpectedly, the Alpha and Zenith special forces, which had practised for weeks at the KGB's training centre at Balashikha, encountered much stronger resistance than had been anticipated and more than a hundred of the elite troops perished in the firefight, among them the leader of the main assault, Colonel Grigori Boyarinov. Kryuchkov's instructions, which must have been authorized by Brezhnev and Andropov, had been to kill Amin and install in his place Babrak Kamal, the Afghan Communist Party's leader, and the plan was executed with ruthless efficiency, despite the heavy loss of life.

As for the general principle of assassination, the KGB's former chief of counter-intelligence, General Oleg Kalugin, says only that:

> [B]y the late 1970s, the KGB had virtually stopped pulling off 'wet jobs', but had retained the services of Sergei M. Golubev of the Operational and Technical Directorate, who ran the *Kamera*, also known as Laboratory 12, which had been created by Stalin to devise methods of eliminating enemies. [Golubev's unit] invented new ways of killing people, from poisons that could be slipped into drinks to jellies that could be rubbed on a person to induce a heart attack.[11]

Allegedly, one such toxin was used against Alexander Solzhenitsyn 'in a store in Russia in the early 1970s, making him violently ill but not killing him'. It had been Golubev, assisted by Yuri Surov, the officer in charge of tracking down KGB defectors, who had gone to Sofia to assist in the DS's scheme to trace and eliminate Markov in London, where he was a broadcaster for the BBC's World Service. Initially this had proved unsuccessful; they opted against treating the handle of his car door with the toxin for fear of killing his girlfriend, and thereby alerting him to the threat; they were unable to smear the poison jelly on Markov while he was at a beach resort in Italy; and they failed to tamper with his food during a trip to Germany. They finally selected the novel method of shooting Markov with a tiny pellet containing a lethal quantity of ricin, and did this in September 1978 as the Bulgarian dissident was walking across Waterloo Bridge, not far from the BBC's World Service headquarters at Bush House. He was shot in the leg by an assassin using a gun disguised as an American-manufactured umbrella, and he succumbed in hospital a few days later, his doctors baffled by his symptoms. By the time the microscopic pellet had been recovered from Markov's thigh, and the ricin discovered, it was too late. Only Oleg Kalugin has acknowledged the KGB's complicity in the Markov assassination, although it is worth noting that when General Ivan T. Savchenko, who was the KGB *rezident* in Sofia between 1969 and 1980, was asked about the Markov case and the subsequent disappearance of Markov's DS file, he replied that its destruction 'would be a completely unprofessional action . . . Such a file would never contain either a murder plan or the names of the killers. Such things are never put down in writing. The standing KGB rule is that if a political removal is planned, it is known of by no more than three people.'[12] Savchenko denies that he ever saw any document relating to the Markov murder, or heard any discussion about it, and makes the improbable claim that the dissident was killed by a Western intelligence agency. Nevertheless, he acknowledges a KGB policy on 'political removal'. Thus Oleg Kalugin is the only witness to the Soviet–Bulgarian collaboration in the Markov assassination willing to speak candidly about the episode. His testimony is compelling, for he attended a meeting chaired by Andropov in which was discussed a request for assistance made by the DS's chief, General Stoyan Savov. Also present were

Vladimir Kryuchkov, as head of the FCD, and his deputy, Vice Admiral Mikhail Usatov, who approved Golubev's assignment in Sofia, so there can be no doubt that there was official sanction for the scheme. There does remain, however, some doubt about the DS's motive. According to General Vlado Todorov, who in 1978 was the DS's deputy chief of foreign intelligence with responsibility for operations in Western Europe, Markov had been a DS agent who had been 'turned' by the British. Speaking from his Moscow apartment, where he took up residence with his Russian wife in May 1991 following a police investigation of the Markov case, Todorov asserted that Markov had reported to the DS 'about his work for the BBC and Radio Free Europe'. Two Bulgarian journalists, Vladimir Bereanu and Kalin Todorov, who investigated the Markov case, have concluded that there was indeed KGB complicity, pointing out that Vlado Todorov's last promotion within the DS had been sanctioned by Savchenko's successor as KGB *rezident*, Vladilen Fyodorov.[13]

With the installation of a democratic government in Sofia, there were several attempts, including two parliamentary commissions, to investigate the DS's misconduct, but they were doomed to failure because of the lack of documentary evidence, most of the archives having been burned as the Zhivkov regime collapsed. General Todorov, having been convicted of destroying files, acknowledged that there had been four large volumes of a dossier on Georgi Markov, but only a single paper ordering their destruction survived. He was sentenced to sixteen months and began his imprisonment in June 1992. His immediate superior in the DS, General Stoyan Savov, who had deputy minister rank and headed the DS from 1972 until March 1989, committed suicide on 9 January 1992, two days after he had been served a court summons regarding the Markov case. Although he left three letters, none explained why he had killed himself, leaving his precise motive open to doubt. Was he seeking to avoid the Markov investigation, or did he have good reason to fear more extensive inquiries, including those being made into the DS's knowledge of the attempt on the Pope's life? The answer was probably known to Colonel General Dimiter Stoyanov, minister of the interior between 1973 and 1989, and member of the politburo, who died in November 1999. He was in overall charge of the political direction of the DS, and was certainly behind the ruthless campaign to rid the country of its ethnic Turks, a charge that he flatly denied in his unrepentant 1997 autobiography. As for the attempt on the Pope's life, no new evidence has materialized to implicate the DS, leaving an international committee of inquiry and an investigation conducted by the new government's Ministry of Internal Affairs to conclude that there was no DS complicity.

The DS's attacks on Kostov and Markov were far from isolated cases, and the organization had a considerable history of intervention in the lives of Zhivkov's opponents overseas. Boris Arsov, editor of the émigré newspaper *Levski*, which he published in Denmark, was seized at his flat in Aarhus and placed on trial in Sofia, where he was sentenced to fifteen years' imprisonment. A newspaper report of his conviction seemed to confirm the DS's involvement, commenting: 'Arsov was playing with fire. The timely intervention of the State Security stopped his dangerous activity. This only shows that the hand of justice is longer than the legs of the traitor.' A year later, in 1975, it was announced that he had been found dead in his cell. In a similar episode in September 1975 three exiled Bulgarians, – Peter Nezamov, Ivan Kolev and Vesselina Stoyova – who were known to organize Bulgarian defections, were shot dead in Vienna. Their murderer, identified by the Austrian police as Stoyan Stefanov, the group's leader, successfully escaped to Sofia. Another defector, Suyko Srednoridski, who was a rocket technician, disappeared from his lodgings in Vienna where he was waiting for an American visa. He was visited by a man calling himself Boris, and the pair were never seen again.

The KGB consistently has taken the view that Agca was a lone madman, and that if anyone was likely to be a candidate for killing the Pope it would have been a Polish communist fanatic. As for a plot, the Kremlin line has been that Agca was probably working for a Western 'special service' because he was known to have been associated with the right-wing Grey Wolves. However, bearing in mind Andropov's ambivalent attitude to assassination, we cannot easily accept Oleg Kalugin's self-serving assertion that the KGB played no part in the plot, and neither did the DS. One possibility considered by the CIA was that the Ukrainian KGB, under the leadership since 1970 of the ruthless hard-liner Vitali V. Fedorchuk, might have orchestrated the assassination bid unilaterally from Kiev. Individual national KGBs had the right to conduct foreign operations if there was a compelling reason to do so, and Fedorchuk, one of Brezhnev's closest supporters, was sufficiently senior to know how Moscow would have reacted to any formal documentation on the topic. Indeed, for a brief period, between May and December 1982, he was to be chairman of the KGB, a post he was obliged to surrender to Viktor Chebrikov when Brezhnev died.

On the question of whether the DS could have acted independently of the KGB, the issue is unresolved. General Kalugin, who travelled to Sofia 'on numerous occasions in the 1970s', acknowledged that the local *rezident*, General Savchenko, 'virtually ran Bulgaria's secret services; no general in Bulgarian Intelligence or in the Interior Ministry dared to do anything of consequence without first picking up the telephone and checking with Savchenko',[14] so it would seem unlikely that the DS could or would plan such a momentous operation without the KGB's knowledge if not active participation. This leaves open the possibility of either a rogue scheme devised by mavericks or that perennial expedient, plausible deniability. Of the two, the latter sounds more likely. Certainly there was plenty of suspicion about both the KGB's willingness to acquiesce in assassinations, and the ability of their surrogates to indulge in murder.

One significant target over many years was Radio Free Europe (RFE), long regarded as a dangerous irritant in the East, and especially by Nicolai Ceausescu and Janos Kador. No fewer than three directors of RFE's Romanian broadcast service died of ailments that could have been artificially induced: Noel Bernard contracted a virulent form of lung cancer and died in December 1983; his successor, Mihai Cismarescu, died in February 1984; and Vladimir Georgescu succumbed to a short illness in November 1988. According to the DIE's former acting director, General Ion Pacepa, Ceausescu had often railed against 'the chatterbox', which is what he called RFE, and had advocated introducing highly toxic radioactive dust known as 'radu' into Bernard's office, supposedly a sure method of getting a target to ingest a deadly carcinogen. The dictator had also ordered the then head of the DIE, General Nicolae Doicaru, to kill a Romanian émigré newsman at RFE

> who had dared to criticize Ceausescu's cult of personality. When he finished giving the order, Ceausescu stopped in front of Doicaru and grabbed his lapels. 'I never want to talk about this again,' he whispered, staring Doicaru in the eye. 'You don't even have to report back to me when he's killed. Let the Western press do that.'[15]

Ion Pacepa was the most authoritative insider to describe the Eastern bloc's links to terrorism, and his sudden defection in Bonn at the end of July 1978 led to far-reaching consequences for the DIE, which was dismantled by the domestic Securitate two months later. Dozens of overseas DIE personnel working under trade or diplomatic cover were withdrawn to Bucharest and a dozen senior officers were arrested on Ceausescu's orders. Twenty-two ambassadors were demoted, including the Romanian ambassador in Washington DC, himself an undercover DIE colonel, who was recalled and imprisoned. Pacepa, who had spent his entire career in first the Securitate and then since May 1955 in the DIE, having been recruited at the age of twenty-two, was easily the most senior Eastern bloc intelligence officer to switch sides, and brought with him a veritable treasure trove of information, including the first details of Romania's secret treaty to exchange ballistic missile research, nuclear technology and even plutonium with Islamabad. This latter disclosure was to lead the Carter administration to suspend aid to Pakistan.

During his debriefing by the CIA, which was to last three years, Pacepa gave a detailed account of how Leonid Brezhnev had decided to support international terrorism. He recalled that in July 1973 he had been informed by Ceausescu that:

> [T]he Kremlin had come to the conclusion that in the nuclear age, when the open use of Soviet military force was greatly restricted, the Soviet Union and its allies should throw the full weight of their support toward international terrorism, for the purpose of creating domestic chaos in the West and thereby facilitating the export of the Communist revolution there.
>
> Brezhnev had decided that the Soviet camp should provide secret help to the West European, Palestinian and other terrorist organizations that were engaged in fighting imperialism. The Soviet leader had called the members of those terrorist organizations 'freedom

> fighters', and their international terrorism 'armed struggle'. The KGB would assume the most difficult tasks, those of providing the terrorist organizations with specialist paramilitary training and false passports. The Czechoslovakian foreign intelligence service would supply them with an odorless plastic explosive that could not be detected by sniffer dogs at airports and other border points. The Cubans would mass-produce concealment devices for transporting the plastic explosive into the target countries. The East Germans would develop remote-controlled electronic detonators for the plastic explosive. The DIE's role in the new joint venture was to reproduce the Western immigration and border stamps needed for the false passports supplied by the PGU to various international terrorist organizations and groups. I was not surprised by the Kremlin's new policy.[16]

Pacepa described a 'Group Z' that had been created in the 1950s, under Soviet supervision, as a *Spetsbyuro*, dedicated to 'neutralizing' the Party's enemies. The letter 'Z' had been chosen because it is 'the final letter of the alphabet – representing the final solution':

> Every punishment operation abroad – that was what this form of terrorism was called – had to be approved by the supreme party leader, because of the potential for political and diplomatic complications. These operations were usually carried out 'under Western flag,' that is, the persons involved were to pose as Western citizens, in order to prevent attribution to any bloc country. Intelligence officers under diplomatic cover involved in a terrorist operation in the West, other than the perpetrator himself, should usually be left in place for a time afterward, in accordance with the KGB principle that withdrawal meant admission of guilt. Assassinations and kidnappings abroad should be kept forever secret. In spite of the Communists' usual penchant for bureaucracy, these cases were to be handled strictly orally, were never to be committed to paper, and had to be kept totally secret from the politburo or any other collective body in the Communist top management – they were to be reported only to the party leader himself. These matters were also never to be discussed in any place where there was the slightest chance of being overheard. After each 'punishment', the bloc services were surreptitiously to spread 'evidence' in the West accusing the

> CIA or other handy 'enemies' of having done the deed, thereby if possible killing two birds with one stone. Regardless of the evidence, no bloc service was ever to acknowledge its involvement in assassinations and kidnappings abroad – the evidence was to be simply dismissed as a ridiculous accusation.[17]

In view of the fact that Pacepa defected almost three years before the attempt on the life of the Pope, it might reasonably be asked whether his testimony is even remotely relevant to that episode. Certainly, one particular recollection seems germane:

> In the early 1970s, the Soviet bloc intelligence community started recruiting foreign professional criminals to carry out terrorist operations abroad, in order to make it even more difficult for Western counter-intelligence investigators to attribute the operations to communist governments. The Spanish communists, who for years were exiled to France, proved to be particularly adept at providing French smugglers and drug dealers. One such French smuggler, who had run foul of Interpol, was granted asylum in Bucharest. When he arrived, he was carrying so many false passports that he could not prove his real name. Codenamed SANDU, he and two accomplices started a new life in Romania. At the time I had defected, they had already been sent to France and West Germany on several terrorist missions.[18]

Pacepa had visited Libya with his minister of the interior to discuss cooperation and, after a ten-hour wait in Colonel Gadaffi's tented anteroom, agreed an arrangement in which the DIE undertook to supply blank passports and intelligence about suitable targets in the West. After their initial four days in Tripoli, Doicaru had reported personally to Vladimir Kryuchkov in Moscow, describing how the Libyans had accumulated the current passport details of more than a million foreigners, mainly Egyptians and Tunisians, who worked locally as expatriates, and every visitor for the past five years. Under the agreement, the Libyans produced the personal data, 'the Soviets manufactured blank Western and Arab passports, and the DIE supplied them with the necessary false entry and exit stamps from all around the world'. Soon they began

> making periodic visits to Bucharest accompanied by small teams of Libyan officers who specialized in providing cover passports for every Libyan intelligence organization involved in terrorist operations abroad. The group never returned to Libya with fewer than a dozen false Arab and Western passports, some of them already complete with the name and photograph of the new owner and all the visas needed for him to enter his target country.[19]

According to Pacepa, the terrorist attack on the OPEC meeting in Vienna in December 1975 by 'Carlos the Jackal' was based entirely on information supplied by the DIE from a source inside the Austrian police who had handed over the building blueprints and details of the protection scheme. Thus the incident which established Carlos's reputation as an international terrorist had been sponsored by Colonel Gadaffi and indirectly implicated Romania and the KGB.

The KGB's willingness to participate directly in terrorism seemed, until early 1985, to be lukewarm, but in that year the CIA's Bonn station was approached by a KGB officer, Gennadi Varenik, who had stolen $7,000 from the local *rezidentura*. Terrified of the consequences, Varenik, who was the son of a senior KGB officer, had offered to spy in return for sufficient money to cover the loss, and in April had disclosed details of a KGB contingency plan which contemplated planting bombs in certain restaurants near US military bases with the objective of creating the impression that the Germans wanted the Allied occupation forces to leave the country, and undermining US-German relations. Horrified that the KGB could develop such a scheme, Varenik had sold the information to the CIA, and in October had volunteered to defect with his wife and two daughters so as to expose the plot which he believed was about to be implemented. However, Varenik was arrested in East Berlin soon afterwards, his name having been betrayed by Aldrich Ames (see Chapter IX).

The extent to which Moscow actively encouraged, tolerated or underwrote terrorist organizations was to become clearer at the conclusion of the Cold War when examination of Stasi files revealed the close relationship between the HVA and the Red Army Faction, whose members were found living under official protection and sponsorship in East Germany. The Stasi had also played a passive role in terrorism by allowing Berlin's Schonefeld airport to be used by fugitives as well as by standing by as attacks on targets in the Western sectors were planned and executed. Similarly, DIE files revealed in 1992 by Romania's newly created Serviciul Roman de Informatii (SRI), headed by Virgil Magureanu, showed that Ceausescu had attempted unsuccessfully to persuade Carlos to kill the hated defector Ion Pacepa. The Securitate had concluded that Carlos was far too unreliable to entrust with such a delicate assignment, but nevertheless continued to give him and his terrorists sanctuary, and to contract him to undertake less sensitive hits. For example, while he was staying in a safe house in the centre of Bucharest in January 1981, the Securitate employed Carlos to kill several of Nicolai Ceausescu's émigré opponents, including the former interior minister, Nicolae Penescu, and the writer Paul Goma, both of whom were living in Paris. They received parcel bombs, and the eighty-five-year-old Penescu's hands and face were badly injured, although both men escaped death, as did three other candidates for assassination.

Scrutiny of intelligence files in East Berlin and Budapest revealed that Carlos, who had attended (and been expelled from) the Patrice Lumumba University in Moscow, had frequently travelled across the Soviet bloc under the sponsorship of first the Iraqis and then the Yemenis and Syrians, who had all provided him and his subordinates with diplomatic passports. However, not a single dossier on Carlos ever showed him to have had any direct contact with the KGB, and there is some evidence that the Hungarians and East Germans in particular grew increasingly cautious about handling such a volatile commodity. The declassified files reveal, for example, that when Carlos took up residence in a rented villa on Budapest's exclusive Vend Street in May 1979 he had been placed under surveillance by the AVH's Colonel Joszef Varga. The AVH chief, General Miklos Redei, had asked the KGB *rezident* in Budapest, General Aleksandr A. Koszov, for advice, but none had been forthcoming. Finally, in April 1981, Colonel Andreas Petresevics had been given the task of asking Carlos and his principal lieutenant, Johannes Weinrich, to move on, and they switched to the Palast Hotel in Berlin where they were assigned a Stasi handler, Colonel Helmut Voigt of the HVA's Department XXII. The East Germans were also to become exasperated by Carlos but were reluctant to move against him as he had powerful Arab protection. They monitored his visits to Moscow, but Markus Wolf, then head of the HVA, acknowledged that Carlos was never a KGB asset, asserting that the organization 'would not have recruited him at a time when he was an active terrorist. Such a move would have been a very great danger for the KGB.'[20]

When in February 1984 Weinrich and another of Carlos's men, Ali Al-Issawa, who was a Syrian intelligence officer, boasted of their KGB connections, the Stasi asked for details from Moscow, but the request went unanswered. However, when the HVA reported that their sources inside the West German government had disclosed that the BND had acquired full details of the facilities made available to Carlos by the Stasi, including the damaging fact that they had supplied Issawa with the Nitropenta explosives with which to bomb the French consulate in August the previous year, Carlos was told he was no longer welcome. By then Bucharest had become increasingly hostile to Carlos, and in April 1985 the Czech StB announced that he was now banned from Prague, thus forcing the self-styled master terrorist to seek sanctuary in the Hotel Frantel in the South Yemeni capital of Aden. Weinrich and Issawa were expelled from Bucharest in September, after the pair had been rejected by Hungary, leaving the group to find a safe haven in a smart apartment block in the Mezzeh district of Damascus, where they were to remain until September 1991 when even President Assad's patience wore out.

Chapter IV

The Target

Karol Wojtyla was born on 18 May 1920 in Wadowice, close to what is now the Polish frontier with Czechoslovakia, and spent the war working as a labourer in a chemical plant and quarry, his university studies having been interrupted by the Nazi occupation. However, in October 1942 he began attending part-time an underground seminary organized by Cardinal Adam Saphieha, the Archbishop of Krakow, and hid in his palace as the Germans retreated. At the end of the war he resumed his theology course at the newly re-opened Jagellonian University and witnessed first-hand the Soviet occupation. Ordained in September 1946, Wojtyla travelled to Rome to take a doctorate at the Angelicum College, working for Catholic war relief across Europe in his spare time, and did not return to Poland until 1948 when he was appointed parish priest in a village close to the Soviet border. Within ten years he was Professor of Ethics at Lublin University and at the age of thirty-eight was the youngest of Poland's eighty bishops, and the author of *Love and Responsibility*, then a highly controversial and innovative study of sexual ethics. In 1967, in a period of unprecedented conflict between the Church and Edward Gomulka's regime, he was appointed cardinal, and was swift to condemn the bloody massacres of striking shipyard workers in Gdansk and Gdynia in December 1970. When he was appointed to the permanent council of the Rome Synod of Bishops the following year, he was committed to confronting communist atheism and set on a course of opposing the Vatican's long-established conciliatory stance of *Ostpolitik*, reaching accommodations with the regimes of Eastern Europe. He began meeting radical anti-communists, including the entire leadership of the Committee to Defend the Workers (KOR) opposition which he met in the apartment of the writer Bohdan Cywinski, having travelled to Warsaw in plain clothes. The KOR had been created by Jarek Kuron and other ex-Marxists, including the nationalists Antoni Macierewicz and Jan Jozef Lipski. KOR was not a political party, but was intended to be a movement committed to campaigning for human rights in the certainty that Marxism had failed. Word spread of Wojtyla's implicit support of the KOR and when Stanislaw Pyjas, a young philosophy student and KOR political activist, was murdered by the SB in Krakow, Wojtyla said a mass for him which was attended by an estimated 20,000 people, and then assigned to the movement that Pyjas inspired, the Student Solidarity Committee (SKS), a special chaplain. Wojtyla also incurred the regime's wrath when, following the strikes and riots of June 1976 caused by Premier Piotr Jaroszewicz's announcement of rises in the price of some basic foods, the archbishop started a fund to support the protestors who had been imprisoned and injured. Whereas some clerics had reached a *modus vivendi* with the supposedly atheist state, Wojtyla clearly was not among them, although he had been criticized for not being sufficiently vocal in condemning some state-sponsored excesses, including anti-Semitism.

Wojtyla's election as Pope in October 1978, the first non-Italian for 457 years, was wholly unexpected, not least because the previous pontiff, Albino Luciani, lived for just thirty-three days as Pope John Paul I before dying alone in controversial circumstances, apparently of a massive heart attack. Although the actual election, conducted in the Sistine Chapel, is supposed to be entirely secret upon pain of excommunication, Wojtyla was never an obvious favourite. Of the 110 cardinals present, allegedly only five voted for him on the first ballot, with Cardinal Giovanni Benelli of Florence establishing an early and clear lead. By the following morning, apparently after a night of reflection and prayer, the frail Archbishop of Milan, Giovanni Colombo, withdrew, leaving the field open for the fifth ballot in which Wojtyla's support, organized by Cardinal Koenig of Vienna, increased to around forty, but with Benelli maintaining a massive lead of seventy, just five short of the number required. On the next ballot Benelli peaked at fifty-nine, and on the seventh, after lunch on the second day of the Conclave, he was overtaken. At the eighth and final vote Wojtyla secured an overwhelming ninety-seven, and was proclaimed the Bishop of Rome and leader of more than seven hundred million baptized Catholics, the largest religion on earth. Predictably, Wojtyla broke with tradition by calling for champagne and leading his supporters in singing Polish songs. As a keen hiker and skier, Wojtyla certainly enjoyed the advantage of relative youth (although Benelli was only a year older) and was hugely fit compared to his two predecessors. The arthritic Paul VI had been beset by chronic medical problems throughout his fifteen-year papacy, and John Paul I had endured appalling circulation and painful phlebitis in his legs. On doctrinal issues Wojtyla was also a safe bet, having written prodigiously on almost every ethical topic imaginable. Copies of all his work were available for scrutiny in the Curia Library, and would have been of particular interest to the conservatives who might have been expected to support Benelli. In Poland, the bishops ordered church bells to be rung across the country, and sent him a telegram of congratulation quoting a Polish poem that had been written 138 years earlier:

In the midst of time of confusion and dissention in the church,
God will send a man who will clarify the confusion,
Sweep the sanctuaries and make clear the truth of God.
See he comes, the Slavic Pope.

Wojtyla had acquired impressive anti-communist credentials and had also developed strong international contacts: he had spent much time at the Vatican during the early 1960s, and had visited the United States for the first time in 1969 when he stayed with the Polish-born Cardinal Krol of Philadelphia; he had also toured Canada, Australia and the Far East, and showed absolutely no signs of intending to become a 'prisoner' of the Vatican. On the contrary, he acted swiftly to transform the power exercised from the Pontiff's twenty-room private apartment on the third floor of the fifteenth-century Apostolic Palace. The so-called Irish mafia, which had run so much of the Vatican for so long, was replaced by forty Polish priests and nuns who reported to his private secretary, Father Dziwisz, and his housekeeper and confidante, Sister Tobiana, Mother Superior of the Congregation of the Heart of Jesus. He also brought in his own private physician, Dr Mieczyslaw Wyslocki and, perhaps to provide some continuity, he retained as his other secretary Father John Magee, originally a missionary priest from Newry, County Down, who had served Paul VI and John Paul I in the same capacity. Most worrying from Moscow's viewpoint was a crucial change in the Secretariat, with the appointment of Andris Backis from Lithuania as the new Pontiff's special adviser on relations with the Eastern bloc. Backis's father had been Lithuania's prewar ambassador to France, and the KGB feared that he would be instinctively 'anti-Soviet'. Moscow also interpreted one of John Paul II's first acts, his decision to send his red cardinal's skullcap to Ostrabrama, the Marian shrine in Vilnius, to be placed on display on the altar of the church of the Virgin of Mary, as an overtly hostile act, and an ominous portent of the future.

The new Pope's initial instinct to break with convention was to become his hallmark, and his determination to avoid being cooped up inside the Vatican was quickly apparent. His first departure, by helicopter on 29 October, was to the Marian shrine at Mentorella, one of his favourite places of worship, and a visit replete with symbolism. The shrine was run by the Resurrectionist Fathers, a Polish order created in the eighteenth century and inspired by the Polish poet Adam Mickiewicz. Clearly, the Slavic Pope wanted it to be known that his commitment to Christ's mother and to Poland remained as fervent as ever.

The Holy Father's supreme authority over the Vatican was centred in three rooms: his private study, next to his bedroom; his official office, two floors below and known as the 'private library'; and the Secretariat of State which administered the city state of the Vatican and the Holy See. As the focus of papal power, these rooms, all dominated by pictures of St Luke's Black Madonna, have attracted unwelcome attention, including electronic surveillance. The Vatican's chief of security, Camillo Ciban, had twice discovered ingenious eavesdropping devices installed in strategic locations, but had never learned who had been responsible. One popular theory was that the professional Italian security men whom he had employed to sweep for bugs had simply replaced the American and Soviet devices they had recovered with their own. Another was that the Swiss Guard had been penetrated by a mole run by the HVA's Markus Wolf. Certainly, the Swiss Guard was an anachronistic organization riven by personal animosities among the senior staff that led to the murder of its commander; as it was in the front line of the Vatican's security, it had undoubtedly been targeted by hostile intelligence agencies. On one occasion, SIS's Nicholas Elliott assisted the Vatican and advised on counter-measures when there was evidence that the KGB had recruited a cardinal, and such suspicions were not unusual. While the KGB believed Cardinal Kron was too close to the CIA, others thought much the same about Cardinal Ratzinger, who enjoyed a close relationship with the West German BND.

Originally hoping for a career on the stage, Wojtyla's life had been dominated by an interest in mysticism and campaigning against totalitarianism. As a priest his doctoral thesis was on the sixteenth-century Spanish poet, theologian and reformer of the Carmelites, St John of the Cross, and he had always taken a strong interest in the Fatima phenomenon and the Virgin Mary. As for covert activities, he participated in an underground theatre group in Poland during the war, and well understood the realities of living under Nazi and communist totalitarianism.

From the Soviet standpoint, Wojtyla had been viewed with suspicion by the KGB since at least 1971 when he had become the target of a sophisticated operation of a type codenamed PROGRESS which focused on potentially dangerous dissidents. The KGB employed an experienced illegal, Gennadi Blyablin, codenamed BOGUN, who posed as Peter Carl Fisher, a West German freelance press photographer, and attempted to cultivate the then archbishop's close confidante, Father Andrzej Bardecki, who was the religion editor of the Catholic weekly *Tygodnik Powszechny*. Although born in Moscow, Blyablin had established himself in East Germany before moving to the West as a refugee in 1959. Three years later he and his wife, whom he had married in Hanover, emigrated to Canada with authentic West German passports. They moved on to the United States in February 1965, remaining there until 1968 when they were hastily withdrawn to Moscow, having attracted the attention of the FBI. Soon after their arrival, Blyablin and his wife were despatched to Prague where their assignment was to penetrate dissident groups while masquerading as sympathetic Westerners and to report on anti-communist activists.[1]

The Blyablins were not the only KGB illegals to concentrate on

Father Bardecki, who was also approached by a French journalist, Ivan I. Bunyk. Codenamed PHILOSOPHER, Bunyk had been born in France but had been taken back to the Soviet Union in 1947 by his Ukrainian parents. In 1970 Bunyk had materialized in France where he established himself as an independent writer and poet, publishing books subsidized by the KGB. In 1977 PHILOSOPHER gained an introduction to Bardecki and began filing reports on Wojtyla, his victim assuming that he was dealing with a sympathetic French journalist. Bardecki in turn introduced Bunyk to Tadeusz Mazowiecki, the editor of Solidarity's weekly newspaper, *Tygodnik Solidarnosc*, and his KGB personnel file shows that this enabled him to make 'numerous contacts within Solidarity'.[2]

As well as the dossier compiled with the help of BOGUN and PHILOSOPHER, the KGB *rezidentura* had access to the routine SB surveillance reports on the archbishop. Those showed that his sermons had been considered subversive to the point that his file had been studied by the state prosecutor. According to the SB, Wojtyla had breached Article 194 of the Criminal Code by making provocative anti-socialist statements during homilies delivered in Warsaw on 5 May 1973, in the steelmaking district of Nowa Huta on 12 May 1973, and again in Krakow on 24 November 1974. Nevertheless, the regime had decided not to take any formal action and limited itself to continuous monitoring. On the day after Wojtyla's election, the Warsaw *resident*, Vitali Pavlov, sent Moscow the SB's summary:

> Wojtyla holds extreme anti-communist views. Without openly opposing the Socialist system, he has criticized the way in which the state agencies of the Polish People's Republic function, making the following accusations;
>
> That basic human rights of Polish citizens are restricted;
>
> That there is unacceptable exploitation of the workers, whom the Catholic Church must protect against the workers' government;
>
> That the activities of the Catholic Church are restricted and Catholics treated as second-class citizens;
>
> That an extensive campaign is being conducted to convert society to atheism and impose an alien ideology on the people;
>
> That the Catholic Church is denied its proper cultural role, thereby depriving Polish culture of its national treasures.

The day after Pavlov's report, his ambassador, Boris Aristov, advised the Kremlin that:

> [The] danger of Wojtyla's move to the Vatican is that it now clearly will be more difficult to use the Vatican as a moderating influence on the Polish episcopate in its relations with the state. The Catholic Church will now make even greater efforts to consolidate its position and increase its role in the social and political life of the country. At the same time, our friends consider that Wojtyla's departure from the country also has its positive side, since the reactionary part of the episcopate has been deprived of its leader – one who has had an excellent chance of becoming Primate of the Polish Catholic Church.[3]

Thus, while the regime was delighted to be rid of the troublesome Wojtyla, there was a fear that his move to Rome would herald a reversal in the Vatican's conciliatory attitude to the Eastern bloc. Certainly, Andropov was appalled at the inauguration of a Polish pope, and demanded an explanation from the Warsaw *rezidentura*, which apparently suggested that the answer lay in Rome. The First Chief Directorate's final analysis asserted that Wojtyla's election had been engineered by the Archbishop of Philadelphia, Cardinal John Krol, who had conspired with Zbigniew Brzezinski, President Carter's national security adviser. While this was far from the case, the KGB did correctly predict that the new Pope would focus on human rights issues in Eastern Europe and thereby pose a significant threat to the entire Soviet bloc.

Once elected, Wojtyla became the focus of attention from the Rome *rezidentura*, then headed by the legendary Boris A. Solomatin who had served as *rezident* in Washington between 1965 and 1968 before switching to New York; he later returned to Moscow to become deputy chief of intelligence for Africa and Asia. Although believed to be a heavy drinker, Solomatin had an impressive reputation as a highly professional, chain-smoking workaholic with strong anti-American opinions, who had supervised the hugely successful handling of the KGB's star spy in the US Navy, John Walker. In Rome Solomatin enjoyed access to the Vatican through Franco Leonori, codenamed FIDELIO, who ran the Adista press agency. Well known as a left-winger, Leonori was extremely well connected and his Catholic news service had the run of the Vatican. Solomatin's other important source was Alceste Santini, the Vatican correspondent of the communist daily *L'Unita*, who wrote *Casaroli: Man of Dialogue*, a biography of the cardinal entrusted since 1963 with the Secretariat's external relations with the Soviet bloc. Santini, who was close to Agostino Casaroli until his death in 1998, was listed as a 'confidential contact' by the Rome *rezidentura*, according to extracts from the Mitrokhin archive, and admits his relationship with Soviet diplomats and journalists was intended 'to facilitate dialogue during the Cold War as the only way to overcome the two opposing blocs'. Through Leonori and Santini, the KGB enjoyed the advantage of a window directly into the Vatican, although this did not amount to influence on policy or advance knowledge of how John Paul II was likely to behave during his papacy.

During his triumphant first, eight-day return to his homeland as Pope John Paul II in June 1979, the Pontiff received a rapturous welcome and celebrated mass in Victory Square in the centre of Warsaw before an estimated one million worshippers. Although the communist regime attempted to play down the visit, restricting local radio and television news coverage to just fifteen minutes, and allowing only 500 of the faithful to welcome him at Okecie airport, he preached thirty-two sermons to a congregation of around thirteen million in six cities. His welcome from Eduard Gierek at the old Belvedere Palace may have been warm, but the Polish government's request, delivered a few days before his departure, that he should wear a bullet-proof vest under his robes had chilled the atmosphere. The Vatican's advice was that, if he chose to do so, this news would be leaked deliberately to the media, doubtless accompanied by the assertion that the Pope did not entrust his safety to his own countrymen.

At Auschwitz and Birkenau John Paul II delivered sermons that resonated with ambiguity, condemning totalitarianism and political extremism, and reminding his audiences of duty, human rights and the responsibility of all Christians. Considering that he was facing the East and speaking to millions of Roman Catholics not just in Poland, but also in the Baltic states and the Ukraine, his message, containing as it did transparent criticism of Polish and Soviet repression, must have been regarded as unwelcome in the Kremlin, but little is known of Leonid Brezhnev's attitude, beyond the muted official reports in the Soviet press of the Pope's progress. The Soviet ambassador in Rome, Nikita Ryzhov, attended Wojtyla's enthronement on 22 October and was granted an audience, and *Pravda* reported that Brezhnev had exchanged laudatory messages with the new Pope.

A campaigning, charismatic, Slavic pontiff must have been an unexpected and disagreeable development for a communist leadership struggling to contain civil unrest in Poland, acutely aware of Roman Catholicism's grasp on the population, exercised by 19,000 priests and 5,000 novices, despite three decades of Communism. According to an official Vatican survey published in March 1978, Poland remained highly religious, with 81 per cent of the urban population and 92 per cent of country folk confirming their Christianity. A survey conducted by Gdansk University in 1979 showed that 51 per cent of Communist Party members regarded themselves as practising Catholics, with a further 22 per cent describing themselves as non-practising religious believers. In other words, the Party leadership saw its own membership as a potential Trojan horse. As for the Pope, he had shown himself to be intensely political, declaring on his first overseas tour, to Mexico, that the liberation theology tinged with Marxism, which had been hitherto tolerated in Central and South America, was incompatible with the Roman Church. The other obvious manifestation of John Paul II's direction was Vatican Radio programmes which had been broadcast to the Soviet Union by the Jesuits on a powerful transmitter constructed in 1957. Although Vatican Radio broadcast in several languages, almost a third of its budget was devoted to the Soviet bloc, and that was to more than double, to a peak of $21 million, in 1989 under the new Pontiff. As the director-general, Father Pasquale Borgomeo, commented wryly: 'Our purpose was not to destroy a political system, but help create a new society.'

The Soviets responded to the perceived threat to the Eastern bloc's stability by extending the KGB's PROGRESS operations in Poland, and in particular by deploying yet another experienced illegal, Oleg P. Buryen, codenamed DEREVLYOV, against a priest, Father Jozef Tischner, one of the Pope's closest and oldest friends. Buryen posed as a Canadian publisher researching a book about Polish missionaries in the Far East and approached Father Tischner, a philosopher and Professor of Social Ethics at Lublin University who had helped found the Papal Theological College in Krakow. Tischner, of course, had no idea that Buryen's sole interest was in learning more about the Pope. As for Buryen, he operated entirely independently of the Warsaw *rezidentura*, although he was equipped with a single contact in the SB, Colonel Jan Slowikowski, in case of emergencies.[4]

The Soviet reaction to the Pope's visit to his homeland was entirely negative, with Pavlov's *rezidentura* making contingency plans in case there was an attempted coup in Krakow, and preparing an escape route for the Soviet trade delegation in Katowice, which was headed by a KGB officer, to the Czech frontier, in anticipation of a general uprising. Gloomily, the KGB advised the politburo that the Pope was embarking upon 'an ideological struggle against socialist countries', and in November a special sub-committee, which included Andropov and his deputy Viktor Chebrikov, set out a plan of propaganda for the Eastern bloc intended 'to show that Vatican policies go against the life of the Catholic Church', combined with active measures in the West 'to demonstrate that the . . . leadership of the new Pope, John Paul II, is dangerous to the Catholic Church'. Their objective was to protect Poland, and to counter what was believed to be a very definite threat to the Soviet Union itself, noting 'the characteristics of Vatican and Catholic Church policies in different regions of the Soviet Union have become more aggressive – above all in Lithuania, Latvia, western Ukraine and Byelorussia'.

While the KGB advised the Kremlin that the new Pope represented a menace to Soviet internal security, it was liaising closely with the SB in the hope of penetrating the Vatican. On 16 June 1980 Pavlov's *rezidentura* informed Moscow that his 'friends' (the SB) had succeeded in placing several assets close to the Pope:

> Our friends have serious operational positions at their disposal in the Vatican, and these enable them to have direct access to the Pope and to the Roman congregation. Apart from experienced agents, towards whom John Paul II is personally well disposed and who can obtain an audience with him at any time, our friends have agent assets among the leaders of Catholic students who are in constant contact with Vatican circles and have possibilities in radio Vatican and the Pope's Secretariat.[5]

The KGB's plan was to exploit the SB's assets inside the Vatican to achieve certain objectives, among them:

> To influence the Pope towards active support for the idea of international detente, peaceful co-existence and co-operation between states, and to exert a favourable influence on Vatican policy on particular international problems;
>
> To intensify disagreements between the Vatican and the USA, Israel and other countries;
>
> To intensify internal disagreements within the Vatican;
>
> To study, devise and carry out operations to disrupt the Vatican's plans to strengthen the Churches and religious teaching in Socialist countries;
>
> To exploit KGB assets in the Russian Orthodox Church, the Georgian and Armenian Gregorian Churches;
>
> To devise and carry out active measures to counteract the expansion of contacts between these Churches and the Vatican;
>
> To identify the channels through which the Polish Church increases its influence and invigorates the work of the Church in the Soviet Union.[6]

That the KGB should contemplate such schemes is not entirely surprising, and increasingly vociferous attacks on the Pope appeared in the Soviet press. Typical was the description of the Pope, published in a Byelorussian journal in March 1981, as a 'cunning and dangerous ideological enemy' and a 'malicious, lowly, perfidious and backward toady of the American militarists' who served his 'new boss in the White House'. Such public statements, undoubtedly approved by the Kremlin, coincided with the Pope's increasing support for Solidarity, which the Soviet leadership regarded as highly subversive and potentially extremely dangerous.

The Solidarity trade union movement had caught the public imagination, it became a focus for dissent that was to lead eventually to the imposition of martial law on 13 December 1981. Certainly Brezhnev could have been in little doubt about the threat posed by the Pope, and according to the secret minutes of a politburo meeting held just three days earlier, on 10 December, he was told by Yuri Andropov that 'the extremists in Solidarity are attacking the Polish leadership by the throat. The Church in recent days has also clearly expressed its position, which in essence is now completely supportive of Solidarity.' It was rumoured that in December 1980 John Paul II had written personally to Brezhnev at the Kremlin threatening to resign and return to Poland to lead resistance to any occupation of the country by Soviet forces, and a month later he had granted Solidarity leader Lech Walesa an audience in the Vatican, making the memorable comment, 'the son has come to see the father'.

The incoming DCI, Bill Casey, was keen to encourage the Pope's interest in Poland, but his initial approach, to Cardinal Casaroli in April 1981, was deftly sidestepped by the wily secretary of state. Casaroli had served four popes and, as the new Pontiff's foreign minister, was unwilling to be compromised by a direct meeting with the DCI at such a critical moment. Instead, he offered a meeting with a senior aide, and this Casey attended on neutral territory, in an administrative office attached to a cathedral in Rome, away from the Vatican. Casey asked about the Church in Poland, and received a depressing briefing. The fiercely uncompromising anti-communist Cardinal Stefan Wyszynski was dying of cancer; he more than anyone held the balance between the government bent on repression and the Solidarity activists likely to provoke an over-reaction. The Pope's principal interest, according to Casaroli, was to avoid bloodshed, and the cardinal had persuaded Lech Walesa to make a tactical withdrawal by retracting Solidarity's threat of a general strike. Apparently convinced by Stanislaw Kania (Communist Party general secretary) and Jaruzelski that the Soviets were on the verge of invading, the eighty-year-old Wyszynski made a highly emotional appeal to Walesa, who reluctantly acquiesced.

Casey was undeterred by Casaroli's caution and left Rome convinced that the Church could play a key role in promoting Solidarity. Rationing had been introduced in Poland in March, and had spread from meat to all sorts of ordinary but essential consumer items. The economy was on the brink of collapse. Upon his return to Langley, Casey urged a new focus on Poland and received a memorandum from his DDI Bob Gates which gave a view of the momentous events taking place in Poland: 'We may be witnessing one of the most significant developments in the postwar period which, if unchecked, may foreshadow a profound change in this decade in the system Stalin created both inside the Soviet Union and in Eastern Europe.'[7] Thus Gates was predicting precisely what the Soviets feared most: inaction would lead to further contamination. Inaction was therefore not an option.

The big questions here are: how far did the Soviets see John Paul II as part of the problem, and to what extent were they involved in the attempt on his life? That the Soviets saw John Paul II as the problem and not the solution is clear from documents declassified since the communist collapse that emphasize the importance Moscow attached to Poland's membership of the Warsaw Pact. In October 1980, Foreign Minister Andrei Gromyko had told the politburo that 'we simply cannot and must not lose Poland', so that even at that relatively early stage there was a deep appreciation of the threat of disintegration. By virtue of Poland's geographical position, it acted as a buffer between Germany and the Soviet frontier, and was a crucial strategic link in Soviet communications, not to mention its role in providing logistical support for the Red Army in Germany and as a base in which to store tactical nuclear missiles. The Warsaw Pact saw Poland as the 'first strategic echelon', so Solidarity's message, that democratization was incompatible with continued membership of the defence alliance, struck at the very heart of the Soviet monolith.

In June 1981 a senior diplomat in the Soviet embassy in Warsaw described the Catholic Church in a cable to Moscow as 'one of the most dangerous forces in Polish society', one which was 'anti-socialist' and replete with 'hostile' elements. Nor was this uncharacteristic. Five months later, Boris Aristov reported that the Church and Solidarity had combined with 'like-minded counter-revolutionary forces' to promote 'an openly counter-revolutionary struggle for the liquidation of socialism' in Poland. They were intent, he insisted, on 'seizing power' from the Party and plunging the country into 'economic chaos'. He predicted 'the collapse of Polish socialism and the headlong disintegration' of the Party, leaving the 'Solidarity extremists in control'. Such pessimism prevailed long after the initial crises had been weathered, with influential Soviet commentators interpreting Solidarity's 'strategy of permanent chaos' as a tactic that would 'threaten not just Poland but the whole of peace and stability in Europe'. Similarly, Mikhail Suslov, one of Brezhnev's principal ideologues, asserted that such deviation would 'entail ruinous consequences for the whole socialist world'. Of particular concern to the Soviet leadership was Solidarity's declared determination to encourage independent trade unions, a campaign that was perceived to have been directly responsible for a considerable increase in labour unrest, strikes and other stoppages in Russia, the Ukraine and the Baltic states. If further encouragement were needed, the Kremlin had come under pressure from other Eastern European leaders – Todor Zhivkov, Gustav Husak and Erich Honecker – in November 1980 to act decisively to prevent a repetition of the 1968 Prague Spring. On 26 November Honecker attended an East German politburo meeting, held at the army's Strausberg headquarters, and urged Brezhnev to intervene without further delay.

> According to information we have received through various channels, counter-revolutionary forces in the People's Republic of Poland are on the constant offensive, and any delay in acting against them would mean death – the death of socialist Poland. Yesterday our collective efforts may have been premature; today they are essential; and tomorrow they would already be too late.[8]

At the Warsaw Pact's emergency meeting held a few days later, on 5 December, the inflexible Honecker declared 'the situation in Poland is much worse and more dangerous' than previous crises, while Husak blamed 'counter-revolutionary intrigues'. In February 1981 they both encouraged Fidel Castro to call for military action 'to thwart the Polish counter-revolution once and for all'. Thus there can be little doubt about the gravity with which the whole of the Warsaw Pact viewed events in Poland, and their increasing hostility to the Polish Pope.

Within the CIA, there were two differing views on the crucial issue of how the Kremlin saw the Pontiff. One was the opinion shared by the DCI, elegantly encapsulated by Bob Gates:

> Those who believe the Soviets were involved [in the assassination attempt] make the case that the Pope was, in substantial measure, the primary cause of the Soviets' trouble in Eastern Europe and especially in Poland. They point to the Pope's election in 1978 and his subsequent visit to Poland as the spark that caused the smoldering

> Polish nationalism and pride to burst into flame and contributed importantly to the emergence of protests, strikes, and eventually the emergence of Solidarity itself in 1980. They point to the Soviets' fear of the Polish Pope's influence in Lithuania, western Ukraine, and elsewhere in Eastern Europe. In short, the argument is that John Paul's election and his actions and public posture thereafter threatened to provoke popular reactions not only in Eastern Europe but possibly even in parts of the Soviet Union as well, foreshadowing the beginning of the unraveling of empire. The danger of such a strategic challenge to Soviet hegemony, the argument went, would justify such a drastic step as trying to eliminate the Pope.[9]

While Casey certainly shared this opinion, he experienced many obstacles when trying to persuade the CIA's analysts to weigh the facts in its favour. The deputy director of intelligence, John McMahon, recalls that 'Casey kept pushing us to the limit. He put different teams on the same job – analysts, super-analysts, insiders, outsiders. He had people who did nothing but sift through every scrap of evidence.' Such behaviour was, of course, pure Casey; he never saw it as his role to be an independent arbiter making recommendations to the president based on advice processed by the DI and DO. He knew that the clandestine service did not share its treasures with the Agency's analytical branch, and he was contemptuous of the bureaucratic tendency to limit the CIA's product to what the academics could justify. Casey was fond of reminding anyone who would listen that it had been John McCone's instinct when DCI that had led him to demand the U-2 overflights of Cuba that eventually, on the third mission, revealed the deployment of Soviet missiles. Had McCone been wrong to insist on further flights when the first two had drawn a blank? To Casey the rhetorical question had only one answer. When your gut tells you there is evidence to be found, keep searching until it *is* found. In the case of the Pope's attempted assassination, that is precisely what happened, even though the Directorate of Intelligence was unable to corroborate the DCI's instinctive belief. Bob Gates informed Casey in September 1982 that 'our analysts and operations officers believed that if Moscow had wanted to assassinate the Pope, Agca would have been too risky an instrument' and prepared a brief for the president which could be summed up with the verdict 'insufficient evidence'. This was delivered on 20 December 1982 and copies also went to George Schultz, Caspar Weinberger and William Clark. Casey, always vulnerable to the accusation that he had deliberately politicized the Agency's analytical work, was under an obligation to submit the assassination report to the White House, but he made his view clear as he did so, expressly disassociating himself from the clinical judgment expressed in the summary of the text. As events turned out, he was entirely right to have done so.

Officially, as the Rome Station monitored the Italian investigation, picking up 'information that had more holes in it than Swiss cheese', the CIA appeared to remain entirely neutral on the issue, as was confirmed by John McMahon and Bob Gates when they both gave evidence to Congress in 1983, the first time that the DDI and the DDO had been cross-examined together by the Senate Intelligence Select Committee. Bob Gates recalled:

> From the time the Pope had been shot, the CIA had straddled the issue of whether the Bulgarians and thus the Soviets had been involved.
>
> The truth was that we really didn't know. The clandestine service worked hard in Western Europe and in Eastern Europe to come up with more information and, hopefully, 'smoking gun' evidence. And we came up with a lot on the trail on the gun that the assailant, Agca, used and on his travels and his arrangements, but nothing on who might have been behind the plot. I had read our own analysis closely enough to know the gaps in the case, and thus remained agnostic on the question. Casey was convinced the Soviets were behind the assassination attempt and frustrated that we couldn't prove it.[10]

In fact there was a growing volume of evidence, but not definite proof, of Bulgarian complicity, even if the Italian investigation of Agca's suspicious intelligence links seemed eccentric to the point of chaotic. Exasperated by the poor reporting from the Rome station, the DI sent David Cohen, as deputy director of the Office of Global Issues, to collect boxes of documents containing the material gathered together by the various, apparently uncoordinated, Italian inquiries, and these were pored over by the CIA's analysts. Cindy Webb and

Nancy Hooper of the DO's counter-terrorist branch wrote a series of papers describing instances of classic tradecraft and had no difficulty in persuading the National Intelligence Officer for the Soviet Union, Fritz Ermarth, that there had been a DS conspiracy even if nothing had emerged actually to prove anything beyond a convincing circumstantial case.

The controversy moved into high gear with the circulation in May 1983 of a DI paper, *The Papal Assassination Attempt: A Review of the Record.* This purported to be a 'comprehensive assessment' and concluded that the tradecraft was not typical of any Soviet or Bulgarian intelligence agencies, and therefore the Soviets were not behind the plot. The document was to come under immediate and sustained criticism for being 'incomplete, poorly coordinated and documented' and served only to confirm to those who held the opposite view that the DI analysts were preoccupied with economic models and tidy order-of-battle assessments, and were unfamiliar both with the Soviet tradition of what was euphemistically termed 'active measures' and with the First Chief Directorate's long history of involvement in mischief.

This situation was to change dramatically in late 1984 when the Directorate of Operations acquired a new source, codenamed GT/MOTORBOAT, who provided a new insight into the KGB's relationship with the Bulgarian DS and claimed that the GRU had been behind the plot. According to MOTORBOAT, an official internal report had acknowledged that Agca had been sponsored by elements not of the DS, but of a network subordinate to the Bulgarian military intelligence service RUMNO, and the arrangements had been coordinated by the GRU, which implied authorization from the highest level in Moscow and the approval of the KGB. This 'for the first time seemed to provide an evidentory base for making a case against them', recalled Gates who ordered the CIA's counter-terrorist branch to reassess the accumulated material. The result in May 1985 was *Agca's Attempt to Kill the Pope: The Case for Soviet Involvement*, written by Beth Seeger, Kay Oliver and Mary Desjeans of the Office of Soviet Analysis, linking Agca to the Turkish mafia and the Bulgarian DS, with contributions by John McCoughlan and Christine Williams, and additional material from Lance Haus, the principal terrorism analyst in the Office of Global Issues.

The document was so highly classified that it was read by only four people outside the Agency apart from the president and the vice president. They were George Schultz and Caspar Weinberger, the chairman of the Joint Chiefs of Staff, General Jack Vessey, and the chairman of the President's Foreign Intelligence Advisory Board, Anne Armstrong. The accompanying note explained to the recipients that this was

> the CIA's first comprehensive examination of who was behind the attempted assassination and the analysis is based upon our examination of evidence gathered by the Italian magistrate's office, the many leads surfaced by various journalists and scholars, independently acquired intelligence information and related historical and background information. While questions remain – and probably always will, we have worked this problem intensively and now feel able to present our findings with some confidence. The paper begins with a very short review of the principal conclusions. This is followed by a several page overview of the findings and evidence, which is keyed to the major sections of the paper.[11]

The reason for the restricted circulation was two-fold. One was the highly sensitive nature of the document, which was so politically charged that the original preface, written by Doug MacEachin, was mysteriously omitted from the version that was distributed (an act that was subsequently used to support the charge that Gates edited CIA reports to make them more palatable to the administration). The second was the new evidence from MOTORBOAT who was to remain a highly-prized source for the DO until he was betrayed by Aldrich Ames on 16 May 1989. Ames had been transferred to Alan Wolfe's CIA station in Rome in July 1986 for a tour of three years as chief of the Soviet branch, and had been entrusted with meeting GT/MOTORBOAT. Although he met GT/MOTORBOAT only a couple of times, Ames knew his true name and he passed this to his regular KGB contact, Aleksei Khrenkov. According to Ames, he had been collected off the street by Khrenkov at a prearranged rendezvous and driven to the Soviet ambassador's residence, the Villa Abamelek, just south of the Vatican. There a soundproofed room in the attic had been prepared for Ames's meeting with his handler, Vladimir

Mechulayev, who paid him around $40,000 in cash for his information. Not surprisingly, GT/MOTORBOAT was withdrawn from Rome and disappeared, only to emerge eight years later.

Nothing in the intelligence business is entirely what it seems, and the GT/MOTORBOAT example is a case in point. The fact that the Bulgarian survived the experience apparently unscathed, suggests that he may have been a double agent, perhaps deliberately despatched to deliver the message that there was an explanation for the increasingly obvious signs of the DS's involvement. The lowest sentence ever known to have been passed on a CIA asset was six years' imprisonment, but only after the person concerned, a GRU lieutenant-colonel, had demonstrated at his Soviet trial that the information he had supplied regarding the organization's structure had been compromised earlier by Vladimir Rezun who had published it in the West in his book, *The Aquarium*. The KGB preferred to use DS personnel as double agents, to avoid having to disclose KGB secrets, and once ran what the FCD regarded as a highly successful case against the CIA in Singapore. In short, GT/MOTORBOAT may have appeared to be a straightforward, useful penetration, but it may equally have been a prepared set-up, developed for the purposes of enhancing Ames's status in Rome, perhaps offering a method of verifying his continued cooperation, and also directing blame for the assassination attempt away from Sofia.

The CIA's secret report into 'the papal plot' was sharply to divide all who read it. Anne Armstrong was appalled by the way the Agency had run its investigation and said so in a rebuke she sent to Casey in June. Similarly, the DI Bob Gates found himself in a maelstrom of criticism from within his own branch when he commissioned an independent review of the report and the way it had been compiled.

> A number of analysts in the office believed that some of their colleagues and managers still preferred not to consider the 'seamy' side of Soviet policy – 'wet operations' (assassinations) and the like. These analysts believed that initially some of their colleagues had dismissed the possibility of Soviet involvement in the assassination attempt, and they consequently welcomed a paper looking at the case for Soviet complicity. At the same time, the evaluation also pointed out that there was another group within the office with a lingering 'malaise'

stemming from the conflict in 1981 between Casey and the Soviet office on the Soviet role in terrorism. In short, there were significant substantive differences and factions within the Soviet office, as well as major differences between some Soviet analysts and the DCI and me on what the Soviets were up to around the world. The paper on the assassination attempt against the Pope published in May 1985 was CIA's last major analytical assessment of that awful event. We never would get additional information from our sources, even after the collapse of the Soviet Union. As a result, the question of whether the Soviets were involved in or knew about the assassination attempt remains unanswered and one of the great remaining secrets of the Cold War.[12]

The ferocity of the debate that raged within the DI was unprecedented. The DCI's special assistant, Herbert Meyer, recalls the treatment given to Claire Sterling's contribution, a veritable hatchet job which he described as 'the filthiest, smarmiest piece of writing I ever saw in my life. They tried to smear Sterling, her credentials, her credibility – everything but her facts.'

Sterling's central thesis had been that the Soviets were the hidden hand guiding international terrorism, but it was only years later, after the Soviet collapse, that the truth emerged. While it was not as simple as a central coordinating role, a picture did develop of the KGB relying on their proxies to undertake some very disagreeable, and deniable tasks. This was especially true in the case of Ilych Ramirez Sanchez, the notorious 'Carlos the Jackal', who was detained by the French in Sudan in August 1994. In his confession he acknowledged having planned numerous atrocities, including the bombing of Radio Free Europe in Munich on 21 February 1981 which had been undertaken by his lieutenant, Johannes Weinrich, who was arrested in the Yemen in June 1995. According to documents recovered from the East German HVA's archive, this particular episode had been organized by the Hungarian AVH, but Oleg Kalugin has confirmed that the overall strategy had been devised by the KGB who had penetrated RFE's Radio Liberty with a bogus defector, Oleg Tumanov. Kalugin regarded both broadcast stations as a menace and had been directed to have them removed from Germany. The bombing had been part of a coordinated campaign which directly implicated the Hungarian premier, Janos Kadar, the Romanian Securitate, the Czech StB and the Bulgarian DS. All these agencies had connections with Carlos; his team responsible for placing the Munich car-bomb outside the RFE building on the Englischer Garten (park) had originated in Budapest and had returned to their safe haven after the explosion. Similarly, as the Stasi files in Berlin were opened to external scrutiny, more evidence emerged of East German complicity in dozens of terrorist incidents.

Agca's Attempt to Kill the Pope was to create a tremendous rift between those who had studied the topic. Gates asked MacEachin to prepare a critique of the very one-sided nature of the document, apparently overlooking the original brief given to Oliver, Desjeans and Seeger, which was to present the best case for involvement. The omission of MacEachin's preface and 'scope note' was vital, for it had cautioned that the paper

> was written for the purpose of setting forth the basis for believing the Soviets may have been involved in the papal assassination attempt. It consequently makes the case for the plausibility of Soviet complicity but does not elaborate fully the counter argument that the Soviets may not have been involved. This draft is not intended to stand alone but to constitute the SOVA contribution to a joint SOVA-OGI paper. The SOVA contribution will examine the particular question of reporting and evidence relating to the papal assassination attempt itself.[13]

The result of this deliberate deletion was the swift preparation of a new paper by the chief of SOVA's Foreign Activities Branch, John Hibbits, setting out the counter-arguments. It was entitled *Agca's Attempt to Kill the Pope: The Case Against Soviet Involvement* and ran to four and a half pages, written over two days and two nights, apparently ignoring the terms of the task given to Kay Oliver, who promptly wrote a rebuttal demolishing it, point by point. The authors, she maintained, had not set out to prove Soviet collusion but had evaluated the hypothesis in the light of the new information, taken with

> evidence developed by the Italian investigation and past Soviet behaviour. Taken together, they concluded that the new information

> strengthens the case for Soviet complicity. The assessment does not draw the conclusion that the Soviets were involved, although the authors do find the available evidence more consistent with the thesis of Soviet involvement than with any alternative scenario that has been advanced.[14]

Thus, Oliver claimed that although she had not set out to prove Soviet involvement, that was indeed the most likely explanation, and that Hibbits had misrepresented many of her key judgments. For example, she had referred to the Bulgarian source that had suggested Agca had been recruited by 'a certain weapons-smuggling network' in contact with RUMNO officers, which was not quite the same as saying that RUMNO personnel had been directly involved with Agca.

A central plank of the Hibbits paper was what he characterized as the general implausibility of the GRU's involvement, noting that this 'would have violated Soviet modus operandi'. The GRU had never been known to indulge in peacetime assassinations, and would never have contemplated such an operation 'without KGB and/or Politburo connivance'. Oliver, on the other hand, made four telling points:

> The case of the Pope was unique and the Soviets would not have been fastidious in observing past operational procedures if GRU officers were in the best position to implement an assassination plan; Many GRU officers are KGB co-optees, their involvement would not imply KGB ignorance of the plot; The GRU has the capability to mount assassinations and has done so in wartime situations, as in Afghanistan; Top Soviet military officers played a prominent role in dealing with the Polish crisis and may have been even more concerned than some civilian leaders to redress the situation there. It is consequently plausible that the idea of assassinating the Pope originated with the military, and this could have increased the possibility of GRU involvement in implementing the operation once it was cleared (probably at the Politburo level).[15]

Oliver accused Hibbits of grasping for straws when he fell back on the classic argument that a competent intelligence agency (such as the DS, RUMNO or the GRU) would never have committed such breaches of tradecraft or other blunders as occurred in this case (Agca was caught, and arrest warrants were issued for three of his Bulgarian contacts). Oliver countered this by admitting that the CIA had insufficient knowledge of Soviet and Bulgarian operations to reach such a judgment. Furthermore, she had never claimed either *direct* RUMNO or GRU involvement, but rather had accepted GT/MOTORBOAT's assertion that both had commissioned a separate organization to execute the plan. In these circumstances, with Moscow anxious to distance itself from the plot, and therefore offering its surrogates a 'wide latitude', it could easily be imagined that one consequence might be 'apparently sloppy tradecraft'.

Hibbits had placed considerable emphasis on the 'ostensible blunders', but Oliver complained that he had not considered the possibility that the 'uncoordinated and unprofessional' episodes in the alleged plot, which he had cited as inconsistent with Soviet practice, might have been intended to enhance the impression that the Soviets had not been involved, and that Agca had 'acted without assistance from a professional service'. In reality, any operational intelligence officer would have known that internationally accepted maxim, 'shit happens'. Furthermore, anyone in the DO could have reminded Hibbits of the essential rule for all operations encompassed by the acronym KISS: 'Keep It Simple, Stupid.'

Hibbits's other assertion, that the Pope was too prominent a figure to murder, was easily dismissed by Oliver who simply listed Moise Tshombe, President Amin and Jan Masaryk as precedents, reminding him that he 'could have thrown in Trotsky for good measure' and recording that before his defection in April 1978 Arkadi Shevchenko had 'picked up rumours of Soviet involvement in a plan to assassinate' President Anwar Sadat. In fact, the Soviets 'may have had particularly strong reasons for wanting to be rid of John Paul' and they 'probably see John Paul basically as an East European defector, rather than a Western leader, more prominent but not different in kind from other defector targets in the past. As for location, the Soviets have assassinated various targets in Western Europe.'[16]

At the time the Hibbits–Oliver debate was under way, the text of the Pope's letter to Brezhnev of December 1980 had not been revealed, but it was widely believed, the CIA observed, 'that the

Pope said he would travel to Warsaw in the event of a Soviet military intervention'. Actually, 'John Paul was *widely rumoured* to have made this statement. The Soviets, like everyone else, heard these rumours and may have believed them – which could have provided an additional incentive.'[17]

On a political level, Hibbits took the view that the Soviets had 'sought to enlist the Pope's cooperation in urging moderation on Solidarity', thus making it less likely that they would want to kill him, but Oliver countered that they 'might in fact have hoped that diplomatic efforts would serve as a foil for an assassination plot. Similarly, Soviet avoidance of direct criticism of the Pope during this period could be attributed to a desire to deflect charges of complicity in the plot'.

Hibbits clearly preferred the option that Agca had either acted alone, or with some of the Turkish mafia who may have planned the attack independently of the Bulgarians or Soviets. Oliver accepted that Agca could have 'used the Bulgarian intelligence connection for drug or arms trafficking, espionage and/or any number of nefarious activities of value to the Bulgarians', but remarked that such an explanation

> is to accept the likelihood that Bulgarian intelligence personnel – presumably unwittingly – dealt with 'loose cannons' in some fairly sensitive activity. Such a view of the Bulgarian services is markedly different from that of many analysts who reject the notion of Bloc complicity in the Papal attack on grounds that the unsophisticated nature of the operation invariably points to the work of amateurs or, at least, non-operatives of professional services. In the absence of the Bloc conspiracy scenario, no compelling or logical motive can be ascribed to Agca – an individual with no apparent personal, religious or political reason to try and kill the Pope.[18]

Both Hibbits and Oliver agreed that 'some sort of conspiracy *was* behind Agca's actions' but while the latter contended that MOTORBOAT's scenario of Soviet–Bulgarian complicity was the most credible, rational and consistent with the other data, Hibbits insisted that 'an equally circumstantial case' could be made for a conspiracy among the Grey Wolves, the Italian mafia and even the P-2 freemasons, a conclusion that was to attract ridicule.

The wrangling reached such a pitch that in May 1985 Robert Gates, who said that he was 'uneasy with the way the Directorate had handled the entire attempted assassination of the Pope', commissioned Ross Cowey to head a team to undertake a comprehensive survey of everything the CIA had done on the subject since 1981. The subsequent Cowey Report criticized the 1983 assessment as incomplete and, while acknowledging the 1985 assessment as 'an impressive compilation of the facts and marshaling of the reasoning for Soviet involvement', said that it ought to have included the missing 'Scope Note', as well as some cautions about the reliability of some sources and certainly ought to have given greater consideration to alternative scenarios. Indeed, apart from Kay Oliver and Mary Desjeans, Cowey was unable to find anyone 'at the working level in either the DI or DO' who agreed with them.

The real controversy was to erupt when Mel Goodman tried to block congressional approval of Bob Gates's appointment as DCI in succession to Bill Casey by accusing him in testimony before the Senate's Select Committee on Intelligence of deliberately skewing his analyst's opinions and rewriting key passages 'to conclude there was Soviet complicity in the attempt on the Pope's life'. Goodman said that Gates had dropped the 'Scope Note' and issued a covering letter to give the wholly misleading impression that the Oliver–Seeger document represented the sum of the CIA's judgments on the issue. In sworn evidence Goodman claimed:

> Casey and Gates believed the Kremlin was behind Ali Agca's attempt to assassinate the Pope in 1981. They tried unsuccessfully for several years to get the DI to find the 'smoking gun' to establish Soviet complicity. On the basis of a new report in 1985 from second and third-hand sources as well as untested subsources, Casey instructed Gates to prepare a DI study to show Moscow's direct involvement in the assassination attempt. Gates ordered that the study be prepared in camera and that there should be no attempt to examine evidence that documented Soviet non-involvement. Three analysts with limited experience in Soviet foreign policy were given the task, and experts on the topic were excluded from preparation and review of the assessment.[19]

These were grave allegations indeed, but Gates was able to call on the support of Seeger, Oliver and Haus to refute them. Seeger described Gates as having given the impression of being an agnostic, and explained that the discretion exercised while preparing the document was in deference to the DO's anxieties about 'source sensitivity'. Oliver reminded the Committee that her paper 'did not simply make the case, but weighed the case concerning Soviet involvement' and Haus stated that 'Gates did not specify or suggest what our findings should be'.

> Mr Gates made no changes to the draft submitted to him other than fairly minor editorial ones. Indeed, I believe he also added a few additional caveats. His concern, if I remember correctly, was that we should not go beyond where the intelligence information would carry us. Let me be very clear on these three related points: Mr Gates did not drop any scope note – I doubt he ever saw the preparatory paragraph eliminated after consultation with Kay Oliver, during my first review of the paper . . . Though he reviewed them, Mr Gates did not draft or redraft the key judgments – I did with help from Beth Seeger and Kay Oliver. Finally, Mr Gates did not draft the transmittal notes – although he certainly reviewed them. Again, I did. This was standard procedure. Fourth, at no point in this process did I feel that the authors of the report or myself were being manipulated to a predetermined end.[20]

Having rejected Goodman's criticism, the Senate Committee expressed surprise that Gates had not tried, in the light of the Cowey Report, to correct whatever misleading impression might have been given to those who read it, but there the matter ended. Kay Oliver was convinced her integrity had been attacked unjustly, and Mel Goodman was equally certain that Gates's political acumen made him unfit to be DCI. In a final salvo she remarked:

> Nothing is more poisonous to the atmosphere at CIA, more destructive to the process of debating issues on their merits, than accusing colleagues of conspiring in or being duped into 'politicizing' intelligence. It is imperative that our substantive discussions take place with an understanding that honest people can disagree, and a

realization that few of us this side of heaven can have a monopoly on truth.

The argument was to have lasting effects in the DI, and lead to Goodman's resignation after two decades devoted to analysing Soviet activities. Deeply suspicious of Casey and openly hostile after he had introduced a Global Issues branch within the DI to pursue what he perceived to be the DCI's political prejudices, Goodman returned to academia and Gates received Congressional confirmation. Perhaps more damagingly, few dared to raise the topic of precisely who had plotted to kill the Pope, and why.

Much later, as the Eastern Bloc intelligence agencies opened their archives, additional material emerged to implicate the Soviets. In particular, the Czechs declassified a batch of StB files, amounting to eight hundred pages, which identified Monsignor (later Archbishop) John Bulovsky, formerly of the Secretariat, as a source inside the Vatican, together with another Czech, Irene Trollerova. Her husband, Marco Torretta, was employed as Cardinal Casaroli's butler and serviced a listening device inside a statue of the Madonna which was placed on the Secretary of State's dining room table. The documents revealed two StB operations, codenamed PAGODA and INFECTION, which discussed the 'physical elimination' of the Pope, perhaps with a virus contained in the lining of a wooden box. While the StB files reveal little in terms of what the organization actually achieved, they confirm the view taken that the KGB's hierarchy had targeted John Paul II.

Chapter V

Kuklinski: the Hidden Asset

American and British efforts to penetrate the Polish *Sluzba Bezpieczenstwa*, or at least recruit sources in Warsaw, proved to be a difficult task in the 1960s and 1970s when Cold War suspicions were at their height. Certainly there had been some useful defections, with Michal Goleniewski in 1961 providing the most spectacular results, for as a self-motivated spy he had supplied information anonymously, and when he finally fled the country he came with an impressive 'meal-ticket' because he had knowledge of KGB operations as well as SB activities. The key to his success had been his dual role as a KGB asset inside the SB, trusted implicitly by both organizations. As a consequence of his information, several spies were arrested in the West, including the SIS turncoat George Blake, and Harry Houghton, then working on highly classified submarine detection systems at the Royal Navy's Underwater Weapons Research Establishment at Portland. Unfortunately, Goleniewski's value rapidly diminished after his arrival in the United States in January 1961, when he demanded to be known as the Czarevich, Prince Alexei Romanov, the Czar's son. Realizing his credibility would plummet if he was allowed to give evidence to the Senate's Internal Security Subcommittee, as had been requested, the CIA humoured his eccentricities and kept him away from Congress.

Thanks to Goleniewsky, the West's knowledge of the Urzad Bezpieczenstwa increased considerably. The UB (meaning 'Security Office') was a shortened version of the official name *Urzad Bezpieczenstwa Publicznego* ('Public Security Office') which was set up in the first week of September 1944 in liberated Polish territory by a team of NKVD agents parachuted into the country. Marceli Nowotko, Boleslaw Molojec and Pawel Pinder established the foundation of the UB, which was led by another NKVD officer, Stanislaw Radkiewicz who was himself closely supervised by the NKVD *rezident*, General Selivanovsky, thereby setting a standard of surrogacy that was to be copied across Eastern Europe as the NKVD inserted its own personnel or nominees into the newly created security structures.

On 1 January 1945 Stalin transformed the Lublin Committee into a temporary government, and the Department of Public Security became the Ministry of Public Security. In April 1945 the Central Committee of Polish Communist Party decreed a target proportion of one ministry officer to 200 citizens.

In July 1946 the Ministry of Public Security was divided into eight departments, five of which dealt with operational matters: I – Counter-intelligence; II – Technical operations and technology; III – Anti-opposition; IV – Protection of the economy; V – Counter-infiltration and counter-Church influence. Early in 1948, Department VII, handling general intelligence, was created and in June the following year a powerful and highly secret Officer's Office (Biuro do spraw Funkcjonariuszy), an internal counter-intelligence section, was set up to maintain surveillance, and to investigate and control ministry personnel.

On 2 March 1950 a Special Office (*Biuro Specjalne*) was set up, which became Department X in November 1951, to provide surveillance and to investigate senior communists and their cronies. At the peak of its power two years later, the security service employed 33,200 officers, with the Ministry of Public Security controlling 57,500 MO Citizens' Militia; 41,000 crack troops of the intensely loyal KBW Internal Security Corps (*Korpus Bezpieczenstwa Wewnetrznego*); 32,000 WOP frontier guards (*Wojska Ochrony Pogranicza*); and an armed industry guard (SP, *Straz Przemyslowa*) to protect industry against sabotage. In addition the regime could rely on 10,000 SW (*Straz Wiezienna*) prison guards and the 125,000-strong ORMO (*Ochotnicza Rezerwa Milicji Obywatelskiej*) Citizens' Militia Voluntary Reserve which consisted of low-level informers who, in emergencies, were armed with batons or guns and deployed against unarmed protesters. All these despised plainclothesmen were referred to as *ubeks* by the general population which did not distinguish between the security service and the rest.

After Stalin's death, the Communist Party decided to curb the power of the Ministry of Public Security and on 9 June 1954 the feared Department X was disbanded. Other changes were limited to the removal of a dozen or so most compromised officers. On 7 December 1954 the Ministry of Public Security was divided into the Ministry of Internal Affairs (MSW, Ministerstwo Spraw Wewnetrznych) and made subordinate to the Cabinet Committee for Public Security (KBP, Komitet do Spraw Bezpieczenstwa Publicznego). Thus the MSW gained control over the MO, ORMO, WOP, KBW, SP and SW, leaving the KBP as a *de facto* security service operating independently and outside the departamental structure of the previous Ministry of Public Security.

On 3 September 1955 the KBP was reinforced by an amalgamation of the Informacja Wojskowa (the military intelligence and counter-intelligence service) and the Wojska Wewnetrzne (an internal military unit designed to prevent mutiny within the armed forces), both of which had previously been subordinate to the Ministry of National Defence. No announcement was made to explain the extension of the KBP's power. An order issued on 17 September 1955 committed the security service to support Informacja Wojskowa, and vice versa.

Following the Twentieth Party Congress in Moscow, at which Khrushchev denounced Stalin, and the Poznan riots, the PZPR (Polish Communist Party) disbanded the Committee for Public Security with effect from 13 November 1956. The various offices of public security were dismantled and the hitherto informal security service was reduced in number and power, streamlined, and incorporated into the Ministry of Internal Affairs (MSW) where it was named officially as the Security Service, thus establishing the SB or Sluzba Bezpieczenstwa; however, the nickname *ubek* was so deeply rooted in the public mind that it survived despite some competition from the new acronym *esbek*.

While Goleniewski may have caused the CIA considerable embarrassment, his information proved authentic, but it was not until August 1972 that another Polish officer volunteered to reveal secrets on the same scale. The offer had been made by an unknown person in a letter addressed to the military attaché at the US embassy in Bonn, postmarked Wilhemshaven and signed 'PV', promising to telephone the US embassy in The Hague a week later. When he did so, a rendezvous was arranged later the same night outside the main railway station, and this was followed by a meeting in a nearby hotel at which Colonel Ryszard Kuklinski identified himself as a Polish General Staff officer who was sailing along the Dutch coast with colleagues aboard the two-masted yacht *Legia.*[1] He had chosen the initials 'PV' because 'V' is rarely used in Polish, and he wished to conceal his nationality in case the offer fell into the wrong hands. Three further meetings were arranged, at Rotterdam, Amsterdam and Ostend, which persuaded Kuklinski's inquisitors of his bona fides. He explained that, having become disaffected by the Soviet invasion of Czechoslovakia in August 1968, he had been persuaded by the events of December 1970, when the Polish army had been ordered to suppress demonstrations in Gdansk and Gdynia, to help the West. He had been particularly impressed by his discovery of Soviet nuclear warheads deployed on Polish territory during a Warsaw Pact exercise, and had determined to make contact with the Americans. Realizing that there would be no chance of reaching the US embassy in Warsaw undetected, he had taken the opportunity to write his letter when the *Legia* docked at Wilhelmshaven. He confided in no one, including his wife Hanka and their two sons, Boguslaw and Waldemar.[2]

The CIA responded to Kuklinski, codenamed GULL, by arranging a series of dead drops in Warsaw, and arranged a meeting with him in January 1973 at the Wolski cemetery at which he delivered nine rolls of film containing classified material he had photographed at work. Six months later, in June 1973, Kuklinski was assigned a new case officer, David W. Forden, who had recently returned to Langley from Mexico. Known to Kuklinski only as DANIEL, Forden spoke Polish, having served previously as the CIA's Chief of Station in Warsaw. The two men met at a safe house in Hamburg so that Kuklinski could be indoctrinated into the tradecraft required to communicate with sources in a hostile environment. Personal meetings were to be avoided, with contact limited to exchanges of exposed film; messages at dead drops were to be indicated by a complex system of signals, each ostensibly innocuous, such as the wheels of Kuklinski's ancient Opel car being turned in a particular direction when parked on a certain street. The CIA had learned from bitter experience that handling agents in denied areas was highly dangerous and two of their star sources, Colonel Oleg Penkovsky and Major Piotr Popov, had both been arrested and executed by an ever-vigilant counter-intelligence apparatus. Ideally, meetings could be arranged in third countries, such as Holland and Germany, but in 1975, after Kuklinski's fourth cruise out of Poland, the *Legia* was confined to Polish waters, so he was obliged to rely on dead drops emptied by the CIA's Warsaw station, with whom he communicated via an ingenious device known as the 'Discus' which could transmit and receive an alphanumeric message. Portable and easy to operate, the Discus was designed to squirt encrypted signals over short distances in a 'burst transmission' lasting less than three seconds, thus minimizing the risk from hostile interception. By constantly selecting new dead drops and varying the times they were used, the CIA hoped to reduce dramatically the chances of detection by Polish counter-intelligence. The CIA also insisted on the tightest possible circulation of Kuklinski's information, always in the top security blue-stripe intelligence folders, so that John Davis, then head of the State Department's Eastern European division, and later the US ambassador to Poland, had no inkling of his existence until after his exfiltration. Indeed, the reaction of several commentators years later, when they had the opportunity to read the veritable wealth of intelligence available to the CIA prior to martial law, was surprise at the Agency's inability to exploit it. Quite simply, the CIA was beguiled by what some believed was an unwritten Polish national commandment: 'Poles will not shoot Poles.' This single tenet explains more than anything the American failure to handle the martial law crisis.

The CIA's poor record at running sensitive sources deep inside the enemy's camp had hugely improved since October 1962 when the brief espionage career of arguably the Agency's best source, Oleg Penkovsky, had ended after less than two years. GRU officer Colonel Dmitri Polyakov had volunteered his services to the FBI in New York in January 1962, following the death of his son whom he believed could have been saved by an operation in America, permission for which had been turned down. He had been run successfully and jointly by the FBI (codenamed TOPHAT) and the CIA (codenamed ROAM) ever since. In 1977, as Kuklinski was mastering his 'Discus' device, Polyakov's CIA handler in New Delhi, Paul L.

Dillon, had taught the GRU officer to use the squirt transmitter so he could send signals while travelling past the US embassy in Moscow on a bus. By this means Polyakov, codenamed CK/BEEP, managed to maintain radio contact with the CIA for two years in the Soviet capital before returning to India as military attaché, with the rank of lieutenant-general. In June 1980, apparently undetected and approaching his official retirement, Polyakov returned to Moscow to reach the peak of his importance, keeping the local CIA station in touch with events inside the GRU's headquarters which, hitherto, had been almost immune to defection and penetration. It was later to emerge that the GRU had come to suspect Polyakov while he was on his final overseas tour, and this had been cut short as a precaution.

By 1980 Kuklinski had also reached a peak, having been promoted to deputy chief of the Operations Directorate. As Poland became increasingly gripped by the civil disorder spreading from the Lenin shipyard in Gdansk, he had access to the Warsaw Pact contingency plans that detailed intervention from East Germany, Czechoslovakia and the Soviet Union. Altogether, Kuklinski was to supply some 30,000 documents on topics ranging from war plans to military exercises, electronic warfare manuals, Soviet General Staff five-year plans for weapons design and construction, military targeting guidelines and even blueprints for command bunkers in Poland, Bulgaria and the Soviet Union. His personal commitment was such that he never accepted payment from the CIA. From the CIA's standpoint, Kuklinski, who signed his messages JACK STRONG, became a key component of a much larger intelligence picture which was later to include General Leon Dubicki, who was to defect in September 1981, Colonel Antoni Tykocinski, who had been recruited some years earlier while acting as a liaison officer in West Germany, Colonel Jerzy Szumanski, and Colonel Wladislaw Ostaszewicz. All four were to help the CIA and their product was circulated within the DI under a single code name (a flower) which gave no clue to the fact that there was more than one source, and was a useful security precaution to conceal the acquisition of a new, highly placed agent, though none matched Kuklinski's extraordinary feat.

Leon Dubicki was the most unlikely spy of all because he had adopted his Polish nationality. Originally a Red Army officer born in Siberia, he came from a Polish family that had been deported after the failed 1905 revolution. He had undergone officer training at Leningrad and had then been posted as an NCO to a parachute brigade in the Far East. He took part in the Khalchin-gor battle and fought behind enemy lines during the Finnish Winter War as a lieutenant. By May 1943 he had joined the Moscow-backed First Polish Tadeusz Kosciuszko Division at Sièlce camp, and ended the war in Berlin commanding the 5th Artillery Battalion. After the war he remained in the Polish army as a Soviet adviser and in 1953 graduated from staff college in the same class as Wojciech Jaruzelski, whom he beat to the rank of general by a year. He had been one of nearly eight hundred Soviets seconded to the Polish army who acquired Polish citizenship between 1954 and 1958 (and invariably gained senior rank). Dubicki retired in 1969 on health grounds, having received several war wounds, two of which had been to the head.

Before his retirement, Dubicki had attended a military intelligence school in Warsaw, and had been posted as a Polish delegate to the neutral Korean Ceasefire Control Commission. His enforced departure from active duty had been precipitated by what was alleged to be 'eccentric behaviour', despite a clean bill of mental health acquired during a check-up at a military clinic in Moscow. Dubicki unsuccessfully appealed his return to the active list, believing mistakenly that he had the support of his old friend Jaruzelski for whom he was to act as a military adviser. By 1981, having been active in the Disabled Veterans' Union and having been awarded a PhD in history, Dubicki travelled to Berlin, on the pretext of making a nostalgic visit to the battleground around the Brandenberg Gate and the site of the Reichstag. Here he defected, complaining to the CIA that his warnings to Solidarity's Mazowsze branch about the imminence of martial law had been disbelieved. Jaruzelski's reaction to the news of Dubicki's defection had been to dismiss him as a mental case.[3]

Initially the Soviets had merely monitored the deteriorating situation in Gdansk but by August 1980 the strikes had escalated. When national security adviser Zbigniew Brzezinski called on the DCI, Admiral Turner, on 3 September to discuss the likelihood of Soviet intervention, the DCI was able to respond in an impressively detailed memorandum dated 19 September describing political concerns in Moscow and military activity on the part of thirty divisions in the three Soviet military districts nearest the frontier which had been placed on 'full combat alert'; this was reminiscent of what had happened shortly before the 1968 invasion of Czechoslovakia. In particular, the Red Army had quietly called up 100,000 military reservists, and had requisitioned 15,000 civilian vehicles. Despite poor satellite imagery, because of dense cloud cover, the CIA undertook to provide two to three weeks' warning of action, relying upon two important sources of information, one technical, the other human. By far the most important was the secret National Security Agency (NSA) intercept facility at Teufelsberg in the British sector of Berlin which was strategically situated on the summit of a man-made mountain constructed over what had been intended as the Third Reich's military academy. Bombed into total destruction in 1945, the location had been used to dump the rubble from 800,000 buildings, and proved to be an ideal site for a joint NSA-GCHQ listening post. Isolated from the city, it offered an almost perfect electronic environment, free from interference; its tall aerials reached to Czechoslovakia and fifty miles into Poland. The 'field station' had been operating since 1957 when it was known as the 280th ASA Company, and had proved its worth by monitoring the military VHF traffic generated by 600,000 Soviet troops during the Prague crisis of 1968. The number of masts and distinctive golfball antennae had increased continuously until 1977 when the site was absorbed into the NSA as the US air force's 6912 Electronic Security Group. More than a thousand Americans and a hundred British technicians from the RAF's No. 26 Signal Unit and the 13 Signal Regiment maintained twenty-four-hour cover in three shifts on East German and Soviet telephone, telex and radio circuits.[4]

The NSA's Field Station Berlin was but one component in a mosaic of Western signals intelligence coverage that had monitored Warsaw Pact wireless and telephone circuits throughout the Cold War; the 1968 invasion of Czechoslovakia had been the event which had proved the importance of electronic interception. On that occasion the NSA had relied on its huge Bavarian facility at Bad Aibling, which had even recorded the radio traffic generated by taxis in Prague as they reported the location of Soviet tanks. The Austrian

Fernmeldeananfklarungs battalion at Königswarte, just outside Bratislava on the Slovakian border, also made a valuable, if unsung, contribution to the NSA. Established in 1955, it acted as a surrogate for the NSA, using American-supplied intercept equipment, but staffed entirely by ostensibly 'neutral' Austrians forty-five miles from Vienna. Further north, the BND's large Asterhig II had also played a key role, operating along the West German borders with Poland and the GDR, and at that time employing more than two thousand personnel at its headquarters at Lauf an der Pegnitz, near Nurnberg, and at twenty intercept sites. Created in 1952, the unit had begun with fourteen operators collecting around two thousand radio signals a month. Under the leadership of Leo Hepp, the organization developed, concealed under commercial cover as Sudlabor GmbH, from its clandestine base at Tutzing in northern Bavaria to give almost blanket coverage to East Germany. By 1980 the BND had combined with the Bundeswehr and the German navy, equipped with three Sigint (signals intelligence) vessels, to coordinate their surveillance with two Danish sites on the Baltic.

As well as hosting British and American Sigint sites, Germany also provided three facilities for the French Groupement de Controlles Radio-electrique (GCR), based at Domme in the Dordogne. Located at Bahrsdorf in the Harz mountains, at Appen in Hamburg, and at Landau, the French did not share their product with the NSA, with the exception of data collected at a station at Berlin's Tegel airport, in collaboration with the BND.

Because of the vagaries of electro-magnetic propagation, some NSA sites were located in unexpected places, among them a network of Norwegian Sigint facilities in the far north of the country which, since the Communications Intelligence Agreement made between Norway and the USA in December 1954, conveniently scooped up the VHF transmissions of Red Army units garrisoned in the Baltic countries. Analysis of routine call-signs and wireless traffic allowed the Norwegians, acting as NSA surrogates, to monitor troop movements, and any sudden deployment to the south and west. Soviet signals were intercepted at Tomaselv on Vadsö Island, Kirkenes and Viksjofjell, and Fasuske, and then sent to the NSA via an American communications relay at Gardermoen, on the outskirts of Oslo, not far from the Norwegian Sigint headquarters at Saeter, or via a tele-

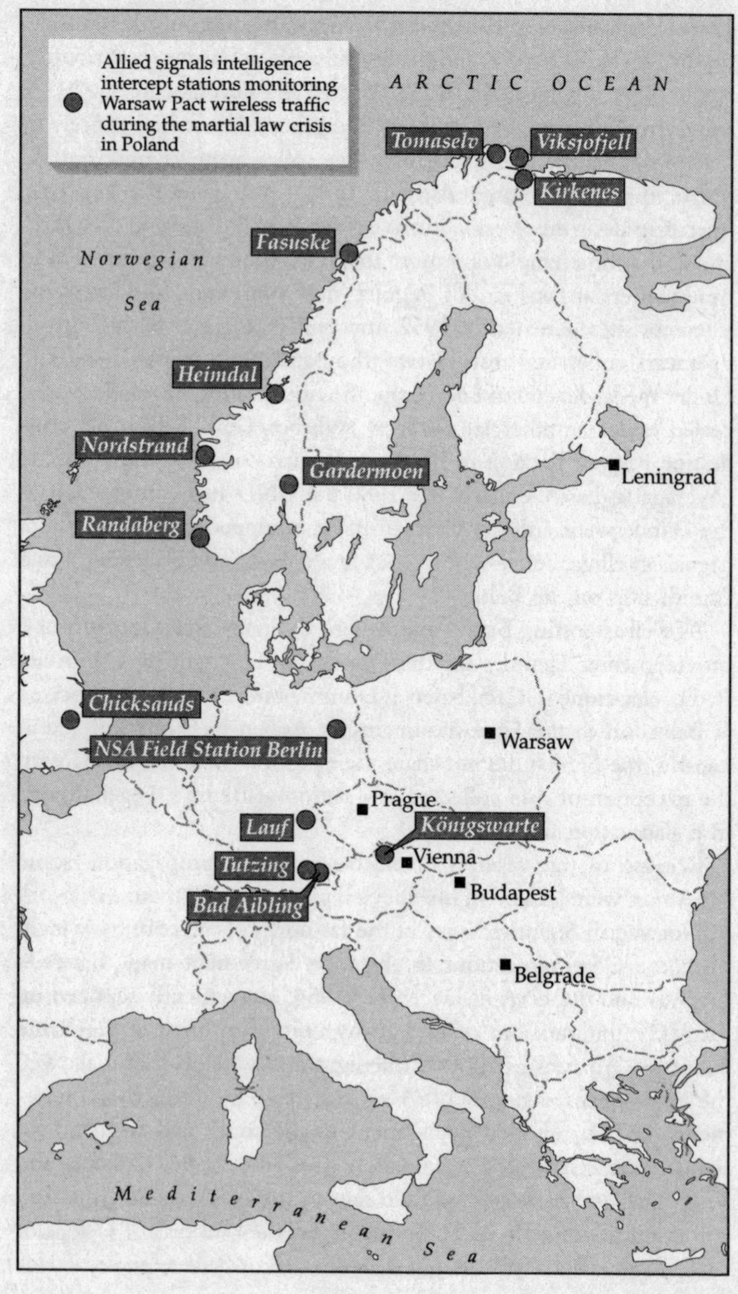
Allied signals intelligence intercept stations monitoring Warsaw Pact wireless traffic during the martial law crisis in Poland
ARCTIC OCEAN
Tomaselv
Viksjofjell
Kirkenes
Fasuske
Norwegian
Sea
Heimdal
Nordstrand
Gardermoen
Leningrad
Randaberg
Chicksands
NSA Field Station Berlin
Warsaw
Prague
Lauf
Königswarte
Vienna
Tutzing
Budapest
Bad Aibling
Belgrade
Mediterranean Sea

printer to Chicksands in England. In addition the Norwegians ran two direction-finding stations at Heimdal outside Trondheim, and at Randaberg, near Stavanger, with a further site at Nordstrand, outside Oslo, which concentrated on the southern Soviet Union and the Warsaw Pact satellite countries. The significance of the Norwegian activity can be judged by the fact that the entire Norwegian intelligence service only ever employed a thousand personnel, of whom more than half were engaged on 'high priority' work, a euphemism for Sigint.

Possibly the most surprising contribution had come from the Dutch, though not directly from the KWR signals organization. Its rival Naval Sigint branch had boasted a source trapped in heavy road traffic on the Czech/Soviet border who had given a running commentary over the telephone about the Russian armour queueing to cross the frontier. The source was a Dutch tulip seller who happened to be a neighbour of the director of Netherlands Naval Intelligence. The tulip seller's car had been caught in the congestion and he telephoned his wife to let her know of the delay. She had then informed her neighbour who had returned the call and scooped his colleagues.

The second important source of intelligence on Soviet military intentions was the BRIXMIS inspection teams deployed into East Germany by the French, American and British occupation forces. Each could, by treaty, move freely throughout the country for the purpose of observing the 400,000 Soviet troops stationed in the zone. Although the teams were small, amounting in total to just thirty-two unarmed officers and men equipped with cameras but no radios, they roamed at will, limited only by 'Temporary Restricted Areas' (TRAs) which had to be announced. By declaring a TRA along the Polish frontier, the Red Army attempted to exclude the BRIXMIS cameras, thereby unintentionally drawing attention to armour and troops assembling in anticipation of an invasion.

When Turner presented his memo to the SCC on 23 September 1980 he also outlined the Soviet dilemma. On the one hand they were anxious to prevent the contagion from spreading, and were under some pressure from Romania, East Germany and the Czechs to stand firm, while on the other they were aware of the probable international backlash and internal resistance. According to Kuklinski, the Polish General Staff instructed General Siwicki on 22 October to create a highly secret planning unit to prepare for all contingencies. By November the crisis had deepened, with Solidarity threatening widespread coordinated strikes if a series of demands were not met by a specific deadline. On 25 November railway workers went on a two-hour 'warning strike', promising a total shutdown, leaving the communists in the apparently impossible position of being unable to make concessions without provoking the Soviets, but unwilling to tolerate the continuing challenge to party authority. The crisis caused Andropov to summon the Polish interior minister, General Miroslaw Milewski, to Moscow to reassure the KGB that the SB had identified 1,200 of the 'most counter-revolutionary individuals' who would be detained as soon as martial law was announced.

According to Kuklinski's information, fifteen Soviet tank and motorized infantry divisions drawn from the Baltic, Carpathian and Byelorussian military districts had assembled on the Polish frontier, with a dozen more divisions standing in reserve as reinforcements, all of which, the CIA said, was 'highly unusual and unprecedented for this time of year', together with two GDR divisions and a token Czech division ready to sweep in, following the model set in Prague in 1968, to support a general declaration of martial law. Furthermore, orders were issued at a day's notice by the commander of Soviet troops in Germany, General Evgenni Ivanovski, for sections of the Polish–German border to be closed between 30 November and 9 December.

Kuklinski's message of 5 December, suggesting eighteen Soviet, Czech and East German divisions were poised on the Polish frontier, had pinpointed Tuesday, 8 December as the day for the Soviet invasion, under the pretext of a large Warsaw Pact exercise, code-named COMRADE-IN-ARMS-80, but the question of what deterred the Soviets remains unresolved. Kuklinski had been prompted to make emergency contact with the CIA following a conference of the Warsaw Pact Council of Defence Ministers held on 1–2 December in Bucharest, attended by General Molczyk deputising for Jaruzelski, which had been followed by an ominous visit to Moscow by General Tadeusz Hupalowski, the first deputy chief of the Polish General Staff, accompanied by Colonel Franciszek Puchala, deputy head of the General Staff's Operations Directorate. New evidence, recently declassified in Poland and Moscow, shows that the Soviet ideologue Mikhail Suslov had been placed in charge of a special commission for Polish affairs by the politburo, and as early as 28 August 1980 had recommended the preparation of a contingency plan for Soviet intervention by three armoured divisions and a mechanized rifle division, to be backed up by between five and seven additional divisions if the Polish army resisted. Certainly, COMRADE-IN-ARMS-80 looked like an ideal vehicle for intervention, as it also included two Czech divisions and one from East Germany, thus accommodating the hard line taken by Gustav Husak and Erich Honecker, as had been advocated to Brezhnev: 'According to information that we are receiving through various channels, counter-revolutionary forces are on a constant offensive in Poland. Any hesitation will mean death – the death of socialist Poland. Yesterday our collective measures might have been premature. Today they are necessary, but tomorrow they will be too late.'

As soon as Kuklinski discovered the plan he called an emergency meeting to hand over a warning. This historic document is one of only three which have been declassified and released, intended to support Kuklinski's successful 1995 appeal to have his conviction and death sentence quashed:

> Very Urgent! At meeting with the General Staff of the USSR armed forces, in accordance with orders from General Jaruzelski's defence ministry, General Hupalowski and Colonel Puchala endorsed the plan to admit into Poland (under the pretext of manoeuvres) the Soviet Army (SA), the National People's Army of the GDR (NVA) and the Czechoslovak People's Army (CLA). Documents and reproduced portions of the plans [for joint intervention] were presented to show that the following forces are to be sent in to Poland: three armies comprising 15 SA divisions, 1 army comprising two CLA divisions, and the staff of one army and one division from the NVA. In total, the intervening group will consist of eighteen divisions.
>
> [A state of readiness to cross the Polish borders was set for 8 December.] At present, representatives from the 'fraternal armies', dressed in civilian clothing, are undertaking reconnaissance of invasion routes as well as the distances and terrain for future operations. The scenario of operations for the intervening armies envisages a regrouping of armies to all major Polish army bases to conduct

> manoeuvres with live ammunition. Then depending on how things develop, all major Polish cities, especially industrial cities, are to be sealed off. According to the plan of the USSR armed forces general staff, the Polish army will remain within its permanent units while its 'allies' are regrouping on Polish territory. The only exceptions will be supervisory officers and military traffic control units, which will ensure a collision-free regrouping of the SA, CLA, and NVA armies from the border to the territories of future operations. Four Polish divisions (the 5th and 11th Tank Divisions and the 4th and 12th Mechanised Divisions) will be called into operation at a later point. Finally, I very much regret to say, that although everyone who has seen the plans (a very restricted group of people) is very depressed and crestfallen, no one is even contemplating putting up active resistance against the Warsaw Pact action. There are even those (Jasinski, Puchala) who say that the very presence of such enormous military forces on the territory of Poland may calm the nation. JACK STRONG[5]

This remarkable message did not actually identify the exact date upon which General Hupalowski had met his Soviet counterparts, but the CIA had its own sources and was aware that General Ogarkov had called the East German General Staff to a conference on 1 December 'to prepare – and on a special order carry out – a joint training exercise' of the Warsaw Pact intended to have 'the goal of demonstrating readiness to defend socialism in the Peoples' Republic of Poland'.[6]

Kuklinski's message was promptly relayed on the morning of 3 December in a telephone call from the DCI Admiral Turner to the national security adviser, Zbigniew Brzezinski, informing him that 'a very reliable source' had told the CIA that 'eighteen divisions will enter Poland Monday morning'. Brzezinski immediately passed the news to the secretary of state, Warren Christopher, arranging to meet him and the secretary of defense the following afternoon; later that afternoon he persuaded President Carter to issue a public 'statement of concern', which was to be preceded by personal calls to various world leaders, including a call late on the evening of Sunday 7 December from Brzezinski to the Pope, warning of a likely Soviet invasion the next morning. According to the CIA, Warsaw Pact troops had been placed on full alert on 4 December, and the visible movement of some cargo convoys through the Baltic region towards Kaliningrad near the Polish frontier had halted three days later, perhaps in anticipation of a swift intervention. The CIA situation report for 6 December cited 'additional evidence of increased Soviet preparedness for an invasion of Poland' and referred specifically to three Red Army divisions based near the East German town of Templin, near the Polish border, which had increased their training activity and prepared vehicle bivouacs. An airborne unit in the Baltic had been seen loading heavy equipment on to pallets, and a mobile hospital had been established in the grounds of a large civilian medical facility in Kaliningrad. This evidence, combined with Kuklinski's dramatic message, convinced Stansfield Turner that 'the Soviets will go in to Poland on Monday or Tuesday'. He predicted that fifteen Soviet divisions would enter Poland from the east within forty-eight to seventy-two hours, setting the scene for a crackdown on Solidarity and widespread bloodshed.

The call was made at 11.30 local time in Rome, and the legendary White House switchboard, not knowing the Pope's telephone number, simply called the main Vatican number and asked for his secretary. By then Brzezinski knew John Paul II quite well, having co-chaired the American delegation to his coronation, and having entertained him to supper at his home during his visit to Washington DC. The Pope was on the line within forty-five seconds, and listened as the national security adviser explained in his native Polish the gravity of the situation. At the conclusion, Brzezinski asked if His Holiness had a private number for future calls, a question which the Pope echoed to his secretary: 'Stanislaw, do I have a direct line?'[7]

By this time General Jaruzelski was already on his way to Moscow to seek approval for the imposition of martial law without external intervention. His purpose was to reassure the Kremlin that Poland could deal with the crisis at home through political measures, obviating the need for a Warsaw Pact invasion, although the politburo was under pressure from the Czech, Bulgarian and East German leaderships to take a hard line. According to transcripts of the Warsaw Pact conference held on 5 December 1980 in Moscow, Erich Honecker had been intransigent, and had led the demands for the re-establishment of orthodoxy, doubtless conscious of criticism he had experienced earlier from Brezhnev, while the Hungarians had taken a more moderate position. The big question that remains is whether General Jaruzelski extracted a promise from Brezhnev not to act without an official request, and thereby saved Poland from 'a greater evil'. In any event, an order was issued at 6 p.m. cancelling a major operation involving fifteen Soviet divisions, two Czech and one East German divisions, with a further nine Soviet divisions acting as a reserve to enter Poland a few days later. Instead, a staff command exercise commenced on Monday, 8 December, and continued for some months.

On 14 December the clouds finally cleared over the western Soviet Union and the satellite imagery showed that three Soviet divisions, which had been monitored since mid-November, had mobilized, apparently in line with the two-phase invasion scenario Kuklinski had described. His plan had revealed a first phase with only three or four Soviet divisions participating, supported by one Soviet division drawn from Czechoslovakia and an airborne division, followed by a second phase which would bring the total military numbers up to fifteen divisions.

President Carter's private call to Brezhnev on the hotline teleprinter, together with pleas from Giscard d'Estaing of France, Helmut Schmidt of West Germany and Indira Gandhi of India, may have influenced the Kremlin, which despatched Vadim Zagladin to the Vatican to reassure the Pope and dissuade him from exercising an implied threat, sent in a letter dated 16 December and addressed personally to Brezhnev at the Kremlin, to return to Poland to rally resistance to a Soviet occupation, but they served merely to postpone the crisis. The Pope's letter, written in French on his personal crested notepaper, used the word 'solidarity' and referred to the Helsinki Final Act which 'proclaims criteria for regulating the relations between states, and in particular the principle of respect for the inherent rights of sovereignty as well as the principle of non-intervention in the internal affairs of each of the participating states'. His meaning, articulated in less than diplomatic language, was clear. Brezhnev was asked 'to do everything you can in order to dispel the actual tension', and the alternative was the Pope's personal involvement, which could mean only one thing.

On 30 January 1981, two weeks after the Solidarity leadership had been received in a private audience at the Vatican by the Pope, the

CIA issued a special NIE predicting 'the most serious and broadly based challenge to Communist rule in the Warsaw Pact for a decade' and reporting a loss of Soviet confidence in the Party's general secretary, Stanislaw Kania. Just ten days later, General Jaruzelski took over as prime minister, and Kuklinski transmitted a message warning that a full dress rehearsal for the introduction of martial law was to be held on 13–14 February. After this date had come and gone, Kuklinski described a secret meeting held on 4 March in Moscow at which First Secretary Kania and Premier Jaruzelski had given the Soviets samples of the official Polish documents announcing martial law. Meanwhile, the country was wracked by disorder, with a strike paralysing Bielsko-Biala for ten days, and the farmers' union, Rural Solidarity, demanding full recognition. Jaruzelski responded with an appeal for ninety days free of strikes, which prompted a general strike on the same day in Jelenia Gora.

Once again, tension was rising, prompting more strikes and demonstrations, and some bloody reprisals, culminating in an incident in Bydgoszcz on 19 March in which a group of Solidarity activists conducting a peaceful sit-in were beaten up by a gang of SB men dressed in plain clothes. Twenty-seven protestors were injured, three seriously, one of them being a regional Solidarity leader, Jan Rulewski. Suddenly the situation deteriorated and Solidarity called a four-hour general strike across the nation on 27 March, to be followed by an unlimited strike on 31 March in support of Rural Solidarity and a demand to punish the SB officers responsible for the Bydgoszcz incident. The 27 March strike, which was the largest protest ever held in Eastern Europe in the postwar era, brought the country to a well-disciplined and total shutdown, an event that was correctly interpreted as a demonstration of what was in store for the regime. The CIA noted that the Bydgoszcz incident had 'raised political tension to its highest level since last November' and asserted: 'In the current atmosphere, such an action could lead to a total breakdown of civil order. If this were to occur, Moscow almost certainly would intervene militarily.'[8]

Kuklinski then reported, ominously, that plans had been made to close Polish air traffic corridors on 28–29 March, apparently pre-empting Solidarity plans to occupy offices and factories. Coincidentally, special instructions were issued to freight terminals in East

Germany to limit the use of all flatbed rolling stock (often interpreted as a prelude to the movement of a significant quantity of armour) and several new Red Army staff units were deployed to Poland, using a communications system that by-passed the existing Polish network, accompanied by an unusual increase in military radio traffic. On 28 March the CIA warned of a 'deepening crisis in Poland' that 'has markedly increased chances that the Polish Government will impose martial law and that the Soviets might subsequently intervene militarily . . . If the Poles request immediate Soviet assistance . . . a limited Soviet force could participate with little or no warning.'[9]

As the crisis weekend passed without incident, Kuklinski announced the arrival in Warsaw of a thirty-strong joint KGB and Red Army delegation, led by Marshal Kulikov and Vladimir Kryuchkov, which had recommended what amounted to a military coup, accompanied by the introduction of Soviet personnel throughout the Polish army. Although some of the Soviet demands were rejected, the domestic situation deteriorated even further, with Solidarity calling a general strike for 31 March, a date which was to act as a significant political deadline. The CIA's analysts noted that the strength of four Soviet divisions, three based in Carpathia and one in the Baltic, had been enhanced with reservists, and that armour and artillery had been spotted in local railway yards, in anticipation of loading on to flatbeds. The Warsaw Pact announced its planned exercises would be 'indefinitely extended' and it was later rumoured that on 28 March the Soviet ambassador in Rome spent two hours in a private audience with the Pope and gave him an undertaking that Soviet troops would not intervene for six months if the strike was called off. Truly, Poland was teetering on the edge of an abyss, and William Casey at least appreciated the implications of Soviet intervention, prophesying:

> economic chaos arising from the debt, a slowdown of the whole Polish workforce, and millions of Poles conducting a guerrilla war against them. If they don't they are open to the West and a political force which could unravel their entire system. Before sending divisions in, they will move heaven and earth to get the Poles to crack down themselves.[10]

Casey's prediction was to be prescient, with Kuklinski reporting on 4 April that the SB had warned of an imminent escalation planned by Solidarity in which activists would take to the streets armed with Molotov cocktails and storm selected government and Party offices. Jaruzelski allegedly had responded by saying that such events would require him to declare martial law on his own authority, adding that a loss of control would inevitably bring Soviet intervention. According to the CIA *National Intelligence Daily* for 31 March, the Soviets could invade with 'as many as twelve divisions' that could be deployed with 'little or no warning' but cautioned, 'The risks to the Soviets would be high . . . because a small force might not be able to cope with potentially rebellious elements in the Polish army and an aroused population.'[11] The CIA analysts also speculated about the impact of a much larger force, amounting to thirty divisions, that had been estimated on the need to overcome armed resistance. In that event, such an invasion 'at the request of the Polish regime or solely at Moscow's initiative would require large-scale preparations lasting 10–14 days. Preparations for a major intervention would exceed those of last December and would include an extensive mobilization of reservists and civilian vehicles and other large-scale logistical activity.'[12]

As the temperature rose, the Soviet ambassador in Rome held three meetings with the Russian-speaking Cardinal Agostino Casaroli and the Pope between 19 and 25 April to urge the Church to use its influence to moderate Solidarity's demands. Meanwhile, the TASS news agency circulated a mischievous report that Solidarity was on the brink of mounting a coup d'état, planning the construction of roadblocks and seizing communication centres. Faced with imminent catastrophe, Kania and Jaruzelski also went to the ailing seventy-nine-year-old Cardinal Wyszynski and asked him to broker a respite. The cardinal described the situation as 'desperate' and, having been shown a poster announcing martial law, agreed to plead with Lech Walesa. He told Walesa that Poland's 'territorial integrity' was under threat. Walesa, very reluctantly, responded to Wyszynski, who was dying of cancer, and called off the general strike on his own authority, without conferring with the rest of Solidarity's leadership. The deal struck by Walesa, which led to resignations within Solidarity, was for an immediate investigation of the Bydgoszcz outrage, and official acceptance of Rural Solidarity until it could be formally registered. To Walesa's critics, this was a climbdown that had achieved rather less than the movement's full demands.

This dramatic episode was widely interpreted as a reluctance on the part of the Soviets to intervene, but in reality it persuaded the Kremlin that a counter-revolution was already underway in Poland. An emergency meeting of the politburo was held in Moscow on 2 April to discuss the crisis, and the following evening Kania and Jaruzelski were flown in a Soviet military aircraft to a secret conference held in a railway carriage just outside the border city of Brest-Litovsk. Present were Yuri Andropov and the Soviet defence minister, General Dmitri Ustinov, who hosted a sumptuous meal and then made demands into the early hours of 4 April, insisting on firm action from the Poles and criticizing them for constantly backing down and making concessions to Solidarity. Allegedly, Jaruzelski offered to resign as prime minister, but whether this was a challenge to the Soviets or simply because he found the prospect of introducing martial law disagreeable remains a matter of interpretation. According to one account, the Polish leaders were presented with the prepared texts of martial law proclamations, complete with blank spaces for the dates to be filled in. Jaruzelski was later to assert that at this encounter he resisted Soviet demands for the immediate imposition of martial law, seeking more time, but certainly a week later, on 10 April, he obtained parliamentary approval for a two-month ban on all strikes.

While the CIA would not learn of this encounter for some time, it was sufficiently concerned about the continuing crisis to have issued an Alert memorandum on 3 April, reporting that:

> Soviet leaders have become convinced by the evident impotence of the Polish party government leaders that military intervention is necessary. They have set preparations in motion and would have the capability to move in considerable force in 48 hours. We believe it likely that they would want to have stronger forces than they could move that quickly and that it would take about another seven days to have the thirty or so divisions needed if the Poles were to resist. We do not know whether they have reached a final decision to act, but this decision could come at any time and the decision could be to

take the Poles by surprise. If this should be the case, there could be a move this weekend.[13]

This document remains one of the most controversial of those declassified by the CIA, and at the time of its drafting was contested by several CIA analysts. Suddenly the twelve divisions referred to in the NID for 31 March had become thirty yet, according to Doug MacEachin, 'there was no evidence that additional divisions had been mobilized beyond the four that had been reported a few days earlier'.

A fortnight later, on 26 April 1981, Kuklinski reported that he had just returned from Sofia where he had attended a two-day conference held by the Warsaw Pact's military council:

> Dear Daniel, After returning from Sofia with several officers from the General Staff, we discussed the current situation in Poland, a situation that, from the military point of view, is hopeless. In this extremely gloomy atmosphere, one of the most committed officers openly said that Poland had to undertake far-reaching political reforms. General Szyszko bitterly accused 'the Americans [of having] sold us out to Russia. Without the Americans' silent assent, the "comrades" would not dare to act this way.' We are now very desperate, but we have not lost hope that General Szyszko is wrong! Appropriate use must be made of the flood of information he is sending to you. We Poles realize that we must fight for our own freedom, if necessary making the ultimate sacrifice. I remained convinced that the support your country has been giving to all who are fighting for that freedom will bring us closer to our goal. Thank you for your most recent, pleasant letter. With heartfelt greetings. Yours, PV.[14]

In the middle of May the Warsaw Pact's supreme commander, Marshal Viktor Kulikov, was back in Warsaw to apply further pressure. This time he was accompanied by those Red Army staff officers who had participated in SOYUZ-81, a dress rehearsal exercise conducted in April, and who had examined the Polish plans for martial law and demanded modifications. According to Kuklinski, General Siwicki drew up a final blueprint which detailed how the borders were to be sealed and the precise command and control system that was to be adopted, and presented it to Kulikov who then returned to Moscow, apparently satisfied. According to Kuklinski, Kulikov also arranged for a group of eighteen Soviet generals to tour Poland to check on local Polish army garrisons and assess the willingness of their commanders to react against 'counter-revolutionaries' should such a contingency arise. With an army strength of 413,000, the largest in Eastern Europe, the Polish army was not to be underestimated. However, while there was a realization in Moscow that Kania had lost the political will to face down Solidarity, there was also concern about how Polish troops would react to an invasion. Certainly, these doubts did not extend to the more reliable senior commanders, nine of whom approached the Warsaw *rezidentura* in June to seek support from Vitali Pavlov for a coup in which the reluctant Jaruzelski would be replaced with a new defence minister, they would seize the government and deport 3,000 detainees to camps thousands of miles from Poland. Their plan then called for Moscow to provide 'military assistance to protect Socialism in the Polish People's Republic'. The offer was relayed by the KGB to the Kremlin, where it was rejected, and instead Pavlov was directed to have 'a straightforward conversation with S. Kania and Jaruzelski on their weak Party and government work, and remind them of their earlier statements of readiness to cede their Party and government jobs if necessary in the interest of saving the Socialist system in Poland and the unity of Socialist co-operation in Europe'.

Little of this was known to the CIA, although Kuklinski and the others in the 'flower' codeword group continued to provide sufficient information to keep the analysts busy preparing highly classified briefs for policy-makers; although the contents of these briefs have been only partially declassified, their titles are revealing. A special analysis distributed with the *National Intelligence Daily* on 29 May 1981 was entitled *USSR: Options for Dealing With Poland*, and the following day there was *Europe: Impact of a Soviet failure to invade Poland* with *Liberalization in Poland: Impact and Implications* circulated on 18 May. Later in the month, or possibly in early June (the exact date of distribution having been redacted, perhaps accidentally) the CIA produced *Implications of a Soviet Invasion of Poland*, announcing:

> there is reason to believe that Soviet leaders may have felt at one time that if Warsaw Pact forces could be inserted into Poland in support of

the introduction of martial law by the Polish regime itself, there might be less resistance.

However, we believe that by now the Soviets, on contemplating military intervention, no longer see any viable alternative to an outright invasion – staged, to be sure, with whatever 'invitational' cover could be arranged. Given the Soviets' likely assessment of the substantial resistance that Pact forces would encounter, we believe they would feel compelled to employ a large invasion force of at least 30, and perhaps as many as 45 divisions.[15]

Although the KGB had advocated the removal of Kania and Jaruzelski, it acknowledged that the vacillating defence minister continued to hold 'authority in the country and especially in the army', so Kulikov held a meeting with him and other generals on 12 August and insisted on 'firmness and still more firmness'. At the same time, the CIA's analysts appeared to back away from seeing martial law as a viable option for crushing Solidarity. As the summer ended, the country was still in turmoil, with no sign that changes in the Party's central committee and politburo had made the slightest improvement. Indeed, the continuing unrest had prompted the new interior minister, General Czeslaw Kiszczak, a hard-liner who had previously headed the military intelligence service, to undertake a concealed increase in the strength of the ZOMO riot troops. On 21 August he flew to Moscow to confer privately with Andropov over the SB's plans for martial law, and told the KGB chairman that the 'Polish leadership has handled Solidarity as if it were an egg which it was afraid to break. We must put a stop to this.' Kiszczak explained that the SB had thoroughly penetrated the Church and that, 'Out of seventy bishops, good contacts are maintained with fifty. This makes it possible to bring influence to bear on the Catholic Church and to prevent undesirable moves.' Apparently unimpressed, Andropov warned Kiszczak that 'the adversary's creeping counter-revolution has long been preparing for the struggle with socialism'.

The Soviet ambassador, Boris Aristov, was especially pessimistic in his reporting to Moscow, warning that Solidarity had combined forces with the Church to challenge the entire Warsaw Pact. Kuklinski then reported that on 9 September General Siwicki confided to a group of senior officers that the moment for introducing martial law was close, and explained that if the Operation WIOSNA ('Spring') seemed to be failing the Soviets would 'help'; in any case, they were arranging for the printing of the necessary leaflets announcing the proclamation. Kuklinski's next message, on 15 September, was prompted by a meeting of Poland's Homeland Defence Committee (KOK), chaired by Prime Minister General Jaruzelski, at which the issue of codewords was discussed. Although not present, Kuklinski had been briefed immediately afterwards, and had been informed that the codeword WIOSNA had been compromised, so a molehunt had been initiated for the source of the leak, and a new codeword, WRZOS ('Heather'), had been selected. The deliberations of the committee were considered so secret that only the secretary, General Tadeusz Tuczapski, had been allowed to take notes. Kuklinski gave the following account to the CIA:

> Warsaw 2030. At an extraordinary meeting of the KOK on Sunday, which Kania attended for the first time, no final decision was made about the imposition of martial law. Almost all the participants supported it. It seems that the tenor of the meeting surprised Kania. Although he did not question that such a development was inevitable, he said, in these precise words, that 'confrontation with the class enemy is unavoidable. This involves first a struggle using political means, but if that should fail, repression may be adopted.' Note-taking was forbidden at the session. During the KOK's meeting, Kiszczak declared that Solidarity knew the details of our plan, including Operation 'WIOSNA' and its secret codename. I should emphasize that this is a codename – the secret title of the operation – and not the codeword needed to put it into effect. The officials responsible for implementing the plans don't know the codename; hence, it will be easy to compile a group of suspects (the MSW was given urgent orders to find the source). The first steps have already been taken. Except for Szklarski and me, everyone was excluded in operational directives from the planning. A counter-intelligence officer visited Szklarski and me yesterday. He spoke about ways of preventing future leaks. At present, Jasinski has taken command of planning at the national level. Szklarski has temporarily withdrawn. Since this morning we have been working, under Jasinski's supervision, and in cooperation with a PUWP CC official, with the KOK secretariat, with

the KPPRM, and with Pawlikowski from MSW, on a unified plan of command for the surprise introduction of martial law. The document is still being put together, so I am unable to give a detailed account of it. (I proposed a break so that I could send this telegram.) In brief, martial law will be introduced at night, either between Friday and a work-free Saturday, or between Saturday and Sunday, when industrial plants will be closed. Arrests will begin around midnight, six hours before an announcement of martial law is broadcast over radio and television. Roughly 600 people will be arrested in Warsaw, which will require the use of around 1,000 police in unmarked cars. That same night, the army will seal off the most important areas of Warsaw and other major cities. Initially only the MSW's forces will take part, a separate political decision will be made about 'improving the deployment of armies', that is, redeploying entire divisions to major cities. This will be done only if reports come in about larger pockets of unrest. One cannot rule out, however, that redeployments of divisions based far away from the areas of future operations will commence with the introduction of martial law or even earlier. For example, it would take roughly 54 hours to redeploy the 4th Mechanised Division to the vicinity of Warsaw. Because the investigation is proceeding, I will have to forego my daily reports about current developments. Please treat with caution the information I am conveying to you, since it appears that my mission is coming to an end. The nature of the information makes it quite easy to detect the source. I do not object to, and indeed welcome, having the information I have conveyed serve those who fight for the freedom of Poland with their heads raised high. I am prepared to make the ultimate sacrifice, but the best way to achieve something is with our actions and not with our sacrifices. Long live free Poland! Long live Solidarity which brings freedom to all oppressed nations! JACK STRONG.[16]

When General Siwicki recommended immediate action in the middle of the month, the politburo rejected the idea claiming that there was still a political solution to the crisis. The CIA's *National Intelligence Daily* for 18 September reflected the regime's shifting position, noting that the euphemistically-termed 'Intelligence Community' (which usually meant the US National Intelligence Council) had

> sensed a qualitative change in the attitudes of Solidarity and the Polish Communist Party. The former has directly challenged the authority of the Polish party and, indirectly, Soviet hegemony. The latter has indicated a determination to confront Solidarity's challenges if necessary with the use of force.
>
> The Polish regime has drawn up a detailed plan of military measures, including curfews, shows of force, total military control of the country, and arrest of Solidarity leaders. The Polish leadership appears to be readying itself for the possible employment of at least some of these measures in the near future . . . The chances of a confrontation leading to the regime's use of force have risen considerably unless the more moderate elements of Solidarity manage to tone down those union actions most objectionable to the government.[17]

This CIA analysis was spot on for, initially mollified, General Siwicki had concluded by 25 September that martial law was the only alternative to continuing chaos and offered the politburo two alternatives, both of which implied support from Warsaw Pact troops. Coincidentally, as Kuklinski reported these events to the embassy station, saying on 7 October that the Russians had now printed the proclamations, the CIA learned in Moscow that the Soviet General Staff was discussing options for intervention in the second half of October. The scenario of the previous December looked ominously familiar; only, on this occasion, Soviet influence had been markedly increased. Both the Polish Interior and Defence ministries had recommended martial law, and Brezhnev had held long and difficult telephone conversations direct with Jaruzelski, excluding the Party's political leadership. In the middle of the month Kania was replaced by Jaruzelski who made an impassioned attack in parliament on Solidarity and the strikes.

Finally, on 4 November, Jaruzelski and Walesa were brought together by the Church's new leader, Archbishop Jozef Glemp, to discuss reconciliation, – in reality a 'Front of National Unity' which would include non-Party members in the government – but it became clear within a fortnight, with the arrival in Warsaw of a high-level Red Army delegation, that the Kremlin had lost confidence in the dialogue and certainly could not contemplate the proposed

Front of National Unity. The purpose of the group, led by General C.G. Nikolaev, was to discuss the exact timing of WIOSNA with his Polish counterparts. Nikolaev was accompanied by eight Soviet General Staff officers, but there was an unexplained absentee on the Polish side: the trusted Colonel Kuklinski had disappeared without trace, together with his family.

The fact that aspects of WIOSNA became known to Solidarity and elsewhere so quickly prompted a meeting in September 1981 at which the Ministry of the Interior complained that there was a serious breach of security. Only about a dozen senior officers had been allowed to know about WIOSNA, yet the highly classified codename had been leaked, so the KGB had reported, to Rome. Two months later, on 2 November, Kuklinski had been summoned to a Chief of Staff's conference with General Florian Siwicki's deputy, General Jerzy Skalski, which was attended by General Szklarski and Colonels Puchala and Witt. It was at this meeting that Kuklinski realized that although he personally was not yet under suspicion, it was only a matter of time before the molehunt now underway, which was concentrating on the only two people with uninterrupted full access to the martial law plans, trapped him because a crucial document had been compromised. The incriminating item was a paper drafted by Kuklinski which had referred to the circumstances under martial law in which the use of deadly force might become necessary. These vital words had been omitted from the final agreed text, but it was clear to the investigation that it was the original version that had leaked, thus narrowing the field to Kuklinski alone. Accordingly, Kuklinski requested another emergency rendezvous and was met by the CIA deputy Chief of Station in Warsaw, a woman who promised an exfiltration for him, his wife and his two sons, and arranged for future communications to be conducted by the sons because Kuklinski feared he was under constant surveillance. However, it proved almost impossible for the local CIA personnel to shake off their surveillance, and on three successive nights the operation had to be abandoned. Finally, two CIA officers under commercial cover flew to Warsaw from Germany to supervise an escape devised by the 'pipeliners' from the CIA's Office of Technical Services. However, by sheer good fortune, the Chief of Station discovered as he drove himself over the Polish frontier from East Germany, after an extended vacation, that he had not attracted the usual SB surveillance. Instead of driving to the embassy or his apartment, he met Kuklinski, his wife and two sons at a pre-arranged rendezvous, and drove them out of the country to West Berlin on 7 November, hidden under cardboard boxes in the back of his Volvo station-wagon. On 11 November they were flown from Berlin in a military transport to Andrews airforce base, where they were met by a jubilant David Forden, who escorted them to a safe house in Warrenton, Virginia, and subsequently had to make complicated arrangements for an unexpected sequel, the exfiltration from Warsaw of Kuklinski's son's girlfriend.

A major concern for the CIA was how the Poles had been tipped off. Kuklinski had heard that the information had come from the KGB, which had attributed it to a source in Rome. Did this mean the Vatican or the CIA's Rome station had been infiltrated? The embarrassing conclusions of the CIA's own internal enquiries suggested that Casey himself had been responsible for the indiscretion, possibly on his visit to the Vatican.

While NATO Sigint could monitor the Soviet military preparations, the Poles had taken care to conceal their plans and ensure nothing leaked via a vulnerable wireless transmission, never realizing that Kuklinski, as one of the handful of indoctrinated officers, had passed every detail to the CIA. However, at the American end in Langley, where Kuklinski's information was circulated on a tightly compartmented basis, not all the political analysts anticipated martial law. Whereas Kuklinski's material was highly valued by the military analysts who consumed it eagerly, recognizing that the source was exceptionally well-placed, and relied on it for their assessments, the DCI's political advisers took the mistaken view that a cataclysmic event such as martial law would occur only if imposed on Warsaw by Soviet *force majeur*, which itself would require a huge, very visible military commitment. Indeed, the DI became so persuaded that such an episode was extraordinarily unlikely that they chose to interpret Kuklinski's data as mere contingency planning, with no direct relevance to the ongoing political crisis gripping Poland. Incredibly, this remained their view even after Kuklinski had been exfiltrated. The difference of opinion centred on the possibility of Polish collusion and was to be the cause of considerable, lasting controversy within the CIA. Some analysts thought the chances of a Soviet intervention had been exaggerated, perhaps deliberately. Kuklinski's reports had referred to a relatively small Soviet force acting in concert with Polish forces, having been inserted under the guise of an exercise. On the other hand, the conventional wisdom was that the Soviets, unable to rely on Polish troops, would have to assemble a force large enough to overwhelm any resistance, which required a ratio of about one-to-one. With only intermittent satellite imagery, the analysts feared that the relatively few Soviet units in a state of readiness merely represented the tip of a much larger iceberg. Finally, as Douglas MacEachin was later to admit, the CIA's 'predictions that intervention was not about to occur were right for the wrong reasons'.

Kuklinski's successful escape was a triumph for the CIA but it effectively eliminated an important source of information about Soviet plans, so that when Kiszczak briefed the KGB *rezident* Pavlov on 7 December, the news failed to reach the CIA.[18] The interior minister revealed that 157 trusted SB officers had been sent across the country by the SB chief, Lieutenant-General Wladyslaw Pozoga, in groups of five to supervise the arrest of Solidarity activists, and confirmed that a special SB unit, headed by Colonel Bronislaw Pawlikowski had inserted agents 'at all levels of Solidarity'. Pavlov subsequently reported to Moscow that the SB had placed suspect Party members, including some of the leadership, under surveillance, and implied that the homes and telephones of several, including Kania, were also the subject of intensive technical surveillance. Kiszczak's briefing had been so comprehensive that Moscow knew much of what Jaruzelski disclosed the following night, on 8 December, when he ran through with Marshal Kulikov the final martial law plan, which included provision of 80,000 security personnel to take 6,000 Solidarity activists into custody before dawn the following weekend.

Even at this late stage Pavlov harboured considerable doubts about Jaruzelski's commitment, and held a trump card up his sleeve. His fallback position was a coup, organized by Stefan Olszowski who would seal the borders, call on Soviet support and take control of the country's food supplies. The situation was balanced on a knife edge, and Vladimir Kryuchkov, the chief of the KGB's First Chief Directorate, flew in to Warsaw to watch Pavlov and Kiszczak in action.

Chapter VI

Martial Law

When General Jaruzelski announced martial law, on a combined radio and television broadcast at 6 a.m. on Sunday, 13 December, the timing came as a complete surprise. Dense cloud cover over Eastern Europe had reduced overhead satellite imagery and industrial action at GCHQ, Britain's cryptographic organization, had temporarily limited the cryptanalytical attack on Warsaw Pact communications. Five days earlier, on 7 December, Kulikov had flown into Warsaw to deliver an ultimatum and an offer of assistance, but his crucial visit had gone unreported because Kuklinski had already left the country. Kulikov remained in Warsaw for ten days, accompanied by his aide General Viktor Anoshkin, who kept detailed notes of the meetings held. These suggest that the Soviets had by then all but abandoned any plans to intervene and were primarily concerned with persuading Jaruzelski to impose martial law. Jarulzelski, however, was apparently uncertain of the loyalty of his own forces and was anxious to obtain a guarantee of Soviet support, which was unforthcoming from either the Warsaw Pact's Chief of Staff, General Anatoli Gribkov or from the KGB *rezident* Vitali Pavlov. Thus there remain two opposing views about General Jaruzelski's strategy, which was either a determination to obtain the support of Soviet troops, or a wish to exclude them. The Anoshkin notes show Jaruzelski complaining that after twelve months of Soviet threats the Kremlin was not prepared to back him with force, and records his Chief of Staff, General Siwicki, threatening that Poland might be lost to the Warsaw Pact unless the Soviets showed 'fraternal assistance' in imposing martial law.

All these manoeuvres had been missed by the CIA which had become wedded to the proposition that Kuklinski's fascinating window had been opened on to an exciting vista of military intelligence, but little with any direct political relevance. The analysts were convinced that he had participated in contingency planning that could not be interpreted as a definite intention to impose martial law, and their opinion was shared by the State Department which found it impossible to believe that the Warsaw Pact could succumb to such political folly. 'The writers were afflicted with denial,' recalls one participant who complained that 'the DCI considered he had his own more reliable sources in the Vatican' which would alert him in good time to Polish intentions. Incredibly, as the CIA Operations Center received the first signs of martial law, William Casey initially declined to authorize a flash report to the White House. One of those present stormed out of a meeting in protest at the DCI's intransigence and waited by the teleprinter just after midnight in Washington DC, six hours behind Warsaw, to seize the news as it arrived and literally throw the announcement across the table in disgust. Doug MacEachin has described (in the third person) how, as the DCI, his executive assistants and the analysts gathered in the Operations Center,

> a debate ensued about how to interpret the events and whether and how to report them to the White House and senior national security officials. The chief of the CIA's unit responsible for analysis of Warsaw Pact military forces and a few of his analysts, who knew the contents of Kuklinski's reporting, were convinced that the actions fit the martial law plan. Other analysts were more uncertain, suggesting that what was taking place was a localized action. They did not want to be seen as sending out a false alarm.[1]

The CIA's failure to predict martial law accurately was hideous, although the scale of the lapse was subsequently concealed by assertions about the quality of Kuklinski's contribution. The problem lay not in the authenticity of his information, but in the reluctance of the CIA's analysts to recognize it for what it really was – advance warning of an occurrence that had been considered close to unthinkable. With the DI and the State Department agreed that the most dangerous moment for martial law had been during the previous April, they considered that the high-water mark of the crisis had passed without incident. Certainly it was true that the Bydgoszcz confrontation had brought Poland very close to collapse, but the Soviets had remained unwilling to fight their way across the frontier and into barricaded factories without a vocal invitation from the regime, and neither Kania nor Jaruzelski had been willing to take on Solidarity at a moment when the organization was at the peak of its power. Some believed that Solidarity's leadership had overplayed its hand and had acted prematurely, but even if this is a criticism made with the benefit of hindsight, it is certainly true that seven months later the scenario was quite different, even if it had been accurately forecast by Kuklinski.

Six hours before Jaruzelski's declaration, 3.4 million private telephones were disconnected at the exchange and 250,000 ZOMO militiamen under the command of the head of the Interior Ministry's counter-intelligence branch (WSW) were deployed to arrest 4,200 political activists overnight, followed by 4,500 the next day, to seal off the frontiers, close down the telephone exchanges and establish roadblocks across the country. Tanks rolled into central Warsaw and a self-styled 'Military Council of National Salvation' (WRON) seized control, taking the West by surprise. The coup had been planned in meticulous detail, masterminded by WRON's seventeen members, but the real power was held by a small committee headed by Jaruzelski consisting of General Eugeniusz Molczyk, the chief inspector of education and training, Czeslaw Kiszczak, the minister of the interior, Tadeusz Tuczapski, the chief inspector of territorial defence and Florian Siwicki.

Perhaps the most devastating dimension to the CIA's failure to predict martial law was the administration's reluctance to exploit the information it had received from Kuklinski. In what must have been a truly bizarre encounter, a fortnight after Kuklinski's exfiltration, the US ambassador in Warsaw, Francis Meehan, held an unusual evening meeting lasting an hour and a half with Jaruzelski who must have known that his trusted former aide would have spilled his martial law secrets to the CIA most comprehensively. Clearly Jaruzelski would have expected Meehan to raise the topic and perhaps deliver a stern warning from Washington about the West's likely reaction to martial law, but in the event Meehan never broached the subject, doubtless leaving Jaruzelski believing that he had received tacit approval from the White House. This view must have been confirmed when Alexander Haig later suggested that the West had been 'caught off guard' by the annoucnement. As MacEachin acknowledged, 'it is clear that there was not a failure of intelligence "gathering":

> There was a failure in the use of the information that had been 'gathered'. And the main problem was not – as has become commonly perceived – overprotection of the source and 'old-fashioned inter-agency rivalry' that caused Kuklinski's information to be restricted to the point that it was 'rendered useless'. The problem was that the CIA's analysis was dominated by the belief that the Polish leaders would not – and could not – impose a military suppression.

Highly critical of the CIA's performance was Bill Casey, who believed he understood why the Soviets had, as he saw it, consistently outmanoeuvred the West. He had taken over a Central Intelligence Agency handicapped by poor morale after a decade of congressional criticism, and a clandestine service that had been decimated by his predecessor, Admiral Stansfield Turner, who had cut 820 posts from the supposedly elite Directorate of Operations (DO). While the Agency had been due to be slimmed down after Vietnam, Turner had wielded the axe over a much shorter period, making the cuts over two years instead of the recommended five. The result was enforced premature departures and twenty outright dismissals, which did nothing to enhance the esprit de corps. However, low morale in the DO was more than simply about job security. After the wretched evacuation of Saigon and the abandonment of so many assets, the CIA had become a target of media and congressional interest, with the Pike and Church committees uncovering past embarrassments that ruined the Agency's liberal elite reputation. Watergate, allegations of botched assassination plots and the revelation of the CIA's illegal domestic operations left the Agency lacking the confidence to confront the Soviets, or so Casey believed.

Casey had not been unimpressed by John McMahon, the DDO appointed by Turner, but he was regarded by some as lacklustre, over-cautious, and lacking a background in operations. Certainly,

McMahon had come from the technical collection side, having supervised the SR-71 aerial reconnaissance programme, but Casey's initial attempt in May 1981 to replace him, by sending him to reorganize the ailing Directorate of Intelligence, went wrong very quickly; his own nominee for DDO, Max C. Hugel, was an outsider, a self-made New Hampshire businessman who was to last only a couple of months before resigning over allegations published in the *Washington Post* of stock market irregularities in his past. Later cleared of insider dealing, Hugel was succeeded by John H. Stein, a DO insider who subscribed to Casey's buccaneering style and supported his political agenda. A Yale graduate, Stein had served in three stations in Africa, and had been Chief of Station in Brussels when Admiral Turner had brought him into the DDO as an assistant to John McMahon.

Badly burned by his first encounters with the DO, Casey characteristically found a way of sidestepping the organization by finding his own independent operator, Richard Lawless, a CIA case officer who reported direct to Casey and undertook his own special assignments. Gates, who mistakenly thought Lawless's surname was actually a cryptonym recalls:

> McMahon, Stein and later I all were extremely uneasy about Casey running this man without checks or supervision. McMahon finally succeeded in corralling his operations – mostly – and bringing LAWLESS and some of Casey's other independent operators back into the bureaucratic tent under a new Associate Deputy Director for Operations, a position established essentially for overseeing Casey's private-sector initiative.[2]

Casey's style was to find a like-minded enthusiast, assign him a special task, and then open a direct line for him to report, thus outmanoeuvring, and infuriating, the bureaucrats. A good example is Dewey Clarridge's unexpected transfer from Rome to become chief of the Latin America Division, even though he did not speak Spanish. 'Casey didn't say I should report directly to him, but he made it happen that way,' recalls Clarridge. 'He phoned me directly and met with me without my superiors, bypassing the deputy director, Bobby Inman, and the DDO, John Stein. Stein knew me and understood that this was simply Casey's style.'[3]

Casey's very distinct agenda dated back to his OSS experiences in Europe during the Second World War, and he was of a generation that believed that friendships and networking could be harnessed to achieve what hitherto had never been considered a realistic political goal, the rolling back of the Soviet empire. Casey's robust politics were shared by President Reagan and his closest advisers who dreamed the impossible: a political and economic offensive to undermine the Kremlin's malign grasp on Eastern Europe and the liberation movements of the Third World. As the first DCI to be appointed to the cabinet, Casey exercised unique influence over the president, and when he took up his post he demanded and received an office suite, 345, on the third floor corner of the Old Executive Office Building, overlooking Pennsylvania Avenue and Seventeenth Street NW, so he could remain within the charmed ring of White House insiders. He was also responsible for maintaining his policy-making role, developed during the highly successful election campaign, by advocating the creation of a new unit, the National Security Planning Group (NSPG), which consisted of just himself, the president, the vice president, the national security adviser (Richard Allen) and the secretaries of state (Alexander Haig) and defence (Caspar Weinberger). Such an innovation was intended to be the fulcrum of foreign policy, neatly sidestepping the National Security Council, not to mention the president's Intelligence Oversight Board. As for the National Security Council, it was to be relegated to relative insignificance; the national security adviser's office, on a first-floor corner of the West Wing of the White House, formerly occupied by Henry Kissinger and Zbigniew Brzezinski, was moved to the basement, beside the situation room and staff canteen, signalling a commensurate loss of direct access to the president. In contrast, the NSPG's status was enhanced, its unpublicized objective to declare war on the Kremlin and avoid the leaks and political flak that would inevitably accompany such a bold public declaration. With the NSPG's support, expressed at a meeting on 30 January 1981, Casey felt free to attack Brezhnev on three fronts.

First, Casey was determined to transform the sterile war in Afghanistan where an estimated 90,000 Soviet troops were engaged in a long but sustainable stalemate against Islamic Mujahadeen guerrillas who had been covertly supported by the CIA to the tune of around $75 million a year. As Casey criss-crossed the globe in the DCI's personal C-141 Starlifter, fitted with a VIP accommodation container, he paid courtesy calls on the CIA's secret partners in the Afghan conflict. The key figures were Prince Turki al-Faisal, the Saudi director of intelligence, who had been persuaded by the CIA station chief, Alan Fiers, to allow his organization to act as CIA surrogates, matching Langley's financial contribution of $60 million and enabling Eastern bloc weapons to be purchased in Egypt and shipped to Pakistan. In Cairo, Casey visited President Anwar Sadat to see if the illicit procurement programme of Eastern-bloc automatic weapons and landmines could be stepped up, and in Islamabad he called on President Zia on 6 April and his director of the Inter-Services Intelligence agency, General Akhtar Abdul Rehman Khan, who supervised the Mujahadeen training camps close to the Afghan border around Peshawar and Quetta. After two days in Pakistan, Casey flew out to Beijing to introduce himself to the Chinese intelligence authorities, who were entranced at being given the opportunity to participate in a mutually beneficial anti-Soviet scheme in Afghanistan. By the time the DCI had left he had concluded a deal in which the Chinese would allow flights across the sensitive and disputed Kashmir airspace to deliver weapons for the Mujahadeen, coordinated by the CIA station in Islamabad.

Despite the scale of the clandestine commitment to the fragmented guerrillas, the war appeared to be having only a marginal impact on the Soviet Union, but Casey saw an opportunity to capitalize on the undoubted goodwill he had discovered in Riyadh, Cairo and Islamabad and to transform Afghanistan into the Kremlin's Vietnam. With Pakistan's willingness to increase the quality of training received by the tribesmen from foreign instructors, and the Saudis and Egyptians willing to improve the hardware, Casey was later to challenge the air superiority exercised by the feared, heavily-armoured Soviet Mil-24 helicopter gunships, designated HIND, which were vulnerable to a new generation of hand-held, heat-seeking missiles. Originally introduced into service in 1974, the Mil-24 was armed with a Yak-B 12.7mm sidemounted cannon or twin 23mm cannon, and became a familiar sight over the rugged terrain of Afghanistan where, with its distinctive 'greenhouse' tandem cockpits, it decimated the Mujahadeen, became associated with terrifying firepower and helped create the refugee crisis in Pakistan. But, despite its intimidatory appearance with weapons pods, gun turret and under-wing munitions, the HIND's size and weight made it an unwieldy battle cruiser, surprisingly vulnerable to attack by heat-seeking missiles.

Either individually or working in swarms, the HIND had established total air superiority by swooping down on isolated groups of guerrillas, raking them with anti-personnel ordnance and then delivering their cargo of up to eight paratroopers to complete the task. Such aggressive tactics had served to enhance the 'ten-feet tall' image of the Red Army infantryman in the West, and filled the Mujahadeen's sponsors with pessimism. The battle cruiser's advantage, fulfilling several different roles, including a combination of anti-tank, ground attack and assault, made it a formidable instrument of death, but its lethality concealed several design flaws, including its lack of passive defence. During a sharp manoeuvre at speed, the main rotors had been known to hit the tail assembly, and the turbine air intakes were prominent and vital targets for snipers. Worse still, the Hind's main oil intake was conveniently located directly under the red star painted on the fuselage.

Initially the CIA had been willing to procure only Soviet-manufactured SAM-7s, but the results achieved were indifferent and far below expectation. The Mujahadeen insisted the missiles were defective, a complaint that was initially dismissed as sheer inexperience, but the real reason was testimony to the KGB's efficiency, as CIA officer Vincent Cannistraro recalled: 'The SAMs weren't very effective for a reason. The Soviets had interrupted the supply channel and had deliberately sabotaged the SAM-7s. The Muj had been right all along.'

Even in unsophisticated hands the new weapons were to pose a potent threat to the Red Army's ability to engage small groups of poorly-equipped marauding insurgents. Armed with the infra-red, heat-seeking Stinger missiles, costing $50,000 apiece, the Pathans were to turn the tables on the Red Army, isolate individual garrisons and make concentrations of armour hard to protect from the air. The missiles were delivered in sealed tubes with re-usable gripstocks and a battery life of just a minute and a half. Having connected the battery cooling unit and identified a target a single flip on a thumb switch started the gyro motors, and then a squeeze on a rubberized button initiated the built-in passive infra-red seeker head and activated the optical sight. As the seeker searched for a heat source the weapon emitted a low growling sound, which changed to a high-pitched buzz as it locked on to a target. Now fully armed, a squeeze of the second trigger fired the missile which would chase the heat source and explode on impact. Once the previously omnipotent HIND-D gunships began to fall prey to the SAMs in September 1986, the morale of the pilots plummeted; they avoided low altitude passes and understandably traded the inaccuracy of height for safety. Although the Hind was heavily-armoured, fast and bristling with weaponry, it was difficult to manoeuvre, especially in the light air of Afghanistan's mountains, and some of its technology was outdated, with the rotor design being adapted from the Mil Mi-8 HIP helicopter which had been introduced in 1961. Its lack of agility, combined with a completely open exhaust, with no attempt at infra-red suppression, made it an ideal target for the Stinger. It took enormous personal bravery for someone to stand up in full sight and engage the target but, confident that Allah was over their other shoulder, there was no shortage of Mujahadeen volunteers.

The intention was to build on Muslim solidarity already expressed by President Zia and President Sadat, and to enhance the Saudi royal family's grip on power by sharing the NSA's wealth of Sigint collected in North and South Yemen, rightly regarded in Riyadh as potentially hostile neighbours and a source of subversion. They had rapidly become Soviet client states, if not actual satellites, backed up by an estimated 2000 military advisers. Thus, with only minimal visible effort, the CIA could strengthen its ties to three key regional powers, promote a major export, worth $8.5 billion, of five defence-orientated airborne early-warning planes to the Saudis, while simultaneously severely undermining Soviet influence. For the NSPG, this was a win-win policy with zero downside and plenty of potential for expansion. The Soviets had made gains virtually unopposed in Africa, Central America and the Middle East, either directly or by using the Cubans as surrogates, as had happened in Nicaragua and Angola. El Salvador, Honduras, Costa Rica, Grenada and Jamaica were now at risk, but Casey wanted to roll back the tide and, as he explained to an NSPG meeting in March, give active support to opposition groups in Libya, Laos, Iran and Grenada. Instead of just taking a stand in El Salvador, and seeking congressional approval for $19 million to defend democracy against Nicaraguan-backed insurgents using Argentine camps and personnel in Honduras, Casey wanted to go for the jugular and start harassing the Soviets in Ethiopia, Mozambique, Somalia and everywhere else where they had deployed military advisers. The costs would reach $20 billion from $6 billion within five years, but President Reagan was undeterred. As Casey reported to him after his Middle East tour in April 1981: 'In the past eight years the Soviets and their proxies have promoted insurgencies in over a dozen countries, five of them successful and seven now underway.'[4]

Casey's second strategy was economic, intended to cut the flow of financial aid and high technology to the Soviet bloc. According to the CIA's Directorate of Intelligence, the entire Soviet infrastructure was becoming increasingly dependent upon external support. Major new investment schemes, such as the controversial Urengoi-6 trans-Ukraine gas pipeline, was entirely reliant on participation by European banks which intended to trade a major injection of capital in return for a guaranteed future supply of discounted fuel from the rich but inaccessible exploration fields in Siberia. Casey intended to apply pressure on the merchant bankers, undermine confidence in the energy barter's viability and thereby strike at the weakness in the heart of the Soviet balance of payments which could amount to $30 billion a year. The DI also focused on the Polish deficit, noting that the country was perilously close to a technical default and required extended credit just to service outstanding loans. A syndicate of international banks had estimated that Poland required around $12 billion in hard currency urgently if the accumulated debt due for repayment at the end of 1981 was to be rolled over. The Polish ambassador in Washington DC, Romuald Spasowski, who was to defect in the aftermath of martial law, later confirmed the scale of the deficit, noting: 'our debt to the West exceeded $25 billion, and thus there was serious concern whether the credits already contracted would ever be repaid to the banks.' Casey advocated exploiting the crisis by offering Warsaw very limited strings-attached aid in return for economic and political reform, while actively encouraging the finance houses to take a firm line, confident that Moscow was in no position to bale Warsaw out.

In terms of assets inherited by Casey, three were of particular significance. Kuklinski in Poland had opened up the Warsaw Pact, and similar sources inside the KGB and GRU had destroyed the prevalent myth of Soviet ubiquity in the intelligence field. However, it was also clear that both organizations had been directed to concentrate on the illicit acquisition of Western technology, and there was growing evidence of Moscow's planners seeking to take shortcuts to the massive investment in research and development that would be required to keep pace with American and European achievements in avionics and electronics. The scale of effort devoted to what amounted to technology theft, in blatant violation of the Coordinating Committee on Multilateral Export Control's (CoCom) restrictions on the export of strategic *matériel*, had been disclosed by a French mole deep inside Directorate T, the scientific branch of the KGB's First Chief Directorate, and run under the supervision of Yves Bonnet of the DST (the French Security Service). Codenamed ADIEU, Colonel Vladimir I. Vetrov had spent five years at the KGB's *rezidentura* in Paris, and when approached by the DST had rejected the 'pitch' in a way that appeared to leave the door open. Later, when posted to the Soviet trade delegation in Montreal in 1978, he had been approached by the Royal Canadian Mounted Police (RCMP) security service, but on this occasion his less than emphatic rejection had been betrayed by a mole, later identified after his death as Gilles Brunet, an RCMP officer. Vetrov became the focus of a counter-intelligence investigation conducted by a KGB expert despatched from Moscow which, although judged inconclusive, resulted in his withdrawal from Canada in 1979. Infuriated by his treatment, Vetrov had subsequently approached the French military attaché in Moscow and had volunteered to document the Kremlin's covert procurement programme, thus revealing the true purpose of the innocuously-titled Military Industrial Commission (VPK) which coordinated the KGB and GRU's new focus on technical data with an economic significance. He handed over the VPK's annual reports for 1979 and 1980 which made astonishing reading, asserting that the organization had saved billions of roubles, had acquired shortcuts to thousands of Western research projects, and had supplied key knowledge and hardware in 5,000 military categories to numerous Soviet schemes. ADIEU's material, which amounted to 4,000 documents, was supplied until November 1982 when the hard-drinking Vetrov was charged with the murder of his mistress and another colleague with whom she was also having an affair. The documents were circulated within NATO under the codename KUDO and revealed that the Soviet RYAD computer was actually a counterfeit IBM 370, and that the radars of the F-14, F-15 and F-18 had been copied and fitted to Soviet fighters; it was even claimed (somewhat improbably) that the *Kirov* class nuclear battle-cruisers had been designed and built from American blueprints. According to a DIA report circulated in 1980, before Vetrov had come into play, 70 per cent of Warsaw Pact weapons were reliant on components from the West.

Vetrov's information had been used as a bargaining chip by President François Mitterrand to gain favour with NATO and President Reagan at the 1981 Ottawa Summit, and to demonstrate that although France had elected a socialist to the Elysée Palace, and had four communists in the cabinet, the administration was no longer susceptible to communist influence. Since Vetrov had also obligingly identified the KGB *rezident* in Paris as Nikolai Tchetverikov, and his deputies as Gennadi Korepanov, Yuri Bykov (in charge of the Line N illegals), Yuri Zevakine (Line X, scientific and technical) and Vitali Ioudenko (Line PR, political intelligence), President Mitterrand authorized their expulsion, together with forty-two other Soviet personnel masquerading as diplomats.

While ADIEU supplied solid evidence of what was to become known as technology transfer, he also exposed a further flaw in the Soviet structure. Casey became convinced that by tightening and stringently enforcing the CoCom rules, the VPK could be put out of business, thereby increasing the technology gap in Moscow almost to crisis point. Once again, the risks were minimal, for the Paris-based CoCom regime, well-established since 1949, needed only the political commitment and the necessary resources to close off the clandestine channels that had allowed the Soviets access to data-processing equipment, solid state circuitry, pumps, drills and precision hardware that kept its creaking infrastructure in operation.

CoCom, administered from an unmarked building next to the US embassy in Paris, operated bans on three trade categories – industrial, military and atomic energy – and extended the embargo beyond the Warsaw Pact to Vietnam, North Korea, Mongolia, Albania and China, with an additional list of suspected countries known as 'diverters'. Although far from an ideal mechanism for restricting exports to the Soviet bloc, because the European membership in particular was keen to promote trade, CoCom proved highly effective, with individual states strengthening their regimes under American pressure. In Britain, for example, this was manifested in 1985 through an amendment to the Export Administration Act 1979, requiring US consent for all re-exports of goods of American origin. Virtually unnoticed in the parliamentary timetable, this single item of legislation was to have a significant impact on Soviet imports.

The third strand of Casey's destabilization strategy centred on Poland, judged to be the weakest link in the Warsaw Pact. The objective was to beef up the collection effort in the capital and give covert assistance to any political movement that could mobilize public opinion and campaign against the communist regime. Such intervention was obviously far more risky than the other routes approved by the NSPG, especially if the vigilant and ruthless local security apparatus detected external interference, as happened in May 1982 when two embassy diplomats, James Howard and John Jerolis, were detained as they met a former detainee, Dr Ryszard Herczynski, in the scientist's apartment. This incident led to the expulsion of the two Americans, and encouraged the CIA to take an indirect approach, cultivating links to Solidarity offices in Paris and London, and making a renewed initiative in the Vatican.

Immediately following the imposition of martial law, the climate changed, and on Saturday, 19 December the Polish ambassador, Romuald Spasowski, defected, fearing that he would be abducted if he returned to his chancery. He, like his deputy, had been recalled to Warsaw, and he believed he had been placed under surveillance by Slawomir Lipowski, the SB *rezident*, who suspected him of disloyalty. Rather than fly back to Poland as ordered, Spasowski called the State Department and applied for political asylum for himself and his wife.

Chapter VII

William J. Casey

Apart from President Reagan, the single person most directly responsible for many of the events leading up to the Soviet collapse was William J. Casey, the DCI appointed in January 1981 whose career has been the subject of much speculation. Commentators who either never met Casey, or misunderstood his objectives, have claimed that he was a reluctant DCI, having really set his sights on the State Department. In reality, succeeding Stansfield Turner was Casey's sole ambition, and it was the single post he had set his heart on, probably long before the election campaign in which he played such a pivotal role.

To understand Casey one has to appreciate his initiation into the world of espionage in the Second World War when, as a young naval lieutenant handicapped by poor eyesight and stagnating in the Office of Naval Procurement where he dealt with the construction of landing craft, he used his connections with Washington's law firms to get an invitation to join the Office of Strategic Services (OSS). If ever there was an event that shaped a man's life, it was Casey's introduction to William J. Donovan late in September 1943. At the time Donovan, a partner in Donovan Leisure, and the charismatic former leader of the 'Fighting Irish', the 69th Infantry Regiment, with whom he had ended the First World War as America's most highly decorated war hero, was a hugely successful corporate lawyer. In 1942 he had been President Roosevelt's choice to head the OSS.

Casey, aged twenty-nine, and Donovan, aged sixty, at the time of their meeting, were both sons of Irish immigrants, devout Roman Catholics, Wall Street lawyers and shared the same first and second Christian names. Casey joined Donovan's OSS secretariat, a group of other young, well-connected lawyers, but within a couple of months had acquired a posting to London to run David Bruce's secretariat. In fact Bruce had no need of a large administrative office filled with lawyers and allowed Casey to become indispensable around headquarters. Nineteen days after the Normandy landings, Casey was at Bruce's side as he stepped ashore in France on an inspection tour. Later he was to visit Algiers while ANVIL, the invasion of the south of France, was being planned, and was in Grenoble soon after the Maquis seized the city. Although Casey's official duties were vague, he appears to have acted as Donovan's eyes and ears, visiting OSS units and writing reports. One such report was the result of a study undertaken by an OSS committee, for which Casey had acted as secretary, into America's postwar intelligence requirements. Casey drafted the document and then hand-delivered it to Donovan in Washington for presentation to the president. Later to be dismissed as essentially a plea for OSS's job security, the paper concentrated on the Soviet Union and the need to collect, collate and distribute intelligence, a crucial function of government that had been wholly neglected by the administration prior to Pearl Harbor.

Upon Casey's return to London, enhanced by a growing reputation as a blunt, impatient and very sharp staff operator with a direct line to Donovan, he produced a new study, running to eight pages and completed on 12 October, on the OSS's role in running agents into Germany. Hitherto, operations in the Reich had been avoided by the British who had also actively prevented the Americans from engaging in this most dangerous region. SOE's X Section had a disastrous record; it was almost wholly reliant on refugees and turncoats as agents who suffered an appalling rate of attrition for no perceptible advantage. SIS had cultivated a few sources in what was left of the German underground opposition, but the secret source codenamed ULTRA supplied far more reliable information than an army of spies, and at minimal risk. Not surprisingly, neither SOE nor SIS was keen to encourage OSS's ambitions, but Donovan visited London at the height of the Ardennes offensive and concluded that the war was far from over. He did not approve of the complacency of the Secret Intelligence (SI) branch, concentrated in the more fashionable bars of Paris, and unexpectedly appointed Casey as the new chief of SI in Europe. The vacancy had arisen after John Haskell had finally wangled a long-sought combat role, and his deputy, Alan Scaife, failed to win sufficient friends to succeed him. Casey was not an obvious candidate for the post, but turned himself into a civilian by obtaining a transfer to the inactive reserve and then getting himself rehired, so as to avoid having to lobby for the appropriate rank.

Casey had been with Donovan in Lyons in August 1944 when he had given Allen Foster Dulles a lift on his plane to London, in anticipation of the latter's new appointment to Wiesbaden as OSS's chief in Germany. Dulles had spent almost the entire war in Switzerland, cultivating German émigrés and some key anti-Nazis, and his version of events contrasted sharply with what seemed to be an inexplicable British reluctance to infiltrate agents into the heart of the Reich. Dulles knew it could be accomplished, but he had never been indoctrinated into the secrets of ULTRA. Casey must have been impressed with Dulles' tales of recruiting senior figures inside the Nazi foreign ministry, and certainly gained the impression that it should be possible to infiltrate agents into Austria and Germany, thereby confounding the British who believed that such undertakings could be accomplished only with the help of reception committees drawn from a resistance organization of the kind that had never existed in the Reich. Undeterred, Casey prepared his memorandum to Donovan on the 'immediate penetration of a fighting Germany'.

The months that followed were unquestionably Casey's finest. He had been given *carte blanche* by Donovan to recruit and train volunteers for perilous missions into Nazi territory, and he had to work from scratch with several handicaps, such as the unwillingness of the USAF to fly north of Stuttgart, and the fact that the only four OSS agents behind enemy lines in December 1944 had no means of communicating with their bases.

By March 1945 Casey's first team, a pair of Belgian SOE agents, were ready to be dropped into Kufstein in the Austrian Tyrol from Dijon in Operation DOCTOR. There followed more than a hundred missions which, according to his own after-action report dated 24 July 1945, divided up as twenty-nine failures, eleven unknown and sixty-two successes, with a casualty rate of 5 per cent, which compared very favourably with SOE's experiences in France or the attrition suffered by Bomber Command, which was considered a standard benchmark for high-risk operations. Casey's subsequent war reputation was to be enhanced first by the publication in 1979 of Joseph Persico's *Piercing the Reich*, which documented OSS's SI operations in Germany and Austria, and second by his own book on the Second World War, *The Secret War Against Hitler*, published in 1988, a year after his death. There remains, however, a strong suspicion that Casey's July 1945 report may have painted a characteristically over-optimistic picture of what had been achieved. It certainly contrasts sharply with the official OSS *War Report* prepared in 1947 by Peter Karlow who recorded critically that, regarding Germany,

> SI/London recruited, trained, and dispatched agents on a mass-production and insufficiently personal and selective basis. Out of 34 teams safely infiltrated, only seven came on the air. Austria, on the other hand, was being built up as the final Nazi 'redoubt' and had become the most tightly controlled enemy territory in Europe. OSS casualties ran close to fifty percent, but, of only thirteen teams from SI/Mediterranean Theatre of Operations, five provided Allied Forces Headquarters with valuable Brenner Pass and 'Redoubt' coverage.[1]

Clearly, there is a discrepancy between Casey's version of events and Karlow's research, and this is most evident in the differing accounts of those missions which were equipped with the lightweight walkie-talkie JOAN-ELEANOR system that allowed agents on the ground to communicate over an innovative voice channel with a Mosquito aircraft circling directly overhead in a tight orbit at an altitude of 30,000 feet. One of the advantages of the J-E was that it was directional, and therefore its signals were virtually impossible to intercept. Karlow reported that fifteen J-E teams were despatched to enemy territory between November 1944 and the end of the war, but contact was established successfully with only four of them, of which the most prolific, with a total of sixteen contacts, was BOBBY in Ultrum, Holland, who in fact was operating under the control of the Gestapo. BOBBY, former SOE agent Anton Schrader, was arrested in February 1945 (shortly before he was due to be murdered by a resistance cell which had mistakenly identified him as a traitor) and agreed to cooperate with his captors, thereby ensuring he survived the war. Curiously, although Casey acknowledged that BOBBY had become a double agent, Persico had omitted to mention it in his earlier account.

At the end of the war in Europe, Casey had intended to go to the Far East, but his plans were dashed when the atomic bomb brought about the Japanese surrender. Casey, already a civilian, resigned from the OSS in August 1945, thus narrowly avoiding having to share Donovan's humiliation the following month when President Truman signed the executive order to wind up the organization. He returned to his law practice in Washington DC and prospered, relying heavily on the many contacts he had developed during the war. It became a characteristic of his shuffling, slightly shambolic appearance that anything was possible and there were people who could fix just about everything. He developed an extraordinary collection of intensely loyal friends, mostly veterans of OSS like Geoffrey M.T. Jones and the oilman John Shaheen.

Casey's networking brought him plenty of business, and ultimately brought him tremendous support behind the scenes as he took over the DCI's desk at Langley on 28 January 1981, having received unanimous approval from Congress. One of his first actions upon arrival was to place an autographed portrait of Donovan on the wall, leaving no doubt about how he wanted to run the CIA. As it had had no fewer than five DCIs in the past eight years, he believed the Agency lacked only strong leadership and a renewed sense of confidence. He wanted to reinvigorate the Agency, free it from bureaucratic and legalistic shackles, and give it a renewed sense of purpose. If this sounds slightly too dynamic and ambitious for a man of his years, Casey was unwilling to compromise and set a punishing pace that left his staff gasping. During his first two years he called on twenty-three station chiefs, cramming in eleven during one particularly hectic fortnight. Even in terms of political influence, the contrast with Admiral Turner could hardly have been more marked. Initially, in 1977, Turner had briefed President Carter three times a week, but by the end of the administration the DCI was visiting the White House once a fortnight, having been adroitly outmanoeuvred by the shrewd national security adviser, Zbigniew Brzezinski. Casey was not only to have instant and continuous access to the Oval Office, but he was also a member of Reagan's cabinet. This latter development placed Casey in a curious constitutional position, for traditionally the DCI had always been part of the executive, carrying out the president's policy. Casey's status in the cabinet made him a policy-maker as well, which was unprecedented but broadly welcomed at Langley. Nor was this his only advantage for, unlike his predecessor, Casey became immensely popular with his troops, beguiling his station chiefs on his frequent whirlwind tours by calling informal staff meetings to introduce himself, and whispering in his host's ear, 'How am I doing?' The easy Irish charm rarely failed to work its magic, and his extracurricular demands, such as always wanting to know the location of the nearest bookstore so he could drop in to make a few purchases, served to endear him to his subordinates, who were often bemused by his shambolic appearance, or his habit of picking his teeth, seemingly distracted, with a paper-clip.

Once at the helm, Casey's style and strategy could not have been more different. He discovered, for example, that following the loss in Moscow in July 1977 of Aleksandr D. Ogorodnik, codenamed TRIGON, and the occurrence of a fire in the embassy, Turner had ordered the Chief of Station, Gardner (Gus) Hathaway, to close down his operations, claiming the environment was too dangerous for clandestine operations to be conducted. TRIGON's case officer, Martha Petersen, had been detained while servicing one of TRIGON's dead drops, and the KGB had seized some of his espionage paraphernalia, including two cameras and some sophisticated miniaturized communications equipment. Ogorodnik, a Foreign Ministry official recruited in Bogota four years earlier, after having sought the CIA's help when his Colombian girlfriend became pregnant, committed suicide using a cyanide pill concealed in a fountain pen while under interrogation, but Petersen was released and expelled because she had diplomatic immunity. Over-reacting, Turner had demanded that Leonard McCoy, the deputy chief of counter-intelligence, conduct a detailed investigation into how Petersen and her agent had been compromised, and then suspended all activities pending an inquiry into whether Gus Hathaway's station on the seventh floor had been compromised in August 1977 when Soviet firemen had entered the building and attempted to penetrate the secure areas. Turner was eventually persuaded to authorize a resumption of operations as the station staff were simply twiddling their thumbs, but Casey's instinctive reaction would have been to order the Directorate of Operations to redouble their efforts and develop techniques to outwit hostile surveillance. McCoy concluded, with a hint from Moscow, that TRIGON had inadvertently drawn attention to himself, although evidence later emerged that he had been betrayed by Karl Koecher, a CIA linguist who was actually part of a Czech husband and wife 'illegal' team.

Far from being deterred by the arrest of an important agent, or the attempt to force entry into the embassy's highly sensitive Communications Programs Unit, Casey regarded such incidents as both occupational hazards and incentives to tighten up lax procedures. While TRIGON's loss was a big disappointment, he was almost instantly replaced by Adolf Tolkachev, codenamed AE/BLIP, who volunteered hugely important aeronautical data from 'Phastron', the Research Institute of Radiobuilding, to Hathaway's deputy by leaving a note in his car. Tolkachev was ideologically motivated and initially had limited himself to distributing subversive literature. When ordered to improve the MiG-25's avionics, following the defection of Lieutenant Viktor Belenko with his Foxbat Mach 3 high-altitude interceptor to Hakodate in Japan in September 1976, he seized the opportunity to inflict some real damage on the regime by compromising all the fighter's new electronics, among them the advanced Fox Fire radar fire control system, the ground-mapping Doppler radar, and the Sirena 3 warning and electronic counter-measures device. Belenko's escape from the Chuguyevka airbase in eastern Siberia gave American analysts total, if temporary, access to his plane, thus forcing the Soviet air defence service to adopt new equipment and standards, every detail of which Tolkachev was ideally placed to reveal to his CIA handlers.

Later codenamed AE/VANQUISH, Tolkachev was paid the equivalent of more than two million dollars, mainly in antique Russian jewellery which he pretended he had inherited from his grandmother, in return for details of Soviet radar, electronic counter-measures, and stealth technology, a veritable haemorrhage of secrets that effectively neutralized the feared Foxbat superfighter. Tolkachev's rather unsubtle initial approach could easily have been a KGB provocation, but with Casey's encouragement Hathaway took the risk and assigned a senior Russian-speaking case officer who had a Russian background (and was impressively experienced, having worked in London on the Berlin tunnel material, and having transcribed the Penkovsky transcripts in 1962) and he ran the source with two successive case officers with great skill until May 1985 when the engineer was arrested, having been betrayed by an embittered former CIA officer, Edward Lee Howard.

For all his eccentricities, Casey is remembered by those who worked for him for his voracious consumption of facts, often acquired by reading up to three books a day, his impatience, and his religious commitment. He was a devout Roman Catholic, rarely missing the opportunity to attend mass, even in strictly Muslim Riyadh where the CoS made arrangements for a private service on Easter Sunday 1981, and had endowed a Catholic school with so much money that he had been elected a Knight of St Silvester. He arrived at Langley with a set of preconceived ideas, and was absolutely determined to make a difference. 'His personal interest was the clandestine side of the business,' recalled his DDCI, Admiral Bobby Ray Inman. 'He expected to run that himself. He'd be supportive of everything else that went on. But he didn't want to be bothered about the rest.' The fact that others around him, including William Clark, General Haig and Vernon Walters were also devout lay Roman Catholics, the latter two having been elected Knights of Malta, gave him a strong sense of community of purpose. When asked whether this Catholic cabal had any political significance, General Walters acknowledged that 'it helped eliminate the fuzziness' found among too many politicians and State Department officials. Certainly the joke inside the beltway was that the initials CIA no longer stood for 'Caught In the Act' but were now 'Catholics In Action'.

What bound the Catholics together, and indeed to many others inside the new administration, was a particular view of what was so memorably labelled 'the evil empire'. What made their perspective different was the inside knowledge that power gave them access to, and the confirmation of that perspective it appeared to provide. Very little mention had been made in public about the colossal signals intelligence facility that had been constructed by the GRU at Lourdes in Cuba, or the thousands of Soviet technicians employed at similar intercept sites in South Yemen and at the old US naval base at Cam Ranh Bay in Vietnam. The expansion had been gradual, but the implications were potentially daunting, giving the impression that the Soviet Union was attempting to develop a signals capability to challenge American domination in the field.

Casey actively distrusted the CIA's estimates on Soviet military spending and demanded a wholesale review of how they were prepared, including the sources relied upon and the methodology adopted by the analysts. He was especially critical of the system of national intelligence estimates (NIE) that were really documents drawn up by committee for the National Security Council and, as a consensus, inevitably tended to level down to the lowest common denominator. Casey was particularly conscious of the 1978 NIE that, two months before the Shah fled from Tehran, predicted his occupation of the Peacock Throne for a further decade and asserted that he possessed sufficient power to see off any challenge to his leadership. Convinced that the Directorate of Intelligence had not produced anything of worth throughout the Carter era, Casey told the DDI, Bruce Clarke, that it was time for him to retire, and established an Office of Global Issues to look at topics of his choice. Nor was he thrilled with the DO. When Casey discovered the DO's 130-page guidelines, a kind of rulebook for the Clandestine Service drawn up by cautious and gun-shy lawyers in the aftermath of the Pike and Church committees, he had every copy shredded and replaced with the admonition, 'use your common sense'. Instead of being advised to reject 'walk-ins' as probable provocations staged by a hostile security apparatus, case officers were assured they would not be penalized for taking the initiative and accepting defectors at face value.

Casey's frustrations and suspicions about the CIA's estimates eventually led to the creation in 1984 of a 'Team B' group of economists to make an independent comparison between the Agency's statistics and those available elsewhere. A similar exercise had been conducted on the 'missile gap' controversy as an external audit to determine the accuracy of the official statistics, and on this occasion Bob Gates gathered together a panel headed by Dr Charles Wolf from the Rand Corporation, assisted by Harry Rowan, who had moved from the CIA to the Department of Defense, Rick Erickson from Columbia, Gayle Johnson, who was an expert on Soviet agriculture, Dr Bournstein from Michigan State University, and Steve Meyer from the Massachusetts Institute of Technology (MIT). Their secret objective was to assess whether the CIA had erred, and they received several briefings from the DI's Maurice Ernst. They were encouraged to consult widely, and their task was made easier by access to some Soviet data made available in the early days of Mikhail Gorbachev's policy of *perestroika*. However, even the most fundamental figures were elusive, and judging the Soviet Union's real gross national product, its growth rate, and the size of the military budget, proved a complex undertaking with plenty of methodological and statistical obstacles. Even judging unit production costs and exchange rates, usually a fairly routine exercise in most economic models, proved to be fraught with problems. Eventually, in the autumn of 1985, Team B reported that the CIA's estimate that the Soviet economy was 50 per cent of the American economy had erred by a factor of 20 per cent, and that the growth rate between 1980 and 1984 had also been exaggerated, as had the size of the military burden, which was calculated to be roughly 12–15 per cent of the economy.

The Wolf Report, which remains classified, was partially leaked to imply that the CIA had failed to assess the Soviet economy properly, but the effect was to enhance the status of those critics who had taken the unpopular view that the communist edifice was flawed, if not actually in a state of slow, progressive collapse. Those such as Zbigniew Brzezinski and the economist Charles Gati, who had fled Budapest in 1956, had often been accused of being Eastern Europeans with an anti-Soviet prejudice which had coloured their judgment. Wolf's conclusions appeared to suggest that they had been right all along, and that the entire Soviet bloc was not just in decline, but in real danger of total collapse, opinions that neatly coincided with those of the DCI.

Casey found long meetings boring, lengthy briefing papers indigestible and complicated statistics hard to grasp, yet he had a voracious appetite for facts, especially when they conformed to one of his deeply held opinions. Dangerously, he had retained an OSS wartime view that the media were potential opponents, and that Congress inhibited good intelligence work, and in his determination to get his way he bruised a great many egos in the intelligence community. Like his mentor, he behaved like a bull in a china shop, but he was also anxious to achieve, just as he believed Donovan had been, and even commissioned a statue of Donovan to stand in the CIA's lobby as a permanent reminder. However, his handicap, and ultimately his undoing, was the legislation that Congress had demanded to rein in such free spirits. Casey's sympathy would have been entirely with the molehunter James Angleton when he had been recorded inadvertently after testifying to the Church Committee in September 1975 that 'it is inconceivable that a secret arm of the government has to comply with all the overt orders of the government'. Angleton, until recently chief of the Counter-intelligence Staff, had served in the OSS and was imbued with what he perceived to be the realities of clandestine warfare; he partially withdrew his unwise comment, but it unquestionably remained his private opinion. A secret intelligence service conducted secret operations and could not be expected to share them with outsiders. This view led Angleton's DCI, Dick Helms, to plead *nolo contendere* on a charge of perjury when he testified to Congress that the CIA had not plotted to bring down the Allende government in Chile. Caught in the dilemma of whether to protect the Agency's secrets or give misleading sworn evidence to an open session of the Senate Foreign Relations Committee held to approve his appointment as Nixon's ambassador to Tehran, Helms opted for less than the truth. As a consequence of the CIA's 'abuses' of Watergate, domestic operations, assassination plots and what some believed amounted to an independent foreign policy, President Ford signed the Hughes–Ryan Amendment which required the Agency to obtain a written approval for each secret operation, and to report it to Congress 'in a timely fashion'. Without such an authorization or 'finding', any money spent by the Agency or its staff would be unlawful. Accordingly, Casey's role would not be limited to setting the CIA a new direction, but would require him to win friends on Capitol Hill and persuade fickle politicians that his operations deserved to be funded. While Casey's initial approval was unanimous, his freebooting style was to create a huge problem for the Agency, easily matching the supposed misconduct that had so enraged previous congressional committees. Even some of those closest to him, including his first deputy, Bobby Inman, found his disingenuous replies to questions put by congressmen hard to swallow; Inman was accused of disloyalty because he fidgeted when the DCI fudged an answer. Inman's self-conscious behaviour, especially fiddling with his socks while Casey gave a less than straightforward account of a secret operation, became a cause for comment on Capitol Hill and Casey suspected his deputy was deliberately sending signals to his inquisitors. 'Bill Casey was a freelance buccaneer,' Inman said. 'If I had to sum the man up in one sentence, I'd put it this way. If it's not specifically prohibited by the law, then it's okay. Do it.'[2]

Gates, however, soon realized what made the DCI tick:

> Casey's approach to clandestine operations was shaped almost entirely by his experience in World War II. In that stage of American intelligence, he wasn't dealing with careerists, with people who had grown up in the business. He was remembering the guy who had been a Wall Street lawyer and a year later is doing brilliant things inside occupied Belgium. Dealing with the bureaucracy that had developed since then drove Casey crazy.[3]

The intelligence bureaucracy that Casey had outmanoeuvred with such ease in 1944 had grown into an aggressive animal, backed with legal sanctions, by 1981. Every new plan of any significance had to be approved by the president, and the House and Senate intelligence committees had to be informed within an undefined 'timely' period, generally held to be about forty-eight hours. Casey regarded this requirement as a potentially dangerous burden, with the congressional committees and their staffs vulnerable to politically-motivated leaking. However, the CIA professionals had come to terms with the oversight requirements and actually found some comfort in getting formal political sanction for activities that might otherwise land them in gaol. The easy-going days of pre-Watergate administrations were long gone, mourned only by a few who had been part of that buccaneering culture. According to Gates, Casey could not abide the new culture and 'was fed up with the DO. It was just too cautious, too bureaucratic, too slow, too timid and too unimaginative. Too much a closed shop. Not at all like the OSS.'

Another significant change in the way foreign policy was created was the growth of the White House bureaucracy centred on the National Security Council. A staff of over a hundred prepared drafts of position papers on every conceivable policy issue. Although Casey was to be equally contemptuous of this monolithic structure, he was to discover that it did possess the remarkable advantage of being entirely free of congressional scrutiny. The extent to which Casey actively exploited this loophole has never been determined, but there is more than a suspicion that he quickly sniffed out the opportunity to mount clandestine operations in the Middle East and Central America that his own organization deemed too risky.

While Casey came to the DCI's job with an agenda, his first task was to redirect the CIA towards what he considered to be the key strategic targets. On 24 February, within four weeks of taking over, he proposed a new covert action programme to interdict the flow of weapons from Cuba and Nicaragua to the guerrillas in El Salvador. President Reagan approved the new Intelligence Finding on 9 March and thus set in motion a plan to confront the Soviets around the globe. As far as Central America was concerned, Casey produced an NIE entitled *Cuban Policy in Latin America* on 6 April, which explained the new approach to policy-makers and asserted that the Sandinistas had expanded their ambitions and were now receiving aid from Bulgaria, Czechoslovakia, Hungary, Ethiopia, Vietnam and the PLO. However, the real catalyst was Casey's visit to Panama in mid-July when he realized that the Sandinistas had stepped up their subversion in the region. Seventy Nicaraguan pilots had been despatched to Bulgaria to undergo conversion courses on various models of MiG fighters, and it was known that Cuba had been equipped with two squadrons of the impressive MiG-23, the interceptor designated FLOGGER by NATO. Speculation was rife that although the Nicaraguans had performed badly during training, either Bulgarian or Cuban pilots might be posted to Managua, thereby altering the balance of power in the region.

Upon his return to Langley, Casey brought Dewey Clarridge over from Rome, first to become chief of the Latin America Division, and then to oversee the new tactics; from then on, as Gates recalls, he 'would talk, meet and travel privately with Casey. The die was cast.' By October, Casey was arguing for indirect intervention, through an ingenious route; Argentina had access to 500 members of Nicaraguan President Somoza's National Guard, many of whom had been educated and trained in Buenos Aires, and the plan called for arming and supporting a resistance organization from an Argentine camp in Honduras. This force was to become known as the Contras.

The National Security Council backed Casey on 16 November, and then President Reagan signed a new Intelligence Finding, designated NSDD-17, on 1 December authorizing $19 million for them. In between those dates Clarridge flew to Argentina to meet General Leopoldo Galtieri and his director of military intelligence, General Mario Davico, and gain their agreement to the scheme, which was instantly forthcoming although little was to come of it.

Casey's new stand against Nicaragua paid its first dividend in February 1982 when Dewey Clarridge flew to Acapulco to negotiate the defection of Eden Pastora, the revolutionary leader and former deputy minister in the Sandinista regime known as 'Commandante Zero', and agreed to maintain and arm him in Costa Rica. Although Pastora was more interested in regaining power in Managua than in stopping the export of Sandinista mischief, his broad objectives coincided with Casey's, and thus won his support. The only problem with this approach was a legal one, which Casey characteristically ignored, and it centred on Pastora's motives. If he was receiving the CIA's aid, and he intended to seize power, then the CIA had involved itself in toppling a foreign government, which made the entire undertaking illegal and outside the terms of the President's Finding. There was also another complication, that of complying with Pastora's unexpected condition that his followers in Costa Rica should receive an airdrop of weapons and radios. Despite the legalistic objections of Bobby Inman, Casey authorized the drop and even received Pastora at his office in Langley.

On 29 March 1981, three weeks after the president had signed the Finding on Central America, Casey asked his DDCI, Bobby Inman, and the DDO, John McMahon, for a detailed analysis of the current status of key Third World countries vulnerable to Soviet influence. He then set off on a personal tour, visiting Tripoli, Islamabad, Mogadishu, Khartoum and Muscat, which led Gates to conclude: 'Casey would remain obsessed with Soviet and proxy subversion in the Third World for the rest of his life. Here was the Soviet challenge he had taken the job at CIA to counter and defeat.' Casey returned from his tour convinced that he had finally grasped the Kremlin's objectives, which were to control the region's principal strategic sites: the Straits of Hormuz by eliminating the pro-British Sultan of Oman; the Red Sea and then Suez by grabbing Somalia and North Yemen; the entrance to the Mediterranean by establishing a base in Morocco to challenge Gibraltar. Casey's solution was a crusade to free the West's oil supplies from what he believed was a concerted conspiracy to encircle and then simply cut them off.

Part of Casey's crusade had been started by Zbigniew Brzezinski in February 1980 when he visited President Zia in Islamabad to restore relations strained by the Carter administration's suspension of aid in April 1979, following the discovery that Pakistan was developing an atomic bomb. Carter had been committed to nuclear non-proliferation but the Soviet invasion of Afghanistan in December had altered the regional geopolitics. During a visit to the Khyber Pass, Brzezinski offered a resumption of economic and military aid, which was to amount to $3.2 billion, if the Pakistani authorities allowed a few of the two million Afghan refugees camped on their territory access to Chinese and Soviet weapons donated by the Saudis in a *jihad*, a holy war against the Russian occupation. The weapons, costing $15 million in 1980, were to come from the huge stockpiles that had accumulated in Egypt before President Sadat had expelled the Soviets, or purchased from the Czechs who were anxious for hard currency, and were to be subsidized by the Saudis in an arrangement Casey had inherited from Brzezinski, on a trip to Riyadh in April 1981. It was reinforced a year later, on 6 April 1982, when Casey met Zia at his unassuming bungalow home in Rawalpindi's military cantonment, followed the next month by a further visit to Crown Prince (later King) Fahd. Although Casey was to build on this foundation, which had begun modestly enough with consignments of old (often rusty) British Lee Enfield 303 rifles sold from Egyptian armouries, it was Brzezinski who was responsible for President Carter's Finding, dated 3 July 1979, starting the CIA's clandestine support for the Mujahadeen, *six months before* the Soviet invasion. However, Casey and Zia really took to each other, meeting again at Brezhnev's funeral in Moscow in November 1982, and they remained close thereafter.

The CIA's failure to predict the Soviet invasion, despite reporting on the military build-up, eventually several times a day, was a lapse that went to the heart of Casey's suspicions about what was wrong with the Agency, and especially the DI. Turner's advice to President Carter had been prepared almost in the face of the strong opinions expressed by the intelligence community warning staff whose function it was to assess conflict indicators and submit objective judgments. The problem arose when the warning staff set out their arguments and were overruled by the analysts who, governed by Western standards of common sense, pointed out that nobody would be daft enough to jeopardize SALT II and intervene in a country with a history like Afghanistan's. The warning staff could see what was happening on the ground, but the analysts showed, correctly, that the political implications mitigated against such a hazardous enterprise. The unanticipated dimension was the Kremlin's willingness to indulge in an undertaking that, by Western standards, was entirely foolhardy. The fact that subsequent tactical intercepts were full of such comments from Soviet military commanders as 'What folly have those idiots in Moscow got us into?' cut absolutely no ice whatever with those who preferred not to be reminded of what they had advised weeks earlier. Stung by what was unquestionably a major intelligence failure, Jimmy Carter signed a further secret President's Finding immediately after Christmas 1979, escalating the non-lethal aid authorized the previous July to 'harassment' of the Soviet occupation forces.

The true architect of many of Casey's schemes was actually Zbigniew Brzezinski, the Polish immigrant who had been taken to Canada at the age of three by his father, a diplomat. Always committed to dismantling the Soviet bloc, Brzezinski had warmed to his lifelong belief that 'there is no supranationalism in the Soviet Union' while preparing his dissertation at McGill University. He saw the crushing of the Prague Spring in August 1968 as 'the beginning of the end' and in his thesis, *Inability to Renovate*, he expanded on this theme. As President Carter's national security adviser, Brzezinski had regarded detente as simply a method of getting Moscow to lower its guard, and had masterminded numerous secret President's Findings, the most significant of which was a still-classified covert action programme aimed at the 'delegitimization of the Soviet Union', by which was meant detaching some of the component states by encouraging nationalism and separatism. As well as channelling money to émigré organizations, this policy also meant developing conduits into the most vulnerable regions to fund dissidents and opposition groups.

Ten months after President Sadat of Egypt was assassinated in

October 1981, Casey flew to Cairo, en route from Pretoria, and resumed negotiations with his successor, President Hosni Mubarak, to extend the procurement beyond small arms to include rocket-propelled grenades and Egyptian 122mm rocket-launchers, amounting to 10,000 tonnes. Casey was to inherit the covert action and in future years expand it dramatically with General Rehman Khan's successor at the ISI (Inter-Services Intelligence), General Hamid Gul, but he was to be limited by the stricture, apparently imposed at the outset by General Zia, that none of the hardware should be of American manufacture. By 1983 the Afghan weapons appropriation had reached $40 million and, emboldened by congressional support and increased enthusiasm from President Zia who no longer feared Soviet reprisals as much as he worried about ancient Russian ambitions to acquire a warm-water port on the Indian Ocean, Casey pressed for more sophisticated weaponry. Hitherto the CIA had placed some value on deniability, working through intermediaries and cut-outs, limiting the hardware to the obsolescent Egyptian inventory and restricting the CIA Chief of Station in Islamabad, Phil Piekney, to discreet liaison, such as having access to Soviet defectors through the Tolstoy Foundation. The objective of the CIA's Near East (NE) Division, then headed by Charles Cogan, had been to find a way of harassing the Soviets using the seven leading Mujahadeen groups as surrogates, without provoking an invasion of Pakistan. Far from creating a political hazard, the CIA had gathered some unlikely allies, among them the Chinese who had been persuaded by Brzezinski to allow the NSA to establish intercept facilities at Korla and Qitai to monitor Soviet wireless traffic after the Iranian bases, authorized by the Shah, were closed down by the Ayatollah Khomeini's Revolutionary Guards. The Chinese had also been willing to supply large quantities of transport mules and locally manufactured Soviet weaponry. Brzezinski had developed a close personal relationship with Chinese Leader Deng Zhaoping, and had seized the opportunity to encourage his anti-Soviet anxieties. For the People's Republic of China, the invasion of Afghanistan had served to extend its frontier with the Soviets, a situation viewed with considerable misgiving in Beijing. The American proposals boasted the added advantage of cultivating Pakistan, which was India and China's natural, historical enemy. On the ancient principle of 'my enemy's enemy is my friend', the Chinese effectively joined a Western Sigint alliance against the Soviets.

The American intercept sites in China were to be run in conditions of the utmost secrecy, and remain in operation to this day, their full story being one of the strangest episodes of the Cold War. The original purpose of the Iranian sites was the interception of telemetry data from Soviet missile tests at Kaputsin Yar and Tyuratam, with the ground stations picking up the wireless traffic from the range that necessarily heralded a test. Once the firing had occurred, the flight would be monitored by Sigint U-2 aircraft flying in parallel along the border collecting the telemetry transmissions. The Chinese solution was to offer Korla and Qitai, with a third facility at Pamir, close to the Afghan 'finger' that extended into China. They were staffed by the NSA, with German BND and Chinese personnel, until 1991 when the Americans left. Although the site was known to the Soviets, and was the target of several KHAD (Afghan security service) penetration attempts, all the Kabul regime succeeded in acquiring was some of the base's shredded waste paper.[4]

For all of Brzezinski's preparation, Bill Casey found himself under pressure from the Saudis who, feeling increasingly isolated, had asked for some of the top-of-the-range hardware that recently had been distributed to US troops in Germany. The newly enthroned King Fahd wanted more sophisticated equipment, and in the spring of 1984 invited Casey to stay with him on his sumptuous estate overlooking Marbella to argue for more help.

Casey and Fahd agreed that the tide was turning in favour of the Mujahadeen, although few external observers knew the reasons why. One was the dramatically improved quality of intelligence reaching the guerrillas through the CIA, and a breakthrough in developing tactics to defeat the Mil-24 gunships. Two Afghan pilots had defected to Pakistan, bringing with them an example of the Mil-25 and its rather more sophisticated variant, the Mil-24. Naturally, the Soviets were pressing for the return of the helicopters, but Vernon Walters flew to Rawalpindi to see President Zia and persuaded him to let the CIA load them on to a C-141 Starlifter and spirit them out of the country. Although Walters had struck up a close friendship with Zia, and paid special attention to his handicapped daughter, he had no expectation of success. To his surprise, Zia authorized the operation, on condition the Mujahadeen were given 'some means of countering this death from the skies'. The result was that the United States acquired a Mil-25, and the Soviets were informed that both helicopters had been destroyed in a hangar fire.

The CIA's tactics had also begun to pay off on the ground where the Mujahadeen had been unimpressed by Spetsnaz troops, and had trained snipers to zero in on Soviet officers. Every strategic review came to the same conclusion: the Mujahadeen were not lacking in bravery or the will to kill Russians, only the means to achieve this objective.

Chapter VIII

The Kremlin's Vietnam

With growing domestic political support, Casey felt sufficiently confident to increase the stakes in 1985 by giving the Mujahadeen up to 65,000 tonnes of the kind of mortars, anti-tank guns, Chinese 107mm rocket-launchers and anti-aircraft artillery that they really needed if they were to do more than harass the enemy. Casey had made a further visit to Riyadh and Islamabad in the spring of 1985 and had been easily persuaded to escalate the shipments to 100,000 rounds and 200,000 artillery rockets. The plan was to stage hit-and-run attacks in the many vulnerable gorges along the winding Salang Highway, linking the Soviet bases over the frontier with the Afghan capital Kabul, where most of the troops were concentrated, thereby increasing Soviet reliance on air transport. The other strategy was to sabotage the underground pipeline carrying natural gas from Shibarghan into the USSR, acts which invariably drew indiscriminate retaliatory air-raids on the civilian population. Far from cowing the villagers into submission, the bombing created immense ill-will, numerous recruits for the Mujahadeen, and even more desertions from the less than reliable Afghan army. To ensure the best deployment of the ragtag guerrillas, the CIA shared overhead satellite reconnaissance photos with the Pakistan ISI and produced imagery-based accurate maps of a notoriously uncharted region so each attack could be planned with precision rather than with what had hitherto been little more than guesswork. 'This was a tremendous help,' recalled the head of the ISI's Afghan Bureau, Brigadier Mohammad Yousaf. 'The CIA would show us the maps and help us target vital areas. CIA satellite information would include exact targets, location of posts; it would also indicate the strength of the enemy and show possible routes to get in and out of the area. This satellite information played a major role in the victory.'

For Casey, this was a vintage OSS logistical problem of allowing the resistance to fight the hated occupation on somewhat more equal terms; the first solution attempted was the purchase from the Swiss arms manufacturer Oerlikon-Buhrle in 1983 of forty modern 20mm anti-aircraft cannon. The person pressing for this particular procurement was a congressman from Texas, Charlie Wilson, who became the cause's most enthusiastic exponent; there was later to be a suspicion that his advocacy of the Mujahadeen was not unconnected with his business relationship with Joe Christie, an arms dealer and former state senator in Texas whose company, Marine Resources Inc., handled the transaction. Although the Swiss guaranteed discretion in such sales, the easily traced banking papertrail – through a Panama-based company, Tremona Investments, that instructed the Interallianz Bank to pay Oerlikon – was later to embarrass the CIA and lead to allegations of corruption in Switzerland.

The Oerlikon procurement represented a major change in policy regarding the clandestine nature of the CIA's support for the conflict, but Howard Hart, the CoS in Islamabad, pronounced the guns unsuitable for deployment with highly mobile guerrilla units constantly scaling mountains. Each weapon cost a million dollars, and with its high rate of fire and enormously expensive 20mm ammunition, could loose off another million in shells in practically no time at all. It was also heavy, weighing 1,200 pounds, and required nearly two dozen hardy mules to carry it into combat. In the end, predictably, most were siphoned off by commission-conscious middlemen long before they came close the Afghan frontier. While this may not have been the wisest investment of $50 million, it did allow Casey in April 1985 to get National Security Decision Directive 166, entitled *Expanded US Aid to Afghan Guerrillas*, in which the president sanctioned the CIA to rid Afghanistan of its unwanted occupiers 'by all means available'. This vague phrase was defined in a sixteen-page appendix, signed by the national security adviser Bob Macfarlane, which recommended classic demoralization tactics, such as the targeting of Soviet officers, and authorized Mujahadeen access to a higher level of American technology, including frequency-hopping radio equipment to baffle Soviet interception, sophisticated timers for delayed-action sabotage, and satellite imagery to assist in planning. Having achieved NSDD-166, which set up an NSC working group to dismantle potential bureaucratic roadblocks within the administration, Casey took off for the CIA's Far East stations, making a special visit to Manila to talk personally to an increasingly beleaguered President Ferdinand Marcos.

In practical terms, NSDD-166 translated into 50,000 tonnes of *matériel* slipping into Afghanistan, five times the amount delivered in 1983. On the ground, this meant a long-range wireless network linking Pakistan to Mujahadeen hideouts in Parwan, Kandahar, Paghman and Mazar-i-Sharif, with tactical circuits on frequency-hopping equipment enabling local guerrilla units to coordinate their activities. Whereas in the past the Mujahadeen had tended to concentrate on poorly defended outposts which the Afghan soldiers were as likely to desert as defend, they now were sufficiently emboldened, armed with plastic explosives, accurate mortars and the latest sniper's rifles, to attack harder targets. Success in the Panjshir valley and at the battalion headquarters at Peshgohor led to an almost continuous barrage on the airfield at Kandahar, and there was even an attempt in Kabul to assassinate Mohammud Najibullah, director of the feared KHAD security apparatus which made ruthless but ultimately futile efforts to enforce the Afghan army's diminishing loyalty. Back in Washington, NSDD-166 produced a hitherto unseen level of inter-agency cooperation with the State Department, the Department of Defense, the US Information Agency and even the US Agency for International Development, previously exempted from national security strategy issues, meeting regularly to apply pressure on the Soviets.

Casey's enthusiasm for the Mujahadeen, combined with that most elusive of attributes, bipartisan domestic American political support for the guerrillas, and blessed with an almost unprecedented consensus of foreign backing for challenging the Soviet invaders, led to the creation of what amounted to a complete, self-contained army staff within the CIA. Despite institutionalized resistance to dedicated task forces, which in the unhappy example of the Central American experience had appeared to some in management to have exercised rather too much independence, Casey commissioned Jack Devine to write a proposal for an Afghan task force. Having recently returned

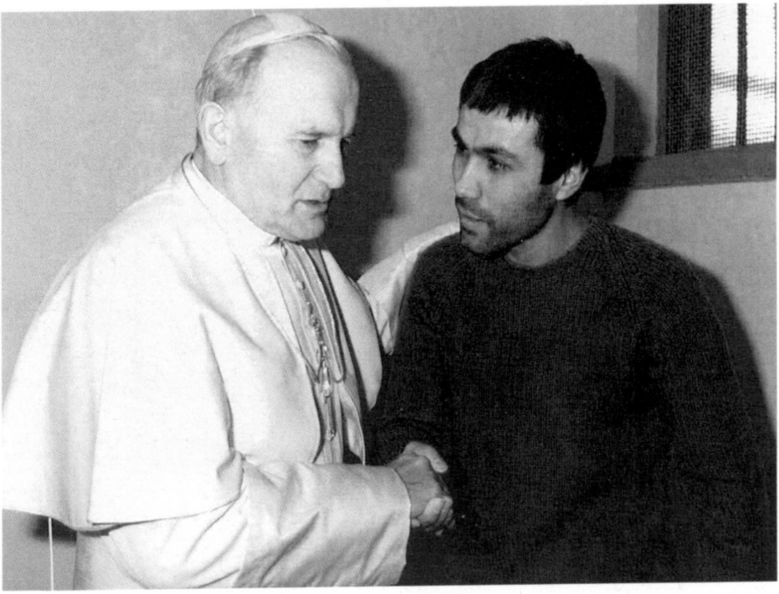

Mehmet Ali Agca meets John Paul II at Rebibbia prison. Baffled by how, as an experienced gunman, he had failed to kill the Pope, Agca became convinced that his target had been saved by divine intervention.

Pope John Paul II meets Sister Lucia, the sole surviving witness to the 1917 apparition at Fatima when she was entrusted with three secrets. This picture was taken on 13 May 1982, exactly a year after the assassination attempt.

Colonel Ryszard Kuklinski, one of General Jaruzelski's most trusted aides, standing at his shoulder *(above)* at a Warsaw Pact conference in Budapest in December 1977 and *(below)* flanked by the Soviet Minister of Defence Marshal Dmitri Ustinov (left) and Marshal Sergei Akhromeyev in Warsaw on 4 December 1979. Codenamed GULL, Kuklinski had passed highly classified documents to the CIA since 1972, but was exfiltrated when he was inadvertently compromised by a leak from the Vatican.

A midsummer Solidarity demonstration in Krakow when the Pope returned to his native city in June 1983. The CIA secretly funded the movement and smuggled printing and video equipment into Poland.

Martial law is imposed across the country, and here ZOMO troops arrive at the Polish Academy of Science in Warsaw to arrest Solidarity members.

Above Lech Walesa receives holy communion from John Paul II. The charismatic electrician from the Lenin Shipyard at Gdansk was later identified as having been a source for the SB.

Below Robert Gates succeeded Bill Casey as DCI but his appointment was challenged by a CIA analyst, Melvin Goodman, who told Congressional investigators that Gates had deliberately skewed information about the Pope's assassination to implicate the Bulgarians.

Above Bill Casey was the original 'true believer' who was always convinced the Soviets had been behind the plot to kill the Pope. Struck down by a brain tumour before he could complete his testimony to Congress on the Iran-Contra scandal, Casey died in May 1987 and took many of his secrets to the grave.

Left Zbigniew Brzezinski, Jimmy Carter's National Security Adviser, who began the clandestine support for the Afghan Mujahadeen.

Right Vladimir Krychkov, chief of the KGB's First Chief Directorate, who arranged for a network run by the Bulgarian DS to plot the Pope's assassination. In August 1991 he was imprisoned when his coup against Mikhail Gorbachev failed.

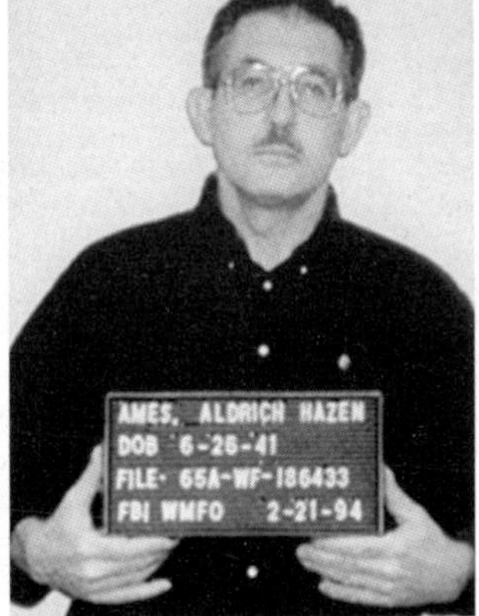

Left Aldrich Ames was posted to Rome between July 1986 and July 1989, where he met and ran GT/MOTORBOAT, an officer in the Bulgarian DS. GT/MOTORBOAT revealed details of Bulgarian involvement in the plot to assassinate the Pope, not realising that Ames had been haemorrhaging secrets to the KGB since May 1985.

General Vernon Walters (left), deputy Director of the CIA from May 1972 to July 1976, was appointed President Reagan's roving ambassador to brief John Paul II in the Vatican, and was authorized to show him classified American satellite imagery to demonstrate the scale of the Soviet threat. Hugh Montgomery (right), formerly the CIA's Chief of Station in Moscow, was brought back from Rome by Casey to run the State Department's intelligence division. Anne-Marie Montgomery, Hugh's wife (centre), drove General Walters into St Peter's Square to witness the announcement that Cardinal Karol Wojtyla had been elected the first Slavic pontiff.

The National Security Agency station at Teufelsberg in Berlin. Established in 1957 in the British Sector to intercept Warsaw Pact signals in East Germany, the intercept facility reached into Poland and played a key role during the months leading up to the imposition of martial law.

Milton Bearden, the Station Chief in Islamabad and the first CIA officer to make a clandestine entry into Afghanistan, dressed in white and standing on a captured Soviet armoured personnel carrier.

Casey's choice as Chief of the Afghan Task Force was Jack Devine, pictured here (fourth from right, back row) in Afghanistan, another 'true believer' who recognised that the introduction of the Stinger missile would eventually drive the Red Army out of Afghanistan and thereby exacerbate the Soviet collapse.

Surrounded by Mujahadeen guerrillas, Milton Bearden was fêted in Afghanistan as the person responsible for masterminding the CIA's largest covert war, and for introducing the Stinger anti-aircraft missile which dramatically altered the course of the war.

from being station chief in Buenos Aires, his fifth tour in the Latin America Division, Devine had switched to the Agency's Middle East Division, and envisaged bringing all the various different officers working in separate divisions under a single organizational roof, which would amount to a staff of almost a hundred. This figure would eventually double, but it was an astonishing escalation from the early days of 1981 when fewer than a dozen personnel stretched across various country divisions, supervising the uncoordinated response to the Soviet invasion.

Ultimately, the Afghan task force, which was to have three chiefs in all before it was wound up, effectively ran and supplied an army of 125,000 Mujahadeen, and became the largest unit of its kind in the Agency's history. As well as provisioning the troops, which meant managing logistics covertly on a gigantic scale, with some 9,000 mules, and supplying around 10 million pounds of munitions a month, the task force was obliged to commission the manufacture of suitable weaponry in third countries, since insufficient quantities of, for instance, the AK-47 assault rifle were available from the usual 'grey market' sources.

That the Soviets were taking their military losses seriously became clear when Spetsnaz special forces were deployed in Afghanistan, a move which heralded a major counter-offensive. New troops, supported by air power, were to accomplish significant gains at Zhawar and Khost, but in the long term these achievements served only to highlight heavy Soviet reliance on strafing tactics, and reveal a fatal flaw in their strategy. Elimination of low-flying helicopters and ground-attack aircraft would transform the relative inequality in firepower, but before the USA agreed to release the weapons demanded, Moscow unleashed a sustained military campaign, led by General Mikhail Zaitsev, widely regarded as an impressive representative of a new generation of Red Army staff officers. Zaitsev had previously commanded the Soviet forces in Germany and was considered a rising star, so his appointment was not without significance and coincided with a combined KGB and KHAD operation to undermine Pakistani support for the Mujahadeen by subverting key Shinwari and Afridi villages close to the border. Despite these efforts, the issue was whether the Kremlin would be able to continue to resource the Afghans in the face of the CIA support which had escalated to become America's most expensive covert action anywhere, ever. The Afghan cause had been adopted by numerous agencies, including the SIS, who had despatched Anthony Hawkes to Islamabad to supervise British liaison. In 1986 he was to be replaced by Mark Heathcote, formerly the station commander in Buenos Aires until the Falklands invasion. Later, this would result in a training cadre of the 22nd Special Air Service regiment adopting the Mujahadeen and even conducting joint exercises in remote areas of Scotland.

The Afghan conflict was to become a veritable playground for numerous intelligence agencies, all anxious to benefit from sight of the battlefield which was strewn with Soviet missile pods, bomblets, ordnance and hardware which merited examination in the West. Almost every interested party was represented, but while the French limited their involvement to military personnel working under medical or journalistic cover, the British, with the enthusiastic support of the SIS Chief Colin McColl, his deputy Gerald Warner and the Prime Minister Margaret Thatcher, went on to the offensive, albeit in a minor role compared to the American commitment, and ran a series of operations supervised in London by the SIS regional controller, Michael Thompson, recently returned from the Hong Kong station.

British involvement in Afghanistan, operating virtually as surrogates for the CIA, led to the adoption of guerilla leader Ahmed Shah Mahsoud by SIS which initially supplied his groups, concentrated in the Panjshir valley, with communications equipment and some training in Pakistan. Later, SAS personnel accompanied some of the Mujahadeen into Afghanistan but this risky practice was abandoned following a Soviet ambush in which the British soldiers escaped unscathed, but their passports were captured, causing a protest in Moscow and an embarrassing diplomatic incident. Thereafter members of the SAS training cadre were 'debadged', officially leaving the regiment temporarily to give them a reasonably plausible cover, and despatched to British-sponsored camps outside Peshawar where they functioned ostensibly as mercenaries employed by SIS intermediaries acting as 'cut-outs' to give deniability, as Sergeant Gaz Hunter has recounted. They also infiltrated Soviet-occupied territory with Mahsoud's men to advise on tactics and, having completed their assignment, returned to Hereford to resume their military careers. Another long-serving SAS NCO, Ken Connor, described how selected Mujahadeen were flown in to the military airfield at Balivanich on the remote island of Benbecula in the Outer Hebrides to undergo training. Benbecula is connected by a narrow causeway to South Uist, the site of a large Royal Artillery firing range and an ideal environment, approved by CIA inspectors, in which the guerrillas could develop their skills far from prying eyes.

> They were well armed and ferocious fighters, but they lacked battlefield organization. Training in the use of communications enabled the junior commanders to deploy their men much more effectively in combat. They were also trained in the planning of operations, the use of explosives and the fire control of heavy weapons – mortars and artillery. There was a strong sympathy between the ex-SAS men and the Mujahadeen. They could discuss specific battlefield problems and provide constructive solutions based on their own combat experience. The Mujahadeen's greatest fear was of being attacked by aircraft, so it was arranged for them to do helicopter flights, just to show them how difficult it was to spot people on the ground when you're a couple of hundred feet in the air.[1]

The SAS contribution remains 'one of the deepest and darkest secrets of the Cold War' but its effectiveness was quickly apparent as the Mujahadeen gained the upper hand, as Connor acknowledges. His colleagues showed them how

> to stage incidents to lure ground-attack aircraft into narrow valleys where they could be destroyed by crossfire from the valley walls, and we taught them to mount linear anti-armour ambushes as well. They later showed their tremendous bravery by standing within fifty yards of columns of Soviet tanks to destroy them with rocket-propelled grenades.[2]

With greater discipline and a grasp of insurgency tactics, the Mujahadeen posed a serious challenge to the Soviet occupation forces but developed a demand for more sophisticated hardware. This need was accommodated within the NSDD-166's vague expression 'all means available', which came to mean selling an initial 400 heat-seeking infra-red Stinger missiles, manufactured by General Dynamics at Ponoma, California, to the Saudis (who had asked for three times that number) and arranging, with President Zia's consent, personally obtained by Casey in January 1986, for their onward transmission to the Mujahadeen (after 100 had been retained for use by the Pakistanis, together with some air-to-air Sidewinders, to protect against the threat of Soviet retaliatory incursions). The deployment of the Stinger meant a significant change from the established policy of supplying only non-US government hardware, but the main resistance had come from the US army which argued, at length but finally unsuccessfully, that foreign sales would compromise their technology and deplete their own stocks of the valuable weapon. The Joint Chiefs of Staff (JCS) claimed to have an inventory of 3,000 Stingers which, they advised, was to be considered an absolute strategic minimum, and they were joined in their opposition by some within the DO, including Tom Twetton, the influential deputy chief of the NE Division. From Islamabad, Chief of Station Phil Piekney warned that the weapons could fall into the wrong hands: 'When you put a highly sophisticated, technologically advanced weapon like Stinger into Afghanistan, the high side is that you start knocking down more planes; the low side is that you don't know where it's going to end up.' Actually, Piekney's assertion about knocking down planes was sheer speculation for, as the JCS noted, the Stinger had never been fired in anger, even in the Falklands, and to that extent was an entirely untried weapon. Even Casey's DDCI, John McMahon, had reservations about the deployment, warning of Soviet retaliation, thus attracting the criticism that he was one of those who perpetuated the myth of the 'ten-foot-tall' Soviet soldier.

The arguments against deployment diminished when the deputy DDO, Norman Gardner, obtained President's Zia's personal approval for the plan, and the DO, under the leadership of Clair George, formerly the chief of the Africa Division, played a devastating trump card against the Joint Chiefs. According to information given to Burton Lee Gerber, the DO's chief of the Soviet/Eastern Europe Division, by Colonel Sergei Bokhan, the Stinger's technology had already been acquired by the GRU. Codenamed GT/BLIZZARD by the CIA in 1977, Bokhan was the GRU's deputy *rezident* under diplomatic cover in Athens, and he was to be hurriedly exfiltrated from Greece in May 1985. At the time of Bokhan's escape, the CIA could not understand how he had fallen under suspicion or why he had been recalled unexpectedly to Moscow, for Ames would not be arrested until February 1993, but it had been his tip to the KGB that had confirmed to them their suspicions about the existence of the CIA's source in Athens. During his debriefing, Bokhan confirmed the substance of a message he had sent to his handler in 1984, that the Stinger's design and components had been compromised and were to be copied to manufacture a clone, later designated the SAM-14. News of the leak conveniently undermined the Joint Chiefs who were then obliged to withdraw their opposition to the deployment.

The view that prevailed finally was Jack Devine's chilling strategic analysis that without removing Soviet air domination the Mujahadeen would falter and that, perhaps within five years, would be driven from their own country, thus making the refugee crisis in Pakistan a permanent human catastrophe. Devine's prediction had been based on a study of the devastating Soviet offensive of April 1984 which had demonstrated how vulnerable the Mujahadeen were. On 20 April 200 Tu-16 medium bombers had begun saturation bombing before an advance up the Panjshir valley by an estimated 20,000 troops, backed by 400 tanks, covered by a rolling artillery barrage. Heliborne infantry leapfrogged ahead of the main column to secure strategic positions while gunships and Sukhoi 25 ground-attack aircraft picked off the resistance. These tactics proved costly for the Soviets, who suffered 500 casualties, but they had achieved all their objectives within a month, and were to repeat the performance in September, capturing the rebel-held town of Zhawar and breaking the siege of Khost. If the Soviets could sustain such large-scale operations, the Mujahadeen most certainly could not, with the villages depopulated and about half the country designated as refugees. Despite their losses, the Soviets continued to pour troops into the country, to a high point of about 118,000 in 1985, with an estimated 30,000 in reserve just over the frontier in Soviet Central Asia, which was calculated to be the practical maximum, considering the primitive transport network in the region.

Devine's pessimism and his depressing prediction were shared by plenty of others, and were sufficient to win the debate with the support of the DCI, who invariably reverted to asking the question,

'Should we help the Muj die in ever greater numbers, or should we help them win?' His plea of 'Let's not fight to the last Afghan' finally won the day.

The debate about allowing the Stinger to be deployed in Afghanistan was to last almost twelve months, with those opposed arguing that the escalation would cause the Soviets to raise the stakes. There was also concern about the weapon's sophisticated circuitry falling into enemy hands, or maybe reaching terrorists in the West.

Unquestionably it was the Stinger which drove the HIND gunships from the skies, and was responsible for the probable destruction of an estimated 350 Soviet aircraft, with losses, at one point in the conflict, running at one a day. The official CIA statistics, based on verified intelligence from satellite imagery, show 269 helicopter kills in 340 engagements, which amounts to an astonishing attrition ratio of 79 per cent. According to Bob Gates, three out of four targets were hit on the first day the lethal weapon was used. As Edward Juchniewicz, then the ADDO supervising the Afghan operation, remarked, 'A near-sighted, illiterate Afghan could bring down a few million dollars' worth of Soviet aircraft' with a Stinger costing $30,000. Actually, this was a slight exaggeration, for the CIA developed a three-week Stinger training course and installed a sophisticated simulator at the Ojhiri Camp military base five miles outside Rawalpindi to teach Mujahadeen instructors how the weapon worked. Its principal advantage was its simplicity, and, as the manufacturer boasted, the Stinger was the ultimate 'fire-and-forget' missile which contained sufficiently sophisticated circuitry to ensure it was not diverted by electronic interference or any secondary heat source such as the flares which the Israelis had developed in combat over the Lebanon to defeat Syrian SAMs. What took skill was the operator's willingness to wait with the five-foot-long weapon, weighing 34 pounds, on his shoulder until a target had come well into range, in defiance of the vibrator which throbbed against his cheekbone and emitted an audible signal. Resisting the temptation to initiate the firing sequence too soon took considerable self-discipline, but the Mujahadeen were to prove brave students.

Jack Devine was an articulate exponent of equipping the Mujahadeen with Stingers, and he was supported by Milt Bearden, Casey's inspired choice as the new Chief of Station in Islamabad. Bearden had joined the CIA in 1964 after four years in the air force, and spoke fluent German and Mandarin. After his first posting in Bonn he subsequently completed two tours in Hong Kong and one in Berne before going to Lagos in 1981 where Casey, on his first overseas visit of his stations, was impressed by the risk-taker whom he recognized as a kindred spirit, the kind of intelligence officer the DCI approved of. A fellow Catholic, Bearden moved to Khartoum in 1983 where he had an exciting two years, coping with a Marxist revolution, saving four Mossad officers under non-official cover who went on the run from the regime and hid in the CoS's house for a month before he had them flown out of the Sudan as diplomatic cargo. What really attracted Casey to Bearden was his cool handling of the Falasha operation, in which he supervised the dramatic air evacuation of the entire black tribe to Israel, allowing Mossad to take the credit. Bearden's compelling commentary, over a satellite link to Langley, demonstrated to the DCI and to Vice President George Bush, who had taken a very close personal interest in the operation, that the CoS kept a cool head in a crisis but was also a man of action.

Bearden made one advance reconnaissance to Islamabad before his formal posting in July 1985, and then took control of the sharp end of the Afghan task force. Fortuitously, Bearden's arrival coincided with an astonishing success in Kabul, when a guerrilla named Ghafar ('the forgiver') launched a 107mm rocket attack on the capital and managed to hit an ammunition dump. An estimated hundred tons of ordnance blew up with spectacular results, recorded by a BBC news crew filming from the roof of the British embassy, and the pyrotechnics continued for twenty-four hours as secondary explosions detonated. Broadcast around the world, the footage proved that the Mujahadeen were a force to be reckoned with, capable of striking right at the enemy's heart.

The first consignment of 200 Stinger gripstocks were delivered via Dhahran in July 1986, and they were deployed to engage a flight of eight HIND gunships coming in to land at Jalalabad's airfield on 25 September. Although the missiles had a ceiling of around 10,000 feet, these targets were low and slow; at an altitude of 4,500 feet and a range of 7,500 feet, they were unable to outrun the warheads closing at 1,200 mph, and were wholly unable to drop decoy flares or take other counter-measures. Three of the helicopters were destroyed and the others abandoned their approach and fled the scene. This was recorded on videotape by an excited Mujahadeen and subsequently used by Bearden as the basis for a scene in *The Black Tulip*, his 1998 novel named after the rare Afghan flower which became synonymous with the flights carrying Soviet corpses home. In his book, Bearden, who was the first CIA officer to venture into Afghanistan, describes three Mujahadeen firing their weapons at Jalalabad's airfield; two missiles streak towards their targets at twice the speed of sound, while the third falls to the ground harmlessly, the rocket failing to ignite after its initial twenty-foot launch flight. After reloading, another Stinger is despatched, to devastating effect. The missile hits a HIND-D in the midsection, causing a catastrophic explosion, the helicopter falling on the south-east end of the runway. A second missile blows two rotors off another helicopter, which drops like a stone 500 yards away, leaving the remaining five survivors to take evasive action and flee.[3]

Bearden's supposedly fictional account was, much to the discomfort of the CIA's publication review board, entirely accurate, although he omitted to mention that the CIA acquired excellent imagery of the still-smoking wreckage, taken by a KH-11 KEYHOLE reconnaissance satellite which passed overhead soon after the incident. The effects were 'immediate, drastic and lasting', according to one of those monitoring the conflict. Morale was restored among the Mujahadeen, and the Stinger came to be regarded by the tribesmen as a kind of talisman, bringing the 'soldiers of God' good fortune. In reality the CIA was discriminating in whom it selected for Stinger training, choosing engineers and others with mechanical or scientific skills in preference to the majority of enthusiastic fighters who lacked a formal education and would be less likely to handle the weapon properly.

According to the after-combat reports received in Pakistan, and subsequently confirmed by comparison of the satellite imagery of the individual hits and the video footage taken by the guerrillas, the first 187 missiles downed an astonishing 150 aircraft. Hitherto the ancient SAM-7, the Milan and the Chinese wire-guided Red Arrow anti-tank missiles had accounted for less than 10 per cent of Soviet air losses, most of which had been hit on the ground in surprise rocket attacks on vulnerable airbases. The SAM-7 was especially unpopular as it trailed a very distinctive tell-tale white plume which tended to identify precisely the firing position, and also allowed a quick-witted pilot to spot the threat and take evasive action. As for the unwieldy Blowpipe, manufactured by Short Brothers in Belfast, which had performed so badly in the Falklands, it confirmed its reputation as a highly dangerous weapon, posing the biggest threat to the gunner who carried it and was expected to keep an approaching target in his optical sights, remotely guiding the missile to impact by transmitting course adjustments by radio. Even with nerves of steel it was close to impossible for the exposed shooter to maintain his position without flinching until contact, and not surprisingly the Blowpipe failed to score a single kill.

Greatly buoyed by the success achieved by the Stingers, the Mujahadeen developed their own unorthodox tactics for acquiring suitable targets, which included the astonishingly dangerous ruse of exposing a decoy, such as one or two vehicles, to tempt the helicopters into what was intended to look like a one-sided engagement. As soon as the gunships closed for an attack, Stinger missiles would be fired from a convenient concealed vantage point, a tactic that became known as 'shoot-and-scoot'.

Among the first proof of the Stinger's effectiveness, which served to boost Mujahadeen morale and generate further political support worldwide for their cause, was footage shot by a former SAS soldier, Andrzej Skrzypkowiak, who carried a modified 16mm camera over the frontier from Teri Mangal to film a Soviet Su-17 jet crashing into a mountain after having been damaged by the missile. Born in England to Polish parents, Skrzypkowiak had served with 22 SAS in Oman and had befriended Commander Pannah, one of the Mujahadeen leaders operating in the Panjshir valley. Having obtained exclusive evidence he recrossed the border to the relative safety of Parachinar, and then dropped the exposed film in to the British High Commission for immediate delivery by the diplomatic bag to London. Within days, Skrzypkowiak's clip was broadcast across the world on news bulletins, an eloquent demonstration that the Afghan resistance was putting up an impressive performance. The CIA demanded similar evidence be obtained by other teams, so there was compelling visible proof of what had been accomplished.[4]

The Soviets, so widely perceived as aggressors in Afghanistan, were powerless to retaliate, and their initial response was to limit their sorties to night operations. This gave them a brief respite, but the carnage continued when the CIA distributed night-vision image-intensifying equipment to the Mujahadeen. From then on, the pilots were on the defensive, making their bombing runs from high altitude, well above 10,000–12,000 feet, and thereby abandoning accuracy. The alternative was low-level, high-speed approaches, but the terrain made such tactics highly dangerous and very unpopular with aircrews who suffered more accidents and even found themselves under attack from machine guns and RPG-7s sited above them. The Stinger's effectiveness was quickly reflected in the casualty statistics. In 1985, 2,013 Soviet military operations resulted in thirteen Afghan deaths per 1,000 of the population. Two years later the number of operations had increased to 4,450, but the deaths had fallen to just nine per 1,000. For demonstrably more military activity, the Soviets were achieving progressively less. Close ground support from the air became impossible and troops moving up the treacherous valleys were unable to rely on the well-established tactic of dropping advance pickets on to the ridge lines to warn of guerrilla activity. As one of the participants commented:

> I would be more inclined to put even greater emphasis on the impact the Stinger had on Soviet air strategy. It was far greater than just the number count of shootdowns. The Russian decision to avoid the threat of the Stinger and to fly at much higher altitudes triggered the end of the conflict. It freed up the badly needed supplies bottlenecked at the border which were substantial. It allowed a free flow of support to the Mujahadeen. From that point forward, the Mujahadeen comfortably could be assured of receiving the necessary ground weapons to sustain a very long fight with the Russians. The Russians understood this and decided that the escalation cycle had to end with this round. They simply weren't prepared to raise the ante one more time. Thus, the beginning of the end. The impact of this strategic decision cannot be overestimated. As [DCI William] Webster, I believe it had a tremendous impact on the Soviet leadership and the military resolve and morale which greatly helped the unraveling of the Soviet Empire.[5]

The only potential downside in the change of strategy was the proportion of weaponry that found its way to terrorists, drug smugglers and other unintended beneficiaries of the CIA's largesse. Casey attempted to staunch the haemorrhage by sending John McMahon to Peshawar to instil some discipline in the mutually hostile warring factions that constituted the Mujahadeen, but his report was depressing. The guerrillas had never trusted the United States and had 'banked' much of the *matériel* for the day when there was yet another change in the USA's foreign policy.

Despite Afghan mistrust, the Americans maintained the pressure, forcing the Soviets into a corner which obliged the Kremlin to increase its military commitment to an estimated peak of $300 million a month before announcing a phased withdrawal. With 13,000 Soviet troops dead, 35,000 wounded, 311 missing, at a cost of a million roubles a day, Mikhail Gorbachev declared that the Soviets had had enough, and eventually the CIA's Afghan task force was wound down. Jack Devine, who had set up the unit in 1985, was posted to Europe in January 1987; he was succeeded by Frank Anderson and Dan Webster, and subsequently served as chief of counter-narcotics, ending up as the acting DDO before spending his final three years as Chief of Station in London. Milt Bearden left Islamabad in June 1989 to take up a new appointment as chief of the Soviet/Eastern Europe Division, and in 1991 moved to Bonn as Chief of Station. According to Islamabad folklore, Bearden had deliberately kept the lights burning in his office, on the north corner of the US embassy building, twenty-four hours a day throughout his service as CoS, making it clear to the Soviets, whose own *rezidentura* was within direct sight, that the local CIA station was very active. On the afternoon of 15 February 1989, as General Boris Gromov walked over the bridge at Termez, the last uniformed Soviet soldier to leave Afghanistan, symbolically accompanied by his fourteen year-old son, Bearden switched off the light in his room.

Much later, as *glasnost* allowed official Soviet statistics to be released, the true scale of the Afghan defeat and its impact on the Red Army and the rest of the Soviet Union became clearer. The murder of Red Army officers had become commonplace, suicides were accounting for 18 per cent of some 7,000 non-combat casualties per annum, and a high proportion of the 4,300 army deserters were Afghan veterans.

By the time the Soviets started to withdraw, in mid-May 1988, the CIA's Afghan budget had reached $700 million and a total of 900 Stinger missiles had been shipped to the docks in Karachi on non-US cargo vessels or had been flown into the Pakistani airbase at Chaklala from Dhahran. Precisely how many were actually launched, how many had been destroyed in a gigantic explosion at an arms dump near Islamabad on 10 April 1988, and how many filtered back to Islamic extremists in the Middle East remains unquantifiable, but the CIA kept a strict inventory of the batteries required to power the hand-held launchers, and the unique battery cooling units. Prolonged storage results in deterioration of the batteries, thus neutralizing the weapon, so there was some confidence that even if the Stingers fell into the wrong hands, close to the Iranian frontier, they would have a limited potency. In the event, despite considerable criticism, not a single Stinger was subsequently used in a terrorist incident, and the CIA underwrote an expensive $110m repurchase scheme to offer high prices to anyone willing to sell the weapons back to the Agency.

Even after the Soviet withdrawal, the Mujahadeen continued the offensive, thereby causing the Soviets to keep the regime in Kabul afloat with an unsustainably costly air-bridge supplying food, fuel and ammunition. Almost in desperation the Afghan army defended Jalalabad with volleys of Scud rockets, and between April and December 1989 fired over 1,000 missiles, despite the fact that Soviet factories at that time were turning out only about 400 a year. In the six months following the withdrawal, 3,800 Soviet flights were counted flying in logistical support, but no more troops. The political cost, of course, was gigantic, and was sustained across the whole of the Eastern bloc where it was realized that, once the Soviets had been forced out of Afghanistan, they would never mount another invasion. For the clear-sighted on the seventh floor at Langley, even after Casey had been replaced in May 1987 by the FBI director, Judge William Webster, there was a definite link between the destruction of Soviet gunships in the Panjshir valley by Stingers, and the cutting of the barbed wire on the frontier between Austria and Hungary just three years later. Just as Casey had occasionally mused about supporting Mujahadeen raids into the neighbouring Soviet republics of Turkmenistan, Uzbekistan and Tajikistan, but had decided against it because of the political risk, Webster was to contemplate the use of remote-controlled, unmanned drones to attack the airfields at Bagram and Kabul. The CIA produced schemes to destroy aircraft on the ground, aircrew barracks and the 'ready rooms', but Webster also vetoed the proposals on the same grounds.

Casey's crusades in Afghanistan and Nicaragua were but components of a campaign of confronting Soviet proxies everywhere. Another significant target was Libya, where Colonel Gadaffi had been linked directly to terrorism over a long period, having sponsored the shipment of weapons and explosives to various groups in Europe. On 24 March 1986, carrier-borne fighters were attacked by Libyan anti-aircraft missiles in international airspace over the Gulf of Sidra, an area claimed by Gadaffi and challenged by the US Sixth Fleet. In response, the planes sank several Libyan patrol boats and destroyed some SAM-5 sites on the mainland, which prompted Gadaffi to declare war on the United States.

The following month, in April 1986, the Libyan People's Bureau in East Berlin was directly implicated by NSA cable intercepts in the bombing of La Belle, a nightclub in the Western sector popular with US service personnel. Two people were killed and 230 injured, among them fifty Americans. The unexpected American response was an Israeli-style air-raid on 14 April executed by eighteen F-111Bs flying from bases in England, and a dozen navy A-6s from the Sixth Fleet. Although they narrowly missed the Libyan leader's own closely-guarded quarters inside Tripoli's 200-acre El Azziya military compound, the mission effectively ended his participation in international terrorism.

Another major component in Casey's policy of confrontation centred on Poland, although initially Casey had been cautious, anxious not to compromise the fledgling Solidarity movement by making the kind of obvious overtures that would be bound to be spotted by the ubiquitous local security apparatus. Casey's solution, apart from obtaining the State Department's consent for the insertion of an NSA special collection element in the Warsaw embassy to enhance the existing rather limited Sigint facility, was to cultivate the existing AFL-CIO (American Federation of Labor – Congress of Industrial

Organization) link authorized by Lane Kirkland and promoted by Irving Brown, the AFL's long-serving European representative in Paris and director of international affairs. Once dubbed 'the most dangerous man' by *Time*, Brown had collaborated with the CIA since the Marshall Plan was instigated in 1947 and had played a key role in QK/OPERA, the Congress for Cultural Freedom which had acted as a conduit for covert funds directed to anti-communist propaganda operations in Europe. For years Brown was a paymaster, distributing CIA bursaries and grants to subsidize loss-making magazines and journals across Europe, among them *Encounter*, and to support many of their contributors. As the AFL-CIO's constitution prohibited the acceptance of government money, a network of intermediaries and front 'institutes' was created to channel CIA support to Solidarity's office in Brussels. The most useful cover was the International Confederation of Free Trade Unions – formed in 1950 because of communist domination of the World Federation of Trade Unions – which provided Solidarity with equipment.

Also close to Brown was Jay Lovestone, the convert from the American Communist Party (CPUSA) who was to become a fierce critic of the Soviets, and another important CIA asset. Lovestone's activities were coordinated by Jim McCargar, a highly experienced 'cold warrior' who had helped found Radio Free Europe and had written *A Short Course in the Secret War* under the pseudonym Christopher Felix.[6] In 1983 McCargar joined the AFL-CIO as a consultant, a post he was to keep until December 1995. Although he acknowledges Langley's role in supporting Solidarity, Irving Brown took the details of his operations to his grave in February 1989. When the State Department's Philip Habib was asked about Brown's CIA connections, he replied: 'We didn't use the sonofabitch. The sonofabitch used us.' Like Brown and Kirkland, Lovestone was committed to destroying Soviet Communism and saw Solidarity as a means of achieving that objective.

Casey also took the opportunity during his Middle East tour in April 1981 to visit Tel Aviv while en route between Riyadh and Cairo. The purpose of his visit, apart from meeting the director of Mossad, General Yitzhak Hoffi, was to cement a new relationship, offering KEYHOLE KH-11 satellite imagery of the Lebanon and Syria in return for access to sources in Eastern Europe. Hoffi's commitment to collaborate in Poland, where Mossad had developed a resilient organization among docks management, was to prove exceptionally useful when the CIA wanted to import contraband to support Solidarity. Initially, however, the trade appeared to benefit the Israelis, as they demonstrated eloquently two months later when Mirage jets struck the Osiraq nuclear plant outside Baghdad on 8 June. The precision attack destroyed Saddam Hussein's first venture into the development of atomic weapons and had clearly been based on reliable intelligence. Many saw the raid as evidence of a new climate of cooperation between the CIA and Mossad after some awkward years of tension. The 'special relationship' pioneered by Jim Angleton had withered after his dismissal by Bill Colby in 1974, and the liaison had deteriorated to the degree that Israeli military intelligence had mounted a semi-transparent 'deniable' operation to acquire satellite imagery of the Middle East from Jonathan Pollard, a US naval intelligence analyst. Pollard's subsequent arrest, in November 1985, was to be the cause of much mutual embarrassment, not least because the climate of official cooperation had appeared to have improved so dramatically.

Although Casey was determined to challenge the Soviets, his time was not fully occupied by his crusade. His style transformed the Agency, and in recognition of their newfound confidence the DCI became the first, on 6 October 1982, to be awarded the Distinguished Intelligence Medal while still in office. Later in that month he flew to Europe, and was in Norway, on a weekend tour inspecting the NSA's intercept stations at Vadso, Vardo and Tromso, when a Hezbollah suicide bomber drove a van packed with explosives into the US Marines barracks in Beirut, killing 241 and wounding sixty. Upon his return to Langley on Monday night, Casey sat in the CIA's ops room as his sole asset in Grenada, Lisa Flohr, reported in anticipation of a full-scale invasion. Eight hundred Cuban troops were said to be on the independent Caribbean island, and had constructed a 9,000-foot runway; although all this and much more could be seen from a satellite, someone on the ground had to measure the depth of the apron tarmac to see whether it could withstand the weight of the heavy-laden transport aircraft the Americans intended to land. On Tuesday, 25 October the assault began, but soon lapsed into tragic farce. The SEAL reconnaissance mission was a dismal failure: four men drowned as they dropped into the ocean, and the remainder abandoned their assignment when discovered by a patrol vessel. Another SEAL unit, deployed to rescue the island's governor, Sir Paul Scoon, retreated when their helicopter was damaged, and another group, sent to take the radio station, was beaten back and forced to call in reinforcements from the crack 82nd Airborne Division. For the first major American military action since Vietnam, Grenada exposed more than a few command and control flaws, with considerable loss of life from 'friendly fire' around the prison where US Special Forces encountered US Marines and engaged them in a deadly firefight.

For the CIA the minor hiccups, such as the troops having to buy tourist maps upon their arrival because no others were available, were irrelevant. As there were no news crews on the island to report on the episode, it received only retrospective media coverage. In geopolitical terms, the US had confronted and reversed Cuban hegemony, and could demonstrate the capture of a substantial arsenal of Soviet weapons, presumably intended for use in exporting revolution to the rest of the Caribbean. The Grenada crisis, prompted by the murder of Prime Minister Maurice Bishop, was over almost as soon as it began, leaving Casey to continue his crusade.

The following month, November 1982, Casey was in West Germany, paying a visit to the CIA base in Frankfurt which had taken the lead in developing contacts with Solidarity. Although the Warsaw station had been assiduous in cultivating discreet contact with the movement's leadership, great care had to be taken to avoid compromising them. The Polish counter-intelligence branch, Department II, led by General Major Janusz Seredy, caught James D. Howard, whom they had pegged as a CIA officer, at a meeting with a Solidarity activist, and expelled him. Department II officers maintained a close watch on the presumed CIA Chief of Station, John Dobrin, and the British diplomat they mistakenly believed to be his SIS opposite number, David Joy. They also concentrated on Leslie Sternberg, withdrawn after Kuklinski's exfiltration to avoid reprisals, and Michael Anderson, one of the CIA officers working to support Solidarity.

Although there had been a disappointing response to Solidarity's call for demonstrations and strikes on 11–12 October, the station reported a dramatic increase in local reporting, including the appearance of a 'walk-in' volunteer, a deputy minister with access to the government's discussions about internal security measures. As a replacement for Kuklinski, he was to prove invaluable although initially his hesitation matched the Warsaw CIA station's reluctance to deal with him in case he was a provocation. Declaring himself to be disillusioned with martial law he began by supplying details of the Polish order-of-battle, but later graduated to sharing political information. Contact with the source, who was later identified as General Tadeusz Tuczapski, chief inspector of territorial defence and a member of WRON, Jaruzelski's inner circle, was to be intermittent but valuable.

Casey's anxiety to balance his determination to help Solidarity with the fear that a single over-zealous act could taint the entire organization, led him to Stockholm in October 1983 where he sought support from the Swedish government, led by the conservative Thorbjorn Falldin, for importing contraband across the Baltic concealed inside otherwise legitimate consignments of aid. The DCI played a strong hand, fortified by a Soviet propaganda catastrophe the previous month when an Su-15 pilot had shot down a Korean Air Lines (KAL) 747 that had strayed over the Kamchatka peninsula. All 269 passengers and crew had died in what had been a tragic misidentification by Soviet ground controllers of the civilian plane as an American RC-135 reconnaissance flight. The Kremlin was immediately condemned around the world for unwarranted, barbaric aggression, and the KAL flight 007 became another stick with which to beat the Soviets. The atmosphere in Sweden was therefore ideal for the DCI's purposes. Agreement was reached in principle with the SIPO's director, Sven-Ake Hjalmroth, and later confirmed by Casey on another visit to Sweden, immediately after his audience with the Pope the following year. He had been warned by the local station to anticipate a chilly reception on this occasion because the socialist Olaf Palme had been returned to power. Palme had long taken an anti-American stance, dating back to his country's acceptance of US draft dodgers during the Vietnam war. However, to Casey's surprise, the Swedish SIPO sanctioned the CIA's plan, and he even held a brief telephone conversation with the prime minister who agreed that customs should turn a blind eye to exports destined for Gdansk.

In February 1984 Casey undertook yet another of his gruelling world tours, this time flying west to Honolulu, where the CIA ran a domestic station covering the Pacific as far as Fiji. He then went to Tokyo and Beijing, where Chief of Station Ted Price arranged for a banquet hosted by Ling Yun, the minister for state security, before calling on President Zia in Islamabad, and moving on to Tel Aviv and Ankara, arriving in Rome for a meeting with Cardinal Casaroli's deputy, Archbishop Luigi Poggi, the Vatican's roving nuncio for Eastern Europe.

Casey's routine was divided between his world tours, intended to bolster support in the CIA's overseas stations for the campaign to destabilize Moscow through Poland and Afghanistan, and dowsing political crises at home. He was fond of boasting that he 'had visited every country on the globe that cooperated with the United States'. The pattern of globetrotting diplomacy to encourage allies led him to Islamabad and Riyadh twice more, in the spring of 1985, while en route from Frankfurt, and again in early 1986, prompted by his most ambitious and controversial scheme of all, cementing relations for the export of the fighting in Afghanistan over the border into the Soviet Union.

The Mujahadeen had acquired numerous allies over the porous Iranian frontier, and in the overwhelmingly Muslim Soviet republics of Tajikistan, Turkmenistan and Uzbekistan, and there is no shortage of reports describing sabotage raids conducted by Islamic insurgents which were planned, encouraged and sometimes directed by the CIA. Casey enthusiastically endorsed any opportunity to hit the Soviets hard on home territory, provided there were sufficient safeguards to prevent a political backlash. For the DCI to have armed or sponsored groups of guerrillas willing to harass the enemy behind their own lines was entirely in keeping with his OSS philosophy, but it was at this juncture that Casey's status as the CIA's saviour was to go into dramatic decline.

Chapter IX

The Crusader

At the heart of Casey's troubles, which were eventually to kill him in May 1987, were separate but fatally linked schemes. While many argue that the DCI's involvement in Nicaragua was to be his undoing, the background to his fall was, typically, rather more complex. The disclosure that Nicaraguan ports had been mined, apparently without congressional approval, put Casey on a collision course with some of his most ardent admirers on Capitol Hill, and the subsequent revelation that the CIA had sponsored what appeared to be a terrorists' handbook, *Psychological Operations in Guerrilla Warfare*, advocating the elimination of minor government functionaries, ensured that his Central American task force, headed by Alan Fiers, the Chief of Station in Riyadh who had so impressed him, received negative media comment. Surely, advocating murder, thundered congressmen, violated the President's Executive Order 12333 which specifically outlawed assassination? Casey had never in fact seen the booklet, let alone approved of it, but it gave the impression that once again the CIA was acting as 'a rogue elephant', setting its own foreign policy.

Casey had flown to Tegucigalpa, Honduras, in June 1983 to talk to his CoS, Don Winters, and see for himself how Dewey Clarridge's Salvadorian resistance organization was developing. He found himself embroiled in a political maelstrom. The CIA was interested in recruiting, training and supporting guerrillas capable of challenging the Nicaraguan style of hegemony; it was less interested in examining individuals' records as respecters of human rights. Indeed, some of the Contras had some very disageeable pasts, as was almost inevitable, but Congress was unwilling to fund what were portrayed as right-wing terrorists combating left-wing terrorists. However, the mining episode was entirely home-grown, for Dewey Clarridge had taken the initiative based on the knowledge that the Contras were not up to overcoming the considerable technical obstacles involved. With the president's sanction, Clarridge arranged for home-made mines to be sewn in the Atlantic harbour of El Bluff and the oil terminal at Puerto Sandino, as well as at Corinto, the only significant port on the Pacific. The objective had been to create an economic blockade during the export season in the belief that once the Contras had announced the embargo, no merchant ship would take the risk of trading with Nicaragua, or incurring the potentially massive insurance liability of entering a declared war zone. At the very least, the Lloyd's London insurance market could be expected to enforce what would amount to a total ban on all oil shipments. However, this expectation proved false when no fewer than seven ships struck mines in March 1984, among them a Japanese freighter carrying a cargo of cotton, a British P & O steamer, the SS *Iver Chaser*, a Dutch dredger and a Soviet oil tanker, the *Lugansk*. Although the magnetic and acoustic mines were intended to make more noise than destruction, and none of the ships sustained any major damage, there was an international outcry. Suddenly the CIA's plan, endorsed by the president, the State Department and even the House Permanent Select Committee on Intelligence (HPSCI), after a briefing given by Casey on 31 January, became an orphan. Amid angry protests from six countries whose ships had been damaged, senators denounced the operation and refused further funding for the Contras. With tremendous reluctance, Casey was forced to apologize to Congress, and in the aftermath Dewey Clarridge was switched to chief of the DO's European Division, and Clair George was replaced as DDO by the CIA's inspector-general, Charles Briggs.[1]

Casey's remedy to the Boland Amendment, which prevented the US government from spending money on the Contras, was to persuade foreign benefactors to fill the gap, thus allowing the CIA to declare it was in full compliance with US law. This scheme fell apart in October 1986 when the Sandinistas shot down a C-123K cargo plane engaged in an airdrop of supplies to the Contras. The pilot, William J. Cooper, was killed, but he was quickly linked to Southern Air Transport, once a well-known CIA 'proprietary' or front company. Worse, one of his mercenary aircrew, Eugene Hasenfus, was captured alive, and promptly declared in Managua that he was under the impression that he was employed by the CIA. When Washington DC-based journalists found the house in San Salvador where Cooper and Hasenfus had been based, they also turned up telephone records showing calls to Joseph F. Fernandez, then the CIA Chief of Station in Costa Rica, and others to Colonel Oliver North of the National Security Council.

While Casey believed he had weathered the storm of the Nicaraguan fiasco, which he regarded as a classic example of politicians running for cover whenever a hazardous venture goes wrong, it was to be only the backdrop for three much larger dramas that were being played out in parallel: the hostage crisis in Beirut, and the molehunt inside the DO's SE Division. The third was the CIA's covert action programme in Afghanistan which was an unlikely beneficiary of the Iran-Contra affair. Casey's congressional critics, who were determined to fathom the murky depths of how Iranian money that had paid for illegally-exported weapons could have ended up with guerrillas in Central America, were equally keen to demonstrate they were not 'soft on Communism' or anti-CIA, and therefore gave as much support to the station in Islamabad, as they expressed indignation about the sale of weapons for hostages.

On the morning of 16 March 1984 the Chief of Station in Beirut, William Buckley, was abducted from the basement garage of his apartment block, setting off a chain of events that would bring disaster on the DCI and his Agency. An experienced CIA officer and an expert on Middle Eastern terrorism, Buckley had been asked by Casey to go to the Lebanon, despite having been expelled from Damascus four years earlier. The previous CoS, Kenneth Haas, and his deputy, James Lewis, had been killed with five others in the massive car-bomb explosion that had destroyed much of the US embassy on 18 April 1983. Fully aware of the risks, Buckley accepted the assignment but was seized less than a year later. Although the State Department never acknowledged Buckley's true role, asserting that he was merely an embassy diplomat, his kidnappers undoubtedly realized who he was, and when three months later a harrowing videotape was released to the press of him accompanied by two other American hostages, he looked as though his nose had been broken in a severe beating. When Casey played the tape to the president, both men agreed that everything possible should be done to achieve Buckley's release.

The suggestion that Casey took a special interest in Buckley's release has been rejected as improbable sentimentalism by commentators who have claimed that the DCI regarded the Chief of Station as a mere casualty of war, and his terrible ordeal as nothing more than an occupational hazard. In fact, there is some evidence to refute this interpretation, not the least of which was Dick Helms's advice to Casey that the Soviets made a demonstrably public virtue of recovering KGB assets in difficulty. Most recently, the KGB had extracted Oleg Spirine, Valeri Kornev and Nikolai Versky from the Lebanon after they had been abducted by Hezbollah in September 1985. All three had been seized with a KGB officer, Arkady Katkov, who was found shot dead a month later. Reputedly the KGB had identified the Arab gang responsible and, once all Soviet citizens had been evacuated from the city, had started terrorizing their families until the remaining trio had been released unharmed. Casey had asked Buckley to accept the assignment in Beirut, and it would not be unreasonable for him to take responsibility for his fate. As for sentimentality, Casey had been close to tears when eulogizing Robert C. Ames, who had died in the Beirut embassy bombing. Knowing that the president cared deeply about Buckley's fate, it would have been entirely in character for his DCI to pull out all the stops to achieve his freedom. In political terms, Casey could have counted on some private support, not least from the analysts and commentators who felt Iran represented a vacuum into which the Soviets would insinuate themselves unless America attempted to build bridges to the Ayatollah's regime.

Whereas the Agency had taken a low profile in dealing with the not infrequent kidnapping of Westerners in Beirut, who had been strongly advised to leave the city, Buckley's rescue was to become an instant preoccupation for Casey. Morale in the Agency would plummet if he did not make every effort to recover his CoS alive, and the staff would expect him to make it a very obvious priority. Casey responded to the challenge by ordering satellite imagery of the Abdullah barracks, Lebanon, and all the other suspected Shiite bases, and deployed such agents as there were on the ground to monitor suspected Hezbollah activists, but the unpalatable truth was that the tightly-knit terrorist groups that had been waging a civil war by proxy in the Lebanon were virtually impervious to the conventional intelligence tradecraft of surveillance and penetration. Such evidence as there was strongly suggested that Islamic Jihad, which had claimed responsibility for the abduction, was an extremist cell led by Imad Mugniyah, a Shiite cleric with strong links to the Iranian Revolutionary Guards. Accordingly, when the suggestion was made that negotiations with Tehran would be more fruitful using satellites to search the Syrian-controlled Bekaa valley, Casey acquiesced.[2]

The basic problem with the CIA's channel of communication with Tehran was that it depended upon an expatriate entrepreneur, Manucher Ghorbanifar, who had been known to the Agency for more than twenty years, and was regarded, after many polygraph tests, to be wholly unreliable. Indeed, he had even been the subject of a 'burn notice' (a circular warning distributed to all CIA stations alerting them to the dubious nature of the information he peddled). However, it was undeniable that he had a line into the Iranian prime minister's office, and it is a measure of the CIA's desperation at this time that although his first direct approach, in July 1984, claiming to know who was holding Buckley, had been rejected after a polygraph indicated deception, negotiations with him were subsequently opened on the DCI's personal authority. The reason for the change of heart was the involvement of John Shaheen, one of Casey's long-time OSS supporters, who reported that his business connections were in touch with Ghorbanifar, now supposedly acting as an intermediary for the Iranians in some enormous financial transactions. Ghorbanifar was certainly in touch with the hugely rich Adnan Khashoggi, and evidently was regarded as a useful source by Mossad, so when he claimed that moderate elements in the Tehran government were anxious to trade Buckley for much-needed weapons which were the subject of an embargo, Casey obtained the president's permission to begin talks. Remarkably, the president did not immediately sign a finding to authorize Casey's proposal, and when he finally did so, it was retrospective in its coverage, it uniquely prohibited any congressional consultation, no copy was delivered to the CIA and it was written in terms that, when it was finally read, were considered too colloquial to be taken seriously.

On the surface, the deal offered by Ghorbanifar appeared to make eminent sense. Iran was then fighting a protracted war with Iraq and was running out of the weapons supplied by the USA to the Shah. There was a general United Nations ban on exporting any military *matériel* to either side, so the Ayatollah's forces were particularly anxious to buy the wire-guided TOW anti-tank missiles from anyone at virtually any price. Ghorbanifar's proposal was to exploit the Iranian demand by buying a quantity of TOWs from the Israeli army, which possessed a large stock of the formidable weapon, and selling 508 of them to Iran at a vastly inflated price. The Israelis were willing to cooperate on condition their own arsenal was replenished by the USA, and, to encourage the Americans to participate, Tehran was willing to free their hostages. Since technically the USA was not supplying the missiles direct to Iran, there was no breach of the UN embargo or American law, so there was theoretically an advantage to all the parties involved, apart from the repudiation of the president's oft-stated policy that he would not negotiate with terrorists. Ghorbanifar's solution appeared to get round most of the difficulties, and as he did not have the necessary money, he had even negotiated a loan from Khashoggi who was attracted by the handsome profit to be made on selling a commodity worth $3,500 for three times that price. Thus, with Casey's consent, and the CIA's knowledge, Khashoggi lent Ghorbanifar a million dollars to buy a first consignment of ninety-six TOWs which Ghorbanifar flew to Iran on 22 August aboard a chartered DC-8. A week later, after he had been paid by the Iranians, Ghorbanifar repaid Khashoggi and began work on a second flight to make a further delivery of the remaining 408 TOWs.

These deliveries, which were completed on 14 September, created several difficulties for the CIA, not the least of which was news from Charles Allen, then the CIA's national intelligence officer for counter-terrorism, that Buckley had probably died of maltreatment, neglect and torture. Casey was sufficiently concerned about this development that he prevailed upon Vernon Walters to call in a few favours, Walters made a personal telephone call to his friend President Assad of Syria who confirmed soon afterwards that Buckley was indeed dead.

Despite the advice, Casey had opted to proceed with Ghorbanifar's proposal as it remained the Agency's sole opportunity to save

Buckley, but the day after the TOWs had been delivered, it was not Buckley who was released but Benjamin Weir, a Presbyterian missionary who had been seized in May 1984. Ghorbanifar's explanation was that Buckley was too ill to move, but the remaining hostages would be freed if Tehran was allowed to make further purchases, and the next item was the prized Hawk anti-aircraft missile. At that stage in the Iran–Iraq war, Tehran was being hammered in night-time raids by Iraqi Bear bombers, and the Hawk was an effective and much desired antidote.

Casey's interest in freeing Hezbollah's hostages diminished considerably the following month when, on 15 October, Islamic Jihad announced that Buckley had been 'executed' in retaliation for the Israeli air-raid a fortnight earlier on the PLO headquarters in Tunis. Nevertheless, the National Security Council staffer responsible for counter-terrorism, Colonel Oliver North, remained keen to develop the contact with Tehran and arranged for the Israelis to supply Ghorbanifar with 120 Hawks. The plan called for the missiles, disguised as 'oil-drilling equipment', to be delivered on an El-Al 747 to Lisbon where they would be transferred to a pair of chartered Nigerian DC-8s for delivery in Iran. However, the first attempt, made on 21 November, failed because the Portuguese authorities would not allow the El-Al plane to land without a detailed declaration of the cargo.

The second, successful attempt was made on 24 November, largely organized by the CIA's Air Branch which arranged for the El-Al 747 to be met in Cyprus by a 707 chartered from a CIA proprietary company, St Lucia Airways, and flown by a German crew. Once again the crates of weapons were described as 'oil-drilling equipment', and the CIA stations in Nicosia and Ankara were involved in clearing the required flight plans with the various air-traffic control sectors over the eastern Mediterranean. Although the Agency dropped out of the picture thereafter, North continued the trade and found a suitable beneficiary for the profits by placing the cash in the Swiss bank account of a Panamanian-registered company, Lake Resources Inc., which had been set up originally to fund the Nicaraguan Contras. The man behind Lake Resources was Oliver North's confidant, General Richard Secord, who managed the very substantial sums that accrued during the two-way trade, by using the profits from the sales to Tehran to buy weapons that were then sold at huge margins to a force of Contras approaching 20,000; the latter paid with funds donated by foreign benefactors, principal among them the Saudi government. This ingenious scheme, which later became known as 'the enterprise', avoided the embarrassment of any US government agency making a surplus, which would have been contrary to federal law, but also ensured that Lake Resources accumulated a huge, unaccountable income. Unfortunately, it did not anticipate or ameliorate Ghorbanifar's irritation at being cut out of his lucrative role as an intermediary, and his increasingly vocal complaints, articulated through the flamboyant Saudi billionaire Adnan Khashoggi, were to alert the CIA's bureaucracy to the scale and complexity of Oliver North's machinations.

Although North had no background in clandestine operations he was an eager student and certainly learned much from Bill Casey who had probably read every book on espionage ever published in the English language. Undoubtedly North's attraction to the DCI, apart from his personal commitment as 'a fellow true believer', was his ability to operate outside the rigidly institutionalized system of congressional oversight. CIA professionals could not legally participate in activities beyond those specifically authorized by a presidential finding, but the National Security Council, its staff and its more than two dozen working groups had never been written into the legislation. Thus, paradoxically, the CIA could silently monitor a covert scheme run by an NSC staffer, but could not assist in it. However, this was far from a formula to manage rogue operations, for it was accompanied on 18 January 1985 by NSDD-159, a presidential finding which created the Planning and Coordination Group (NSPCG), a formalized version for deputies of the National Security Planning Group set up immediately after President Reagan had taken office. Like President Kennedy's Forty Committee, it was unacknowledged and unpublicized, and was intended to give senior DO personnel monthly access in Room 208 of the Old Executive Building to the deputies of the key policy-makers. All covert action henceforth would be designated a generic codeword, VEIL, which would signify an NSPCG-approved operation. Each meeting was attended by the DDO, Clair George, or his deputy, Norman Gardner, and one of the two senior members of the NE Division, Bert Dunn or his deputy Tom Twetton.[3]

The DCI certainly spotted the opportunity to outmanoeuvre his congressional critics by using Oliver North as a surrogate, but the intrinsic flaw in the scheme was that it never achieved the desired results. While Casey could testify, as he did, that the CIA was completely unaware at the time that Oliver North's consignment of oil-drilling equipment was actually Hawk missiles destined for Tehran in contravention of US law, this was nothing more than the DCI's semantics, for he personally almost certainly did know of the plan long in advance of its execution, and may even have been its original author. Nevertheless, Casey's dubious distinction between what he knew and what his organization knew, and when, provided the CIA with a figleaf defence that was never tested with any rigour. However, the fatal aspect of the entire scheme was that it never achieved its intended purpose of freeing the wretched Bill Buckley. Although it could be argued that North's intervention did obtain the release of two hostages, Benjamin Weir and later Father Lawrence Jenco, it also had the effect of enhancing the status of American captives as a valuable trading commodity. No sooner had Weir and Jenco been freed than another pair, Frank Reed of the Lebanese International School and Joseph Ciccipio of the American University, were abducted on 9 and 12 September respectively, almost as though Hezbollah had decided to restock their inventory. Even worse, the terrorists also seized the British churchman Terry Waite who had acted for Oliver North as a compliant cover for the hostage releases which, under any circumstances, could never be linked publicly to the illicit sale of weapons. Thus, far from enjoying the advantage of success, North's ingenious scheme never accomplished its primary purpose. Indeed, according to some reports, the venture actually served to infuriate the Iranians who had been told by Ghorbanifar to expect a different model of the anti-aircraft missile, and instead had received outrageously over-priced Hawks stamped with the star of David and covered in Hebrew stencils.

The Iran–Contra affair, as it came to be known, and the diversion of the profits from the weapons sales, was a scandal too many for the Reagan administration which became the focus of one of a series of congressional investigations. Casey, just back from a gruelling tour of the CIA stations in El Salvador, Cosa Rica and Honduras, was called to give evidence regarding the CIA's denial of any knowledge that the 'oil-drilling equipment' had been Hawk missiles until months after the transaction had taken place, but on 15 December 1987, while undergoing a medical examination in his office at Langley, he collapsed and was diagnosed as suffering from a massive brain tumour. He underwent surgery three days later, but never recovered and died on 6 May 1987, just as the first witness began his testimony in the Senate. The question about the extent to which the DCI had known, or had approved, of North's illegal diversion of funds to the Contras remained unanswered by him.

Throughout his six and a half years as DCI, Casey knew that in such a high-risk business any success could probably not be advertised, and the media would be sure to concentrate on the failures. They did so in spades, even accusing him of complicity in a massive car-bomb which exploded killing eighty bystanders in the Beirut suburb of Bir el-Abed on 8 March 1985, suspiciously close to the home of Sheikh Mohammed Hussein Fadlallah, the leader of Hezbollah who had masterminded the bombing of the US embassy in Beirut in April 1983. He was also believed to have organized the destruction of the US Marines barracks in October 1983, killing 241 marines, and the demolition of the embassy annexe on 20 September 1984. These incidents made Fadlallah a prime target of the CIA's attention, but not for assassination, and it had trained three official Lebanese government teams to conduct surveillance and anti-terrorist operations. Evidence later emerged that one of the three had probably been responsible for placing the Bir el-Abed car-bomb but, after a lengthy investigation conducted by the HPSCI, the CIA was cleared of the *Washington Post*'s charge of having planned or directed the operation.

Although Casey was able to mount a robust defence against his accusers in the example of Sheikh Fadlallah, he was always vulnerable on an issue that he himself had publicized in September 1985, following the defection of a senior KGB officer, Colonel Vitali Yurchenko. What made Yurchenko so valuable was his previous experience as a counter-intelligence expert attached to the KGB's Washington DC *rezidentura*, and his subsequent senior appointment in Moscow. He was a virtual treasure trove of secrets, and in July 1985 had seized the opportunity to escape from poverty and an unhappy marriage by requesting political asylum in Rome while on a mission to find Vladimir Alexandrov, a Soviet nuclear physicist who had gone missing. Yurchenko was flown to a CIA safe house in Vienna, Virginia for lengthy debriefing, and disclosed fabulous information, including evidence which identified a former CIA officer, Edward Lee Howard, and a former NSA analyst, Ronald Pelton, as spies for the KGB. He was also able to clear up dozens of loose ends on other counter-intelligence cases and reveal the KGB's latest tradecraft, including the deliberate brushing of CIA personnel in Moscow with radioactive dust to enable their movements to be monitored. Unusually, Casey met Yurchenko several times during his debriefings, entertaining him to dinner twice, and was quite unable to resist spreading the good news of the CIA's impressive coup. Unfortunately, the rather unpersonable Yurchenko, who had been promised total discretion, was understandably dismayed by the leaks and disappointed in his treatment by his Security Divison handlers who had failed to show him the respect he felt he deserved, He re-defected to the Soviet embassy in Washington DC on 31 October and called a press conference four days later to complain that he had been abducted by the CIA and drugged.

The post-mortem conducted by the CIA suggested that Yurchenko's considerable personal problems had not been properly appreciated when he approached the Rome station, in the way that they probably would have been had he been recruited and run for a period. Instead, he had simply turned up unexpectedly, demanding asylum and resettlement. The heavy-drinking counter-intelligence expert had an exaggerated view of what was in store for him, and was bitterly disappointed when he was rejected by his former girlfriend, Dr Valentina Yereskovsky, a pediatrician and the wife of the Soviet consul general in Montreal. The CIA concluded that it was highly likely that Aldrich Ames, who had been part of his debriefing team, had tipped off the KGB to Yurchenko's continuing interest in the woman with whom he had previously conducted a lengthy and passionate affair and with whom he remained besotted. Accordingly, when Yurchenko unexpectedly turned up on the doorstep of her apartment in Canada, she had almost certainly been warned to throw him out, which is precisely what she did, protesting that she had no intention of defecting with her two daughters. Yurchenko's ludicrous claim to have been abducted and drugged was highly reminiscent of the assertions made by the journalist Oleg Bitov who had gone unpunished after he abandoned his defection to England. Doubtless Yurchenko had calculated that the prospect of major political embarrassment would persuade the KGB to pretend that his feeble excuse had been accepted. This reckoning proved to be correct, for Yurchenko was never prosecuted and was allowed to live out the rest of his KGB career before falling on hard times and becoming a bank guard in Moscow. The fact that Yurchenko had supplied the CIA with some invaluable information at a particularly critical moment was probably too politically awkward for the KGB to acknowledge, so the defector's improbable tale had been swallowed, albeit with some private scepticism.

Overnight Casey's great triumph turned to dust and his reputation as a shrewd espionage operator was left in tatters, the only consolation being that Yurchenko had not received any of the money promised him, and had publicly announced the figure as a million dollars, thereby effectively broadcasting a tempting advertisement to attract other like-minded KGB colleagues. Casey was especially sensitive on the re-defection as he personally had achieved much to reverse the Agency's poor record of handling Soviet defectors. He had pressed for and obtained the special legislation that allowed the DCI to bypass the usual immigration procedures and grant ten valuable US passports a year to his nominees. Hitherto the CIA had been vulnerable to complaints, often voiced by its own retirees, that many potential defectors had been deterred because of the notoriously poor aftercare and resettlement offered to former KGB officers. According to a political lobby group, the Jamestown Foundation formed to study the problem, some Soviet turncoats had become so disillusioned they had even risked returning to Moscow rather than face the unrewarding realities of scraping a living in an unfamiliar capitalist system, equipped with few appropriate social or employment skills.

The CIA had received two very senior defectors in 1978, Arkadi Shevchenko, who was the second most senior Soviet diplomat at the United Nations, and Ion Pacepa, the acting director of the Romanian DIE. Codenamed DYNAMITE, Shevchenko had been run for months as a CIA source by his handler, based in New York, until April 1978 when he suspected he had been compromised, while Pacepa was an unexpected, opportunist escape via the US embassy in Bonn. Both men were to express considerable dissatisfaction with their treatment, with Shevchenko suffering the humiliation of being provided by his FBI minders with a prostitute from the Yellow Pages, who subsequently wrote a book about their brief romance. As for Pacepa, he gained the impression that he was something of a political embarrassment for the Carter administration which had entertained Nicolai Ceausescu three times, referring to him as one of the world's leading statesmen, with the president describing him as 'a great national and international leader', and even claimed that he had been threatened with deportation on the grounds that he was a a KGB plant. What remains undeniable is that Pacepa was unable to publish his memoirs, *Red Horizons*, for nine years, and remains bitter about his experience.[4] His critics claim that his defection was kept quiet to protect his wife, daughter and son-in-law left behind in Bucharest, and his book was released as soon it was safe to do so. While Admiral Turner mentioned Shevchenko in his 1985 autobiography, *Secrecy and Democracy: The CIA in Transition*, inexplicably he omitted all references to Pacepa, which is odd considering that the general was the highest ranking Warsaw Pact intelligence defector of all time. Quite apart from the information he supplied regarding his own organization, the DIE, Pacepa represented a treasure trove of material about other areas of interest, including the first detailed inside news of the Soviet VPK, which apparently had used the DIE to acquire an advanced IBM-360 computer, the plans to the German Leopard-II main battle tank, and the French Berliet heavy truck. Whereas Shevchenko had been of limited intelligence value after his defection, because he was an authentic professional diplomat, and had been debriefed so extensively during the period he had been run as an agent, Pacepa in contrast was an unprecedented windfall, although the CIA manifestly failed to exploit him to his full potential.

Casey had been an early Jamestown Foundation supporter and recognized that a comprehensive financial package combined with proper post-defection support could help attract high calibre line-crossers. He was quickly proved right, with a dramatic increase in senior GRU and KGB personnel making discreet approaches to see what was on offer. For the right meal-ticket, as Yurchenko had been promised, the down-payment was a new identity, up to a million dollars to buy a home, and a lifetime pension equivalent to the applicant's military rank. The result of the new policy was the recruitment of Sergei Bokhan, the GRU's deputy *rezident* in Athens, Colonel Viktor Gundarev, a KGB officer in Athens, and several other undisclosed defections which served to bolster the CIA's morale and give the Agency a much-needed glimpse into its opponent's camp. Codenamed GT/BLIZZARD, Bokhan had proved his worth in 1978 by tipping off the CIA to the existence of a traitor, William Kampiles, who had sold the Soviets the handbook of the KH-11 satellite for $3,000, and he had also incriminated a retired naval officer. The GRU officer was into his third year on his second tour of duty in Greece, being run by the CIA's Chief of Station, David Forden, but in May 1985 he was recalled to Moscow. Instead of flying home, fearing the worst, Forden arranged for his exfiltration to the United States. Similarly, when Gundarev was recalled in February 1986, he abandoned his wife and took his girlfriend to the United States.

Although Congress expressed an interest in investigating the Yurchenko fiasco, Casey prevailed when he argued that he had already set up an internal inquiry, and that there was little point in washing the Agency's dirty linen in public. He more than most appreciated the scale of the disaster but, as John McMahon observed, in a free society it was impossible legally to prevent Yurchenko from changing his mind and strolling into the Soviet embassy.

There was to be a further unfortunate, unexpected consequence of the Yurchenko affair which was to rebound on Casey personally. The defector had revealed sufficient clues for the FBI to finger Ronald Pelton as a former KGB source inside the NSA. Pelton was arrested, and among the charges was one concerning IVY BELLS, an extremely secret NSA collection programme that inexplicably had been compromised and terminated in 1981. The origin of IVY BELLS had been the NSA's covert use of submarines to intercept Soviet signals by extending an aerial above the surface outside sensitive naval installations. The US navy had then developed an impressive technique of finding Soviet underwater cables and recording their traffic by overlaying them with a special pod which was a combined induction antenna and tape system. Because there was minimal physical interference with the cable itself, the operation was executed at limited risk of discovery, although the entire undertaking was exceptionally hazardous because the actual intercept site was well inside Soviet territorial waters. A dedicated submarine, the USS *Halibut*, already well experienced in retrieving spent test missiles and warheads from firing ranges, specialized in finding these cables on the ocean floor and attaching the listening device. After a designated period the submarine retrieved the equipment and delivered the material to the NSA for processing. A military line stretched across the Sea of Okhotsk from the sensitive Kamchatka peninsula to the Soviet mainland had been a significant target, but the pod had disappeared in 1981 – only to turn up later in a Moscow military museum – when the *Halibut* routinely returned to service it. According to Yurchenko, Pelton had alerted the Soviets to IVY BELLS in return for a few thousand dollars, and they had intervened, tracing and seizing the gadgetry.

Initially the loss had been written off as an occupational hazard, with dozens of possible explanations, but when the betrayal was to be used in the evidence against Pelton the media began to take an interest, much to Casey's consternation. He believed that any public comment on the subject of advanced clandestine collection techniques would jeopardize current projects and give the Soviets confirmation of what had hitherto probably been only speculation. Having failed to obtain a consensus that US national security would be compromised by any public disclosure of IVY BELLS, Casey contemplated criminal proceedings against the newspapers that reported the details. Convinced that Casey was anxious to conceal an intelligence failure that had no implications for current operations, the media rejected pleas to their patriotism and were enraged by the threat of legal action. The DCI's apparent success in landing a defector who had identified and eliminated a spy inside the NSA was transformed into a public relations catastrophe, alienating newspaper columnists and investigative journalists who had always been suspicious of Casey.

Although IVY BELLS did create headlines, two other technical operations which failed around the same time received absolutely no coverage, but were later offered as evidence that the CIA had suffered appalling penetration. Operation TAW had been a recording device placed on the KGB's main underground landline connecting the Lubyanka headquarters with its communications centre at Troitsk, twenty-five miles south of Moscow, and from its installation in 1980 had required frequent servicing by the local CIA station staff who clambered into an access tunnel to replace the tapes. In 1985 TAW was betrayed, together with details of ABSORB, an ostensibly innocent freight container which travelled the Trans-Siberian railway from Japan to Hamburg in West Germany, but actually concealed sophisticated sensors designed to detect Soviet missile sites. On 24 January 1986 the KGB swooped on the flatbed train carrying the container, thus bringing the operation to a conclusion.

The DCI was to clash with the media on many issues, although he certainly understood the need to get a good press. Some of his closest colleagues could not understand his willingness to try and cultivate implacably hostile critics, among them Bob Woodward of the *Washington Post*, when such efforts were inevitably doomed to failure, whatever charm he could exercise on such occasions. Certainly, events often conspired to undermine his overtures, as happened in August 1986 when Nicholas Daniloff, the *US News and World Report* correspondent in Moscow, was detained by the KGB on charges of espionage. Daniloff protested his innocence and the US State Department accused the Soviets of a blatant tit-for-tat retaliation for the recent arrest of Gennady Zakharov, a KGB officer under UN cover in New York. Unfortunately, the truth was a little more complicated, for Daniloff had delivered a package to the US embassy at the request of an anonymous contact, and thereby had unconsciously opened a new lead in a potentially promising but stalled case. Five years earlier another anonymous donor had sent the CIA some extremely valuable information concerning Soviet missile technology and strengths, but contact had not been maintained. A comparison of the handwriting in both packages suggested that Daniloff's source was the same person, so the CIA's Chief of Station in Moscow, Murat Natirboff, had asked for the journalist's help in reaching their mysterious benefactor from 1981. Unaware of the previous history, Daniloff had supplied what he believed to be his contact's telephone number, and thereby set in motion the events that were to lead to his arrest in the act of receiving a further package of classified data. While the CIA had taken reasonable care to avoid embroiling an American journalist in espionage, in contravention of the ban on such activities, Langley had insisted that its CoS reach Daniloff's source, and thus had compromised him. The episode also served to sour relations further between Casey and the fourth estate.

The DCI could take the credit for having supervised the highly profitable revival of the National Collection Division which established representative offices in thirty domestic cities in which to debrief volunteers from private business who traded in, or visited, or had contact with, the Eastern bloc. Casey instituted special gatherings at Langley in which dozens of selected candidates were invited to receive confidential briefings, and offered the opportunity to reciprocate. The 'executive seminars' engendered tremendous goodwill, provided some 'non official cover' openings and generated excellent intelligence at absolutely minimal cost and risk. Casey had also presided over a remarkable transformation at Langley, which had been so been so demoralized at the end of 1979, doubling the intelligence budget, from about $10 billion to $24 billion, of which half a billion had been devoted to the CIA which had employed an additional 3,000 staff, many of them in the DO, thus reversing the decline overseen by his predecessor, Stansfield Turner.

The horrors of the Iran–Contra scandal came to dominate the last years of the Reagan administration on a scale that at times seemed to imitate Watergate's impact on the Nixon presidency, and certainly Casey's legacy, of an enhanced CIA with an increased overall budget approaching $3 billion, with $500 million earmarked for covert action, was replaced by an atmosphere of scandal and criminality. Burdened by an undiagnosed brain tumour, and still recovering from treatment for prostate cancer which he had divulged to hardly any one, Casey's last days at Langley were beset by a war conducted on several fronts, not the least of which were his own cabinet colleagues, Congress and the media.

The CIA's greatest catastrophe, which Casey would have found hardest to shoulder, was the egregious counter-intelligence disaster represented by Aldrich (Rick) Ames. His duplicity dated back to May 1985, while Casey was fighting numerous battles at home and abroad, but it would be misleading even to imply that if Casey had not been distracted he would have devoted more time to the catalogue of failures that beset the DO's Soviet/Eastern Europe Division. Still mindful of the hideously debilitating decade of molehunts conducted by James Jesus Angleton in the 1960s and early 1970s, the CIA had been unprepared for one of its own senior management becoming a turncoat.

Fluent in Mandarin and the son of a CIA officer, Rick Ames had joined the CIA in 1967 and had turned in mediocre performances as a DO officer in Ankara and Mexico City. Nevertheless, he had participated in some significant cases, including those of the Foreign Ministry spy Aleksandr Ogorodnik (TRIGON), and two members of the United Nations, Arkadi Shevchenko (DYNAMITE) and Sergei Fedorenko (PYRRHIC). In September 1983 Ames, by now fluent in Russian, had been appointed chief of the counter-intelligence branch in the SE Division which had given him complete access to the DO's most closely guarded files on its most successful assets. Heavily in debt and convinced that his talents had gone unrecognized, Ames made an initial approach to the KGB *rezident* in Washington DC, Stanislav Androsov, in a letter delivered on 16 April, offering to sell him the names of several CIA spies for $50,000. At a meeting on 16 May, Ames supplied three names, and at a further rendezvous on 13 June he provided an almost complete roster of the CIA's most valued agents in the Soviet Union.

Precisely which names Ames supplied, and on what date, remains a matter of speculation, although it is now generally acknowledged that he was probably not responsible for Tolkachev's arrest, which had taken place in Moscow on 9 June, four days *before* Ames sold his notorious long list. Codenamed AE/SPHERE, AE/BLIP and then AE/VANQUISH, Tolkachev was seized as his wife was driving him into Moscow from his dacha, and his CIA handler, Paul Stombaugh, was briefly detained on 13 June while preparing to meet his contact in a park, and expelled. If Ames betrayed Tolkachev in his April letter, it is likely that his identity had already been disclosed by Edward Lee Howard, a disaffected and somewhat unstable CIA officer who had been briefed for a tour of duty in Moscow but had been sacked in May 1983 for lying about his previous use of drugs while in the Peace Corps. He defected in September 1985, just as the FBI was about to arrest him concerning Yurchenko's identification of him as ROBERT, the man who had sold some information to the KGB, which probably included sufficient data to compromise TRIGON and Operation TAW. Although Yurchenko never knew Howard's name, his description of a man who had been trained for a special mission at the US embassy in Moscow, running TRIGON and servicing the TAW device, was unmistakable. If Ames had contributed anything to GT/SPHERE case, it was probably the arrest of Tolkachev's wife, a communications expert whom her husband recruited and with whom he probably shared the astonishing fortune of 400,000 roubles found in their apartment by KGB investigators. She was imprisoned, and died of cancer a year after her release.

In any event, the damage caused by the Ames list was immense, and severely compromised AE/TICKLE, Britain's star agent inside the KGB's London *rezidentura*. As a direct consequence of the tip from Ames, Oleg Gordievsky was unexpectedly recalled to Moscow on 17 May 1985, supposedly for urgent top-level consultations three days later, but actually for a lengthy, hostile interrogation which included the use of drugs. Originally recruited by SIS in Copenhagen in 1973, Gordievsky had proved to be a hugely important coup for an organization with a depressingly long history of penetration, and his true name was kept a closely-guarded secret at Century House. Unfortunately, the CIA had worked out for itself his likely identity as the only KGB officer who had served in Denmark in the 1970s, and was later gaining access to critical political intelligence material in the London *rezidentura* a decade later. Ames named GT/TICKLE as Gordievsky, and in August Yurchenko confirmed SIS's worst fears by mentioning that the KGB's *rezident* designate in London had been recalled in May as a suspected spy and was still in Moscow under investigation. Incredibly, SIS reacted by pulling off a remarkable achievement, succeeding in exfiltrating their man from Moscow, right from under the KGB's nose. Another lucky escape was made by Sergei Bokhan, the CIA's GRU source, GT/BLIZZARD, in Athens. He had defected at the end of May, a fortnight before Ames had delivered his list.

Other agents, working for the CIA, suffered a rather different experience. Major Sergei M. Motorin and Colonel Valeri F. Martynov, both KGB officers who had been recruited by the FBI in Washington DC, were arrested and later executed. Codenamed GT/GENTILE, Martynov was a Line X scientific intelligence officer under cultural attaché cover who had been recruited as an ideologically-motivated agent in 1980 and had returned to Moscow in January 1985. Motorin, codenamed GT/GAUZE, had been blackmailed into cooperating with the FBI in early 1982 following an illegal bartering transaction; he had been one of Yurchenko's four KGB escorts on his flight home on 6 November, and was arrested on his arrival at Sheremetyevo airport. Although Ames has never acknowledged precisely whom he fingered in his first letter, it is highly likely that he included the names of Motorin, Martynov and Gordievsky, the KGB trio in the best position to warn the CIA of the existence of a well-placed traitor within its own ranks. As a matter of self-preservation, Ames would have been bound to warn the *rezident*, Stanislav Androsov, that some of his colleagues were really working for the West. In his list of 13 June he mentioned Tolkachev, who had just been arrested and was to be executed, and a group of other Soviet intelligence officers who had been recruited while under diplomatic cover in the US: Leonid Poleschuk (GT/WEIGH), recruited in Katmandu in the 1970s, had been recalled from his counter-intelligence post at the Lagos *rezidentura* in May 1985 and was arrested three months later in Izmaylovskiy Park as he emptied a dead drop; a GRU officer, Gennadi Smetanin (GT/MILLION) and his wife Svetlana, who had been recruited in 1983 at a price of $300,000, had returned from Lisbon on home leave in August 1985, but had not reappeared at an October rendezvous as scheduled; Gennadi Varenik (GT/FITNESS), the son of a senior KGB officer, under TASS cover when he had been recruited in March 1985 in Bonn, where he revealed details of a KGB plan to plant terrorist bombs, was arrested in November, and shot in February 1987.

In addition, GT/BACKBEND, GT/GLAZING, GT/TAME and GT/VEST showed signs that they had come under the KGB's intensive scrutiny, a development that indicated the SE Division had suffered a very comprehensive calamity. The scale of the catastrophe was not lost on Burton Gerber or his deputy, Milton Bearden, both incidentally Roman Catholics, who instituted a major review of each case so as to establish whether operational blunders were to blame, or if there was something altogether more sinister afoot. Gus Hathaway, who had returned from Bonn in January 1985 to run the Counter-intelligence Staff, estimated that up to forty-five separate cases had been placed in jeopardy. Fluent in Polish, Russian, German, Spanish and Portuguese, and having fought in France with the US army in 1944, Hathaway had joined the Agency in October 1951 and had served ten years in Germany and nine in Latin America, working against Soviet targets on each assignment. As the losses mounted from May 1985, Hathaway became increasingly convinced that SE had been penetrated at a high level.

The DCI was briefed on the SE Division's losses for the first time in January 1986 by the DDO Clair George, Gerber, Hathaway and Bearden, and Casey promptly instructed the former DDO, John Stein, who was then the CIA's inspector-general, to conduct an urgent investigation. As Stein reviewed each case, the DO suffered more inexplicable losses. On 10 March, Sergei Vorontsov, code-named GT/COWL, who had spied since late 1984, was caught, and his CIA contact, Michael Sellers, was detained while on his way to a rendezvous in Moscow and expelled. Also in March, GT/VILLAGE was recalled from the Soviet consulate in Surabaja, Indonesia, and vanished. Two months later, on 7 May, another member of the Moscow station, Erik Sites, was ambushed while attempting to meet GT/EASTBOUND. On 1 July, Vladimir V. Potashov (GT/MEDIAN), an arms control negotiator at the Soviet Institute for USA and Canada Studies who had spied since 1981, was taken into custody, and three days later Dmitri Polyakov was summoned unexpectedly to the Lubyanka and arrested. Soon afterwards Colonel Vladimir M. Piguzov (GT/JOGGER) who had been recruited in Djakarta and had been assigned to the KGB's Andropov Institute training academy, dropped from sight. This was an especially mysterious and sinister loss, for Piguzov had not been in contact with the CIA since 1979 when he had returned to Moscow, and had proved himself to be an exceptionally useful source by identifying as a turncoat David H. Barnett, a CIA retiree working on a training programme on contract, who was arrested in April 1980 and had been sentenced to eighteen years' imprisonment. It was almost as if, having exhausted the current hot cases, someone was rifling the DO's dormant files to find less valuable spies to betray. Almost as confirmation, Boris Yuzhin (TG/TWINE), who had been the TASS correspondent in San Francisco in the 1970s and had returned to Moscow in 1982, was arrested on 23 December 1986. Virtually simultaneously, Colonel Vladimir M. Vasilev (GT/ACCORD), a GRU officer recruited in Budapest in 1983, who had identified a GRU network in which US army Sergeant Clyde L. Conrad had been active in West Germany, was also caught. Vasilev's loss was significant, for he also enabled the Swedish security police to arrest Conrad's controllers, Dr Sandor Kercsik and his younger brother Imre, and roll up a large Hungarian military intelligence network headed by a retired warrant officer, Zoltan Szabo.

Originally a refugee from Hungary in the 1956 exodus, Szabo had joined the US army and had been decorated for gallantry in Vietnam. According to his confession, he had been recruited by the Hungarians in 1971, when he took his German wife and children on holiday to Lake Balaton. Although Vasilev had tipped off the CIA to the existence of Szabo's huge Hungarian spy-ring in 1985, which extended into Italy, his role had been skilfully concealed, so it was a surprise when he was suddenly taken into the KGB's custody in 1986 and executed the following year. Conrad was allowed his liberty until August 1988, and was sentenced to life imprisonment in June 1990, but Szabo escaped to Budapest.

What made some of the arrests in Moscow so odd was the lengths the KGB went to in order to conceal the exact date on which they had occurred. Uncharacteristically, news of some took more than a year to leak out; for example, Motorin had been taped by the FBI as he telephoned his girlfriend in Washington DC, assuring her he was all right, months *after* he had been detained in Moscow. The pattern that emerged was of sources being recalled to Moscow or disappearing while on home leave, and, for reasons that intrigued the CIA molehunters, the KGB evidently had attempted to conceal the undeniable fact that between May and September 1985 the majority of the SE Division's spies had been arrested. Indeed, the KGB used numerous ruses to distract the CIA investigation into its own losses, which was anyway handicapped by the certainty that Edward Howard had betrayed a wealth of secrets, probably including TRIGON and TAW, and that some of the marine guard detachment in the US embassy in Moscow had allowed KGB personnel access to sensitive areas in the building. Sergeant Clayton Lonetree confessed to having been honeytrapped into helping the KGB, and Corporal Arnold Bracey admitted to a similar affair, so there was a possibility that listening devices had been installed in the embassy's comms equipment. The big question was whether the CIA's 1985 losses were evidence of a dangerous, currently active mole, or could be rationalized by other more mundane explanations. John Stein concluded in a ten-page report that there was no proof of a mole and opted for the opinion that poor tradecraft had been at the root of each loss, a view that was rejected by the counter-intelligence experts. However, it was equally true that not everything could be blamed on Howard's treachery. After all, Sergei Vorontsov's recruitment had occurred *after* he had left the Agency, so Howard could never have been in a position to compromise him to the KGB.

The CIA molehunters were to take nearly nine years to identify Aldrich Ames as the source of the SE leaks, in part because the Soviets laid several false trails, including the initially plausible assertion, made in March 1986 through an anonymous source in Germany who turned out to be a KGB-controlled double agent, that the security of the CIA's communications had been compromised by the successful penetration of its principal radio facility at Warrenton, Virginia. The information, hand-delivered by letter to a CIA officer in Bonn, contained some genuine information about Gennadi Varenik (GT/FITNESS) and correctly named his CIA case officer as Charles Leven. An inevitably lengthy investigation had concluded finally that no such breach had occurred, and that the entire tale had been a skilfully constructed ploy. Similarly, another KGB source, Vladimir Smetanin (GT/PROLOGUE), sold his CIA handlers dozens of supposedly authentic internal Second Chief Directorate documents which seemed to disclose how the KGB's ubiquitous surveillance on US embassy staff had been responsible for identifying the CIA agents lost in 1985. Once again, Smetanin was finally exposed as an elaborate hoax, presumably intended to divert the CIA from the existence of a well-placed mole within the SE Division. Even when the CIA's attention eventually focused on Ames, months of surveillance failed to produce anything incriminating, and it was only when his personal finances were scrutinized belatedly that he was found to be spending prodigiously in excess of his salary, and thus confirmed as quite the worst breach in security the CIA had ever suffered.

In his eventual confession, traded for a five-year prison sentence for his wife, Ames admitted to having betrayed for cash amounting to two million dollars more than two dozen CIA spies, among them a pair close to him who were never arrested. Sergei Fedorenko (GT/PYRRHIC), and a scientist codenamed BYPLAY originally recruited by the FBI in San Francisco, had been handled by Ames personally in New York. Fedorenko was run until his return to Moscow in 1977, and both later reported that they had come under sustained KGB surveillance. Fedorenko, who had worked as a subordinate to Arkadi Shevchenko in the UN Secretariat, had suspended contact with the

CIA following the arrest of TRIGON, who had worked in the same department of the Foreign Ministry, and had taken even more precautions, including the destruction of his secret communications equipment, when his colleague at the Soviet Institute for USA and Canada Studies, Vladimir Potashov, was caught. Despite having been named by Ames, the KGB apparently had been unable to arrest so senior a political figure as Fedorenko, who was to be promoted to become one of Mikhail Gorbachev's advisers. Like GT/BYPLAY, Fedorenko survived despite Ames's treachery, and subsequently went to live in the United States, while the scientist chose to stay in Moscow. Ten others suffered confiscation of their assets and the KGB's traditional execution of a bullet fired at point-blank range in the back of the neck, an unmarked grave and a perfunctory form letter mailed to the next of kin. While the CIA remained anxious to channel financial support to the families of his victims, it was not always possible to do so without jeopardizing further innocent lives; Adolf Tolkachev's son was effectively orphaned and forced to carry the KGB's punishment into the next generation.

The combination of the Beirut crisis, the Iran–Contra affair and the SE molehunt served to undermine Casey's reputation as a crusader set on confronting the Kremlin, but in reality these dramas, while important in their own way, were never going to detract from the DCI's main achievements. The CIA had made Afghanistan an open wound in Soviet society, and had transformed a dispute about union recognition in a Gdansk shipyard into a source of subversion that would undermine the entire Soviet empire.

Chapter X

Solidarity

General Oleg Kalugin, formerly the KGB's chief of counter-intelligence, recalls the moment when he realized that all was not well in Poland:

> It was August 1979, and I was on a delegation accompanying Vladimir Kryuchkov to talk to colleagues in our sister service. As was customary, we made a visit to the great Lenin shipyards, and when we arrived we were greeted by the manager who asked us to leave our big limousines outside the gates. He explained that there was a lot of unrest among the workers and that the sight of our impressive convoy might be too provocative. Naturally we complied, but far from being welcomed by the workforce, or being clapped as was the convention during tours of such places, we met sullen stares and resentment. This had quite an impact on me and during the toasts at a banquet thrown in our honour at the end of our visit to Poland I made a casual reference to the dissent in my speech. To my amazement, the Minister of Security, Nikelsky, reacted as if I had touched a very raw nerve and insisted there was only a handful of troublemakers, and he had them completely under control. I knew then there was a real problem, and this was the moment that I think of Solidarity as the beginning of the end.[1]

From the KGB's perspective, virtually all information about the Solidarity movement came to Moscow from the Polish SB via the head of the official KGB mission in Warsaw, Lieutenant-General Vitali G. Pavlov, whose staff also manned an office inside the Ministry of the Interior building on Rakowiecka Street. Although there was an undeclared *rezidentura* in Warsaw, primarily tasked to recruit foreign diplomats and other targets, the KGB had deliberately refrained from contact with Polish domestic sources since 1956, for fear of jeopardizing the delicate relationship that existed between the KGB and the SB. This liaison was unique among the Warsaw Pact countries, perhaps with the limited exception of Cuba, because the SB demanded an unusual degree of independence, and the direct recruitment of agents within Solidarity was considered much too dangerous. The KGB leadership took the view that the discovery of its involvement with such a volatile group could be open to serious misinterpretation by the SB and lead to very difficult political consequences. Accordingly, the policy decision was taken at an early stage to rely entirely on SB reports for news of what was happening in Gdansk, until a local *rezidentura* was established in the autumn of 1980, with the built-in safeguard of more objective and realistic commentaries from KGB sources recruited from within the SB itself. KGB personnel had the run of the SB's headquarters and there was never any shortage of willing collaborators among ambitious SB officers because a good Soviet reference was considered very helpful for promotions.

The cosmetic deference to Polish sensibilities was, in Kalugin's opinion, a fatal mistake: 'Perhaps if the SB had been tougher at the beginning, if we had given more support, things might have been different, but the Poles were always difficult. They were not like the Czechs and East Germans . . . they had to be handled with care.' In fact, the KGB occasionally circumvented the 1956 ban on the recruitment of Polish domestic sources by running agents under a 'false flag', the KGB handlers masquerading either as SB officers or members of the more trusted military counter-intelligence service.

Vitali G. Pavlov, the KGB's Chief of Mission in Warsaw, was an exceptionally experienced and decorated intelligence professional who had no doubt about his status, judging from the title of one of his books, *I was Rezident in Poland: Who Really Ruled Poland*. His operational life had begun during the Second World War when he had been deputy chief of the NKVD's American department; subsequently he was posted as *rezident* to Ottawa under second secretary cover where he was compromised in September 1945 by the defection of a GRU code clerk, Igor Gouzenko. Although Gouzenko was able to disclose a wealth of information and documents to incriminate the GRU, Pavlov's separately compartmented network escaped relatively unscathed, although he himself was named as the NKVD *rezident*, an episode that might have been expected to curtail any future career in the West, particularly as he only narrowly escaped arrest when the Ottawa police found him smashing his way into the defector's apartment, accompanied by two embassy guards. Hastily withdrawn from Canada, where he had been decorated the previous year for running a well-managed *rezidentura*, Pavlov was appointed deputy head of the First Chief Directorate's American Department; then in October 1952, he arrived in Canberra for a temporary (four-month) tour of duty as a 'repatriation officer' with the rank of colonel; later he headed Directorate S, in charge of all illegals worldwide. He was then appointed *rezident* in Vienna, under diplomatic cover using the name Nikolai G. Kedrov, and his transfer to Warsaw was his last job before retirement. His career, outlined in his autobiography *Operation Snow*, described his recruitment in Washington DC in May 1941 of Harry Dexter White, a key source close to President Roosevelt while he was in the United States, an achievement that was to establish his reputation as a formidable operator. Following this assignment, which he completed while travelling as a diplomatic courier, Pavlov returned to Moscow via San Francisco, Hawaii, Japan and Vladivostok. Forty years later, as *rezident* in Warsaw, he was to play a key role as a hard-liner in advising the Kremlin about developments in Poland.

According to the electrician Lech Walesa, Solidarity was born in the Gdansk strike of August 1980, when 17,000 shipyard workers demonstrated for the right to withhold their labour. Perhaps not entirely coincidentally, the Pope had been visiting Brazil, and in Manaus on 10 July had addressed the sensitive issues of land reform and the treatment of minorities. Controversially, he had also emphasized that one of the principal, inalienable rights of all workers was the right to strike, and while that particular message may not have had much impact in Latin America, beset with other social crises, it hit home hard in Europe and especially in Gdansk, the focus of the labour unrest that had crippled the country during the long hot summer. The strikes had begun in Lublin in June, when railway workers had welded train wheels to the lines, and had escalated to such an extent that Cardinal Wyszynski broadcast a largely futile appeal to halt the protests on 15 August from the holy shrine of Our Lady of Czestochowa.

Although Solidarity became known as a trade union, and was quickly to acquire a membership approaching nine and a half million, it was really a very widely based movement committed to economic, political and social reform. Certainly, the Pope's visit the previous year had encouraged Slavic self-assertiveness and confidence, but Solidarity was much more complex than a mere manifestation of anti-Communism or hostility to Eduard Gierek's regime. Nor, for that matter, was it a tightly organized, centrally controlled organization, but it none the less represented a potent force in a country increasingly accustomed to a spiral of sporadic protest, followed by repression and violence. In previous instances, such as the massacres in Gdansk and Gdynia on 16 and 17 December 1970 which left twenty-seven dead, with further casualties of seventeen dead and 177 wounded at Elblag and Szczecin, the spiral had been abruptly terminated by government intervention which had left the bodies of demonstrators lying in the street. In this particular example, these tactics had rebounded against the regime as rumours circulated about four to five hundred deaths.

In June 1976 strikes in Radom and Warsaw against steep price rises had prompted more suppression, but on that occasion the Party's General Secretary Gierek had conceded a delay in implementing the increases and unintentionally had spawned the Committee to Defend the Workers (KOR), which was formed to press for the release of imprisoned strikers. While not bound by a single ideology, KOR was united in the belief that totalitarianism should be opposed, and that Marxism had failed. This common purpose created a coalition that coincided with wider external pressures for human rights, as asserted by Charter 77 activists in Czechoslovakia, and echoed a theme oft repeated by the Pope. When one of the Charter 77 founders, the sixty-nine-year-old Professor Jan Patocka, died of heart failure on 13 March 1977 after eleven hours of interrogation, the fuse for conflict was lit. Not long afterwards KOR activists occupied a Warsaw church and went on hunger strike, putting them on a collision course with a regime unused to dealing with political dissent.

The regime in Warsaw responded to the unrest by sending Gierek to meet Cardinal Wyszynski in October, and then flying him to

Rome to have an audience with Pope Paul VI in December. The Party's purpose was doubtless to draw in the Church which had long played an ambivalent, almost collaborationist role with the state authorities, invariably advocating passive resistance and acquiescence. At this stage, official strategy was to make friendly overtures to the Church while maintaining comprehensive surveillance on the opposition. Although the Party's headquarters was at Nowy Swiat Street, Warsaw, where the political decisions were taken, it also established a dedicated operations centre in Gdansk, at the SB's regional headquarters at 15 Okopowa Street, headed by deputy interior minister Major-General Boguslaw Stachura, to monitor the strikers, identify and destroy their printing presses and prevent them from developing links with areas of unrest elsewhere in the country. The SB claimed to the KGB's Warsaw *rezidentura* that 'Attempts by anti-Socialist forces to establish contacts with the artistic, scientific and cultural intelligentsia, in order to enlist their support for the demands of the strikers were cut short', but Pavlov was sceptical, and reported to Moscow that actually the SB had failed to

> recognize the extent of the danger in time or the hidden discontent of the working class. The blame lay chiefly with the leadership of the Interior Ministry, and in particular with General Stanislaw Kowalczyk and his deputy Stachura. When the strikes intensified in the coastal region, Kowalczyk simply lost his head . . . in the opinion of the KGB mission, it is time to replace Kowalczyk and Stachura with other officers.

The glue that bound Solidarity's disparate components was the call for free trade unions. The movement's potent message was articulated in September 1981, at Solidarity's first national congress, by Andrzej Gwiazda, who promised support for all independent unions elsewhere in Eastern Europe, and spoke of 'the struggle for a free trade union movement'. The lure was hugely attractive, but also deeply corrosive to the Soviet bloc if allowed to go unanswered, and accordingly was described at the time by the SB as 'a brazen attempt to interfere in the internal affairs of Socialist countries'.

Pavlov and his colleagues had been convinced that Solidarity was externally funded, if not actively managed, by the CIA, the British

SIS and the French DGSE, and to some extent his analysis was correct. American support for the trade union had been initiated by Zbigniew Brzezinski, President Carter's national security adviser, in 1980, with AFL-CIO donations amounting to $150,000 and channelled through Brzezinski's friend Lane Kirkland, who had offered to organize a worldwide boycott of Soviet ships if Poland was invaded. Within five years that figure had reached $8 million, but in February 1981, when the Kremlin authorized a campaign of denigration, accusing the Voice of America and Radio Free Europe of transmitting covert messages to the Solidarity leadership, the CIA had scarcely begun to involve itself in the organization and had limited itself to printing T-shirts and subversive literature outside the country. On 5 March 1981 four members of the Polish politburo travelled to Moscow to be received by Brezhnev, Yuri Andropov, Foreign Minister Andrei Gromyko and Defence Minister Dmitri Ustinov. Although an official bulletin disclosed that Party leader Stanislaw Kania and Prime Minister General Wojciech Jaruzelski had held talks about the situation at home, the real purpose was to issue a stern warning: external influences should not be allowed to endanger the socialist community. The threat was explicit to the Polish delegation, and was intended for consumption further afield, but it was based on a fundamental misconception. The CIA had discussed increasing its support of Solidarity in March 1981 but, according to Bob Gates:

> Casey was cautious about any covert action planning prior to a Soviet invasion. He told Weinberger that US actions prior to Soviet action would be very risky and promised little benefit.
>
> Our people thought that deniability was important for Solidarity, and so we worked through third parties or other intermediaries in Western Europe. Most of what flowed out of CIA and through the intermediaries to Solidarity was printing materials, communications equipment, and other supplies for waging underground political warfare.[2]

The first covert support for Solidarity had been authorized by Zbigniew Brzezinski in the previous administration, when he had approved CIA funding for the monthly *Kultura* magazine published in Paris, and for the purchase of Xerox machines. He had also had a hand in the development, by Bill Donnelly of the CIA's communications branch, of an ingenious television interruptor. The compact device effectively overrode a conventional television broadcast and transmitted a special signal. In Solidarity's case the screen was obscured by a test board printed with the organization's name, in its distinctive print, accompanied by a recorded voice-over, which was transmitted at peak viewing, such as in the middle of a popular football match. Although it had only a localized effect within a radius of about a mile, briefly suppressing the legitimate transmission, it was a potent demonstration of the movement's effectiveness in delivering its message despite the best efforts of the regime. Listeners were asked to indicate that they had received Solidarity's signal by switching their house lights on and off, which created some spectacular night-time scenes with the lights in whole districts flickering.

Following martial law, Casey's enthusiasm for Solidarity increased immeasurably, and as the White House prepared for a trade embargo, which President Reagan announced on 29 December, Casey swung into action, calling Mossad director General Yitzhak Hoffi for immediate access to Israeli contacts, offering to fund the French DGSE's sponsorship of one of Solidarity's external representative offices, and raising the Rome station chief from his bed to demand a renewed attempt at direct liaison with the Vatican. Evidently stunned by the news of martial law given to him at home, Cardinal Agostino Casaroli agreed to meet the CIA to discuss the potential for mutual assistance. Simultaneously, the Polish embassy hand-delivered a note to the Vatican Secretariat, informing the Pope of the 'state of war' which had been declared by General Jaruzelski. What it did not mention was the wave of arrests that had swept through the country, with hundreds of Solidarity activists being detained at the Mokotow prison on Warsaw's Rakowiecka Street, and Lech Walesa escorted to a government villa in a Warsaw suburb.

The internments had been well planned, and much of Solidarity's leadership was seized by the police as they took 5,000 supporters into custody, including Jacek Kuron and Adam Michnik, who were held incommunicado. While temporarily paralysing the movement, with only Zbigniew Bujak and Zbigniew Romaszewski escaping the dragnet to go underground, the arrests hardened domestic and international public opinion against the regime and served to prompt further unrest, with miners occupying their pit near Katowice in protest. A bloody confrontation followed, leaving seven dead and thirty-nine injured, with forty-one casualties among the crack ZOMO units that broke up the demonstration. Other coalmines began 'working to rule' on 2 February. From the Soviet perspective, this episode was especially disturbing as it sparked off sympathy action within the Soviet borders, in the Dombas pits. In Poland the authorities reacted on 17 February with Operation CALM, arresting a further 4,000 suspects, which brought the estimated number of temporary political prisoners to around 40,000, thus leaving the movement in the hands of a small underground network consisting of Bogdan Lis in Gdansk, Zbigniew Bujak in Warsaw, Wladislaw Hradek in Krakow and Wladyslaw Frasymiuk in Wroclaw.

Later, the SB was to report to the KGB's *rezidentura* in Warsaw on what had been achieved in the twelve months following the imposition of martial law. A quarter of a million security personnel had been deployed, and had identified 430 separate opposition groups associated with Solidarity; 10,131 people had been interned; 370 printing presses seized, together with 1,200 other pieces of printing equipment, and 1.2 million undistributed leaflets; a dozen Solidarity radio stations had been taken off the air; and 400 demonstrations suppressed. The SB also believed that it had a hold over the intransigent Lech Walesa who, codenamed BOLEK, had been in contact years earlier with the SB in Gdansk. The officer assigned to liaise with Walesa during his detention was Colonel Adam Pietruszka, and according to Czeslaw Kiszczak who reported the tape-recorded encounter to the KGB, Walesa was also confronted with his former SB handler. Presumably this was an attempt to apply pressure on the uncompromising electrician, but if so it appears to have failed as Walesa remained as uncooperative as ever, much to the exasperation of Archbishop Jozef Glemp.

With the leadership isolated, and Walesa kept under house arrest at a government hunting lodge at Arlamowo, near the Ukrainian frontier, 500 kilometres from Warsaw, Solidarity appeared to be in serious danger, until Walesa indicated that he would be prepared to be conciliatory if he were granted a television interview. The regime seized the opportunity to use the state news channel for what promised to be a propaganda coup, but in the event Walesa delivered an extremely robust and hostile diatribe to his interviewer. The videotape could not be broadcast, and was destroyed, but a copy of the interview's soundtrack was acquired by another sound recordist, Wojtek Harasiewicz, a fervent anti-communist, who promptly passed it to David Ensor, the ABC News television correspondent in Poland. The enterprising Ensor had established a reputation for out-manoeuvring the restrictions placed on the foreign corps to prevent reporting of civil unrest and, despite a mysterious attack on his office in which his equipment and furniture were trashed, was able to obtain advance notice of demonstrations and smuggle his film crew into closed cities, including Wroclaw, at precisely the right time. The ABC TV bureau in Warsaw enjoyed an especially close relationship with Solidarity as a member of the staff was close to one of the movement's leaders. David Ensor seized the opportunity and used the tape extensively in his news despatches, which were intercepted by Radio Free Europe and Voice of America, stations that broadcast Walesa's intransigent and defiant words. When the leak was eventually traced to the sound technician he was arrested and served a prison sentence, with David Ensor supporting his family during his imprisonment. Ensor subsequently developed a close rapport with Walesa, who was released in November 1982 after eleven months detention, to the point that Solidarity often, to Ensor's embarrassment, sought his advice about strategy.

Ensor's coup was but one episode that persuaded the SB that the country was in danger of being engulfed by hostile intelligence agencies, and of the 1,300 foreign journalists based in Poland early in 1981, the SB estimated that approximately 10 per cent were either agents or officers of NATO intelligence agencies who 'were acquiring firm agent positions within Solidarity'.

Although hitherto the CIA had exercised extreme caution in its links with the movement, not so much in fear of routine accusations of America 'meddling in the internal affairs of a sovereign country', but out of concern for compromising Solidarity, martial law was to be the turning point, with two intermediaries travelling to Warsaw on the Chopin Express from Vienna in February to attend a clandestine rendezvous at Zyrardow organized by a contact in touch with Lech Badkowski, the Solidarity spokesman in Gdansk. With the CIA station in Warsaw and the US consulate in Krakow under intense surveillance, this external mission was to be the first, preliminary direct encounter between the union and Agency personnel operating under 'Non-official Cover'. The objective was to offer support and establish a secure, verifiable line of communication, just as had happened in occupied Europe during the Second World War. At Casey's urging the DO invented myriad ways of channelling dollars and zlotys to Solidarity, but few details were put on paper. At the president's behest, Casey confided in Dr Glenn Campbell, then chairman of his Foreign Intelligence Advisory Board, and also obtained secretary of state Judge Clark's approval for a strategy that, as he described it, was intended 'to loosen Moscow's grip'.

When the KOR leadership of Michnik and Romaszewski went on trial before a military court, the proceedings proved to be a gift for Radio Free Europe which described how the defendants had declared themselves to be unrepentant, and had questioned the legitimacy of both the court and the government. Under intense internal and external pressure, the regime offered the men their freedom in return for immediate exile, but they declined, forcing the regime to endure more embarrassment when Lech Walesa demanded entry to the court, and was refused.

At the height of the crisis, according to General Wladyslaw Pozoga, then head of the intelligence and counter-intelligence service, one of his agents inside the US embassy reported that the Americans were anxious to open a back channel to the SB, bypassing the foreign minister, Stefan Olszowski, who was generally regarded as more loyal to Moscow than to General Jaruzelski. Their chosen intermediary was the philosopher Professor Adam Schaff, who was close to the US ambassador John Davis, and economic concessions were offered in return for the immediate release of Michnik, Romaszewski and eight others. After an initial rendezvous, a second meeting was arranged in Vienna with the assistant secretary of state, Lawrence Eagleburger, who apparently proposed the restoration of 'Most Favoured Nation' status for Poland and the creation of a Polish American investment bank in Warsaw if the eleven Solidarity leaders were released. He also mentioned appointing a man the SB wrongly suspected of being a former CIA officer, John Scanlon, as Davis's successor at the embassy, but the talks broke down when it was believed the details had been leaked to Moscow.

The dramatic shift in policy that Casey had pressed for first in February 1982, later to be known as the Reagan Doctrine, was eventually encapsulated in May in NSDD-32, *US National Security Strategy*, which advocated covert support for anti-communist organizations in Eastern Europe and formal authorization to use Voice of America and Radio Free Europe broadcasts in what amounted to a psychological warfare offensive. When Casey had originally proposed this method of communicating with Solidarity's underground network, he had been warned that VOA's charter specifically excluded the type of clandestine signals pioneered by the BBC during the Second World War that had proved so successful. What better way to establish the bona fides of an authentic CIA agent in a country populated by informers and agents provocateurs than a pre-arranged coded message? Casey had seen the system work in Nazi-occupied Europe and recognized its continuing effectiveness. In addition, Casey wanted to back Solidarity with cash and supply the organization with a modern communications network. This latter proposal implied training some selected candidates, and Casey wanted to take this a stage further and have the president's approval for the CIA to indoctrinate these individuals with helpful information acquired by the Agency.

Casey's ambitious scheme was rather more than wishful thinking, for the Agency had by April 1982 put in place a commercial front to act as a conduit for the hard currency needed by the beleaguered movement. Although NSDD-32, which had been drafted by Richard Pipes of the NSC's staff, who was himself of Polish origin, referred vaguely to 'neutralizing' the Soviets in Eastern Europe, Casey had firm plans about how the objective could be accomplished and sought to confront the Kremlin's influence worldwide, and split Moscow from its client states.

Details of the CIA's covert action to support Solidarity have never been made public, and 'once the covert action was under way, Casey paid little attention to it'. There was no need for micromanagement, but he remained entirely committed to the plan. Bob Gates recalls:

> One time Brzezinski complained that funding had been cut off to a very worthwhile project. Casey asked how much it would cost to remedy the problem and Zbig replied, 'About $18,000.' Brzezinski

> later told me that the next day a man showed up at his office without an appointment and asked to see him. Zbig reluctantly agreed and the man handed him a briefcase full of cash – $18,000 to be precise – for the project Brzezinski had mentioned to Casey. Somewhat nonplussed, he nevertheless took the briefcase and passed it on to a visiting Pole associated with the project who was headed back to Europe. This was indicative of Casey's penchant for 'action this day'.[3]

The most obvious and immediate manifestation of the CIA's covert intervention was the continuing existence of Solidarity's publishing arm, *NOW-a*, which survived martial law without any obvious source of financial support. Within a month of martial law *NOW-a* was printing *Tygodnik Mazowsze*, circulated from thirty-seven underground centres across the country, and distributing a magazine, *Krytyka Tygodnik Mazowsze*, in Warsaw.

Another example of the CIA's activities was the unexpected appearance on 12 April of Radio Solidarity, broadcast in Warsaw from vans driving around the city. Coordinated by Zbigniew Romaszewski, the illicit station was actually fifteen different transmitters, all sending the same programme on the identical frequency. This hugely successful experiment prompted a wave of police raids on 30 April, but the network was still in operation on 9 May when Solidarity's surviving leadership, the Provisional Coordinating Committee (TKK), called for a general strike. The TKK had announced itself at the end of April and included Bogdan Lis in Gdansk, Zbigniew Bujak in Warsaw, Wladislaw Hradek in Krakow and Wladyslaw Frasymiuk in Wroclaw.

The second part of NSDD-32 was of an economic nature, intended to maximize the pressure on Moscow and reduce the Eastern bloc's dependency on the Soviets. However, this aspect of the plan was not received well in Europe where several large and lucrative contracts, including the Siberian pipeline, were under negotiation.

On 31 August, large demonstrations were held to mark the second anniversary of the formal founding of Solidarity, and were publicized and coordinated by the TKK which continued to elude the police. The next day, having debated several options with George Shultz (who had replaced General Haig as secretary of state) and Caspar Weinberger, Casey asked Judge William Clark, the relatively new and inexperienced national security adviser 'to schedule a meeting on an enhanced covert action for Poland'. With characteristic energy, the DCI then set off to see eleven countries on an inspection tour of the CIA's stations in Dakar, Ivory Coast, Lagos, Kinshasa, Lusaka, Pretoria, Harare, Nairobi, Cairo, Ankara and Morocco before returning to Andrews Air Force Base eighteen days later.

On 9 October President Reagan suspended Poland's 'Most Favoured Nation' trading status which excluded the country's exports from the usual tariffs, thus eliminating it from the US markets. This was to be a milestone in the country's economic collapse, the severity of which could be seen in the West's own statistics. In 1980 the regime had borrowed up to eight billion dollars a year to finance trade worth $7.5 billion. Five years later these figures had declined to loans of a billion in support of imports totaling $300 million.

By November Casey was back in Europe, visiting the CIA's base in Frankfurt which was in the forefront of the Agency's covert support for Solidarity, and on 12 November, two days after Brezhnev's death, Reagan signed NSDD-66, *Protracted Economic Warfare Against the USSR*, which set out a new, agreed strategy for tackling the Kremlin with the active support of Europe. In future Moscow would have to pay at least market rates for any credit, and henceforth the CoCom regulations would be tightly enforced. To overcome French and German reluctance to jeopardize their gas delivered from the East, President Reagan announced the following day that no further contracts for Soviet natural gas would be signed until a joint study had been completed on the subject of European dependence on external strategic energy supplies.

As it turned out, NSDD-66 was not to be the last word on squeezing the Kremlin, now occupied by the hard-liner Yuri Andropov who previously had been chairman of the KGB. The next stage was to replace the long-standing American policy of 'Soviet containment' with a commitment actually to change the Soviet system. Although a considerable break with the past, which had encompassed peaceful co-existence and then detente, NSDD-75, entitled *US Policy on the USSR*, challenged the fundamental principles agreed at Yalta and was signed on 17 January 1983. It was no longer acknowledged that the influence of the Soviet Union extended beyond its borders, and it made a commitment to terminate exports and other economic support that enhanced Soviet status. In particular, the USA would henceforth take any opportunity to achieve these objectives and impose costs on the Kremlin.

Casey's role in NSDD-66 was the introduction of the Technology Transfer Intelligence Committee, which was to monitor exports to the Eastern bloc and coordinate the activities of twenty-two separate federal agencies that had an interest in the subject. By liaising closely with CoCom, the US administration hoped to corner Europe into tightening the grip on Moscow's jugular. By the end of 1983 the new Defense Technology Transfer Administration, established under NSDD-70 also in November the previous year, reported that 1,400 consignments of banned strategic *matériel* had been interdicted, representing more than $200 million. While this was never intended to close down Soviet industry, it would apply pressure on an inflexible, centrally-planned system that was already creaking at the edges and had no ability to respond. As had been demonstrated in Afghanistan, when an energy supply was cut, the Soviets had no alternatives and simply shut down their consumers. Instead of switching to other suppliers in the market, the rigidity of the Soviet structure forced a disproportionate response that no other economy would contemplate. Starved of energy, raw material or even a critical component, in a monolith devoid of incentives that actually discouraged personal initiative, the Soviets just walked off the job, thereby inflicting further damage on an already weakened economy. NSDD-75 was not intended to make the Soviet predicament any easier.

Despite the deteriorating domestic situation in Poland (or maybe because of it), Jaruzelski's regime announced the wind-down of martial law on 30 December 1982 but did little to reduce the repression of Solidarity. A printing press near Poznan was raided on 1 January, resulting in fifteen arrests, and the police seized large quantities of money and food. Solidarity had seven leaders in custody, and KOR five. Centres for distributing underground literature in Gdansk and Warsaw had been closed down, and the charismatic strike leader in the Szczecin shipyards, Stanislaw Zablocki, had been detained. However, the TKK was better organized than ever, communicating via a frequency-jumping wireless circuit that was difficult to intercept, and protecting itself with an internal security apparatus known euphemistically as the Bureau of Hygiene and Safety, an agency responsible for ensuring safety standards in the workplace. Numerous underground resistance groups had been spawned, including an influential organization of intellectuals based around Wictor Kulerski, the twenty-seven-year-old former president of Solidarity in Warsaw. Providing logistic support to the network, such as false documents, transport and the provision of safe houses, was a mathematician, Konrad Bielinski, and Ewa Kulik, a PhD student preparing a thesis on William Faulkner.

One of the major turning points for the movement was the murder of Father Jerzy Popieluszko, the outspoken curate of the church of St Stanislaw Kostka in the Warsaw district of Zoliborz, on 19 October 1984, while he was driving home from Bydgoszcz. The young priest had become a focus for dissent and nationalism, and his congregations, often of local steelworkers, were always packed, sometimes with several thousands listening to his sermons in the street outside. He was hugely popular and highly articulate, and when his badly beaten body was recovered from the Wloclawek reservoir on 30 October, intense pressure was put on the regime to find the killers, not least because of the widespread belief that the SB had been responsible for several other deaths. Grezgorz Przemyk, the student son of the poet Barbara Sadowska, famous for her dissident verse, had been beaten and killed by the police, and a pattern had emerged of Solidarity activists being grabbed off the street by snatch squads, and winding up dead, their bodies dumped in another part of town. This is what happened to Andrzej Gasiewski, whose beaten torso was recovered near a railway line, and Jan Samsonowicz of Gdansk who was found hanging on a wall inside the shipyard. Also, the murder of the leader of Rural Solidarity, Piotr Bartoszcze, on 7 February 1984, had probably also been the handiwork of an official assassination squad. Eventually, four Ministry of Interior officers, Lieutenant Leszek Pekala, Captain Grzegorz Piotrowski, Lieutenant Waldemar Chmielewski and their section superior, Lieutenant-Colonel Adam Pietruszka, were tried at Torun and convicted of Popieluszko's murder, but that did not end the speculation. The much decorated Piotrowski was suspected of being implicated in Bartoszcze's death, and the involvement of Chmielewski strongly implied an official sanction, as Pekala admitted in his first confession. Chmielewski's father, Major Henryk Chmielewski, had been deputy director of

Department V, the SB branch then responsible for monitoring the Catholic Church. For Chmielewski and Pietruszka to have been involved meant that it was likely that General-Major Zenon Platek, the head of Department IV, would have known of the plot, and that in turn suggested that the minister of the interior, Lieutenant-General Czeslaw Kiszczak, had given his tacit approval. In any event the conspirators, who admitted they had intended 'to teach Father Popieluszko a lesson', acknowledged that they had expected their efforts to be rewarded with promotions.

Had the quartet convicted of the crime acted on their own initiative, or was there a conspiracy that led not just to the politburo, but to Jaruzelski's inner committee? Few insiders, aware of the intensely bureaucratic nature of the Ministry of the Interior, had any doubt about where final responsibility really lay, and this certainty was exploited by the CIA which had 40,000 postcards printed bearing the priest's photograph, with extracts from his most pro-Solidarity sermons, and distributed them in Poland in March. The dual purpose was to enhance Popieluszko's status as a martyr and to prevent the regime from orchestrating a convenient cover-up. By maintaining the pressure, public opinion continued to demand a solution, which created a crisis atmosphere in the Ministry of the Interior and undermined the confidence of its personnel.

The public response to Popieluszko's murder, or martyrdom, was spectacular, and even Cardinal Jozef Glemp, who conducted the Requiem Mass on 3 November, was impressed by the crowds of hundreds of thousands who descended on Zoliborz to pay their last respects. Glemp had often disapproved of Father Jerzy's confrontational style, but there was no denying that his popularity had extended far across the country, and had made him a symbol of Solidarity's resistance, one which had been thoroughly endorsed by John Paul II. Reluctantly, Glemp gave permission for Popieluszko to be buried in his old church, and despite his personal commitment to detente with the regime, conceded that the priest who had acted as Solidarity's chaplain would inspire many others to follow in his steps.

The first cracks in the regime's response to Solidarity can now be said to have appeared in July 1984 when a conditional amnesty was announced, freeing within five months those prisoners who agreed to abandon their protests. By the New Year, only 350 activists had accepted the terms on offer, and once again Solidarity had succeeded in broadcasting its defiance. However, six weeks later, on 13 February, Lech Wałesa was caught in a police raid on an apartment in Gdansk's Zaspa district. Also present were several of the movement's leaders, including Stanislaw Handzlik of Krakow, Adam Michnik of Warsaw, Wladyslaw Frasymiuk of Wroclaw and Bogdan Lis of Gdansk.

Later in the same month the movement suffered another blow when a Solidarity courier, Jacek Knapik, was searched at Warsaw airport and found to be carrying an ostensibly compromising letter from Jerzy Milewski of Solidarity's representative office in Brussels to Bogdan Lis, describing his recent discussions with American State Department officials. While the regime extracted what propaganda value it could from the episode, it was soon replaced by other events, including the expulsion of the US defense attaché from Warsaw, and the detention and harassment of two diplomats from the consulate in Krakow who were also PNG'd. The regime's purpose was to increase the pressure on the movement, directly and indirectly, but the strategy failed, and on the May Day holiday Solidarity organized large simultaneous demonstrations in Gdansk and the capital.

By 1986 Solidarity was receiving $500,000 in voluntary donations, with a rather larger amount coming through a variety of CIA conduits. The AFL-CIO was contributing $300,000, the money filtering into some unusual projects. Dozens of illegal presses were churning out protest literature; one of them, known as CDN, was headed by a dissident architect, Czeslaw Bielecki, who distributed a Solidarity newspaper for the army and a series of pamphlets entitled *The Little Conspirator* (it was an ironic title – Bielecki was exceptionally tall). With all this activity, the only setback was an apparent leakage of information which led to the confiscation off the Swinoujscie ferry of a lorry-load of offset litho printing presses, forty-nine Xerox photocopiers, sixteen fax machines and some IBM computers. This was followed by the loss of a container unit packed with contraband, discovered by Polish police on a ferry, which suggested methodology not luck. An inquiry conducted by the Swedish secret police established that the SB had recruited a Swedish customs official who had been put on the payroll to tip off the Polish authorities to suspect consignments. To maintain secrecy, the suspect was switched to a better-paid job and removed from access to future bills of lading.

The smuggling of contraband was financed by Solidarity's office in Brussels which from the outset had received financial support from various French trade unions, coordinated by René Salan, including the FO, CFDT, FEN, CFTC and CGC, and later from the American AFL-CIO and the National Endowment for Democracy. One of the most successful channels was a lorry with a secret compartment driven by a French volunteer, Jacky Challot. Officially sponsored by *Kultura* in Paris, and converted by Mirek Chojecki, the vehicle was registered in the name of a non-existent Pole and driven into Poland by Challot who claimed that the owner had fallen ill and was booked to fly direct to Warsaw. A flight reservation was made to back up the story, and the truck's registration number was altered on each trip to make it appear as though it was the first. Challot was arrested and imprisoned on his eleventh mission after suspicious customs officers measured the vehicle's internal and external dimensions and discovered the hidden contraband.

The Polish authorities' crackdown at the beginning of 1986 led to the arrest of 320 activists, and they also scored a success on 5 June 1986 when Zbigniew Bujak was caught in a police raid. Bujak had been on the run since martial law had been introduced and his detention was to prove a severe blow to the movement, not just in terms of morale, but administratively because he had been so responsible for supervising Solidarity's logistics and secret finances. However, he was to remain in custody for a relatively short period because on 22 July 1986 the regime declared a general amnesty and released the remaining political prisoners.

In October 1986 the Solidarity leadership gathered in Gdansk to debate future tactics, and made the momentous decision to campaign overtly. Inevitably, this gave a huge boost to dissident groups and human rights campaigners in Czechoslovakia, East Germany and Hungary. With Vaclav Havel in Prague and George Konrad in Budapest issuing joint statements with Lech Walesa, the scene was set for protest across much of Eastern Europe, gleefully encouraged by broadcasts from Radio Free Europe and Radio Liberty.

Chapter XI

The Vatican Pipeline

For much of the twentieth century the Holy See had been regarded as a highly competent intelligence environment in which the Vatican operated a truly global collection system with lines of communication reaching directly into some of the most obscure troublespots. Often protected by diplomatic status, the Pope's spies were deployed throughout Europe and the western hemisphere, reliant on a network of priests, convents, monasteries, voluntary groups and religious institutions that was the envy of rival collection agencies. Like such structures, it was vulnerable to penetration, and over the years there had been numerous attempts made to plant moles in positions of influence.

The CIA's entrée in the Vatican had been prepared by Hugh Montgomery, the Chief of Station in Rome at the time of John Paul II's election. He and his Viennese wife Anne-Marie had been in St Peter's Square as the white smoke had risen skywards, accompanied by General Vernon Walters, their house-guest, whom they had persuaded to stay an extra day in order to witness the extraordinary event. As a devout Catholic, Walters needed no persuading to alter his schedule. Anne-Marie, who was well known to the Vatican's Swiss Guards, used her fluency in German and the CD plates on her car to negotiate a strategic vantage point from which to witness the historic event.

General Walters is an intelligence phenomenon who adores to tease those he meets by demonstrating his remarkable gift for languages. His Italian is fluent, having served as military attaché in Rome; having spent the early years of his life in France, his French was good enough to impress President de Gaulle; his Spanish enabled him to be accepted by his Argentine contacts when he was military attaché in Buenos Aires, and later by General Augusto Pinochet in Chile and Fidel Castro in Havana; his Russian surprised the Soviets, especially when he addressed the UN Security Council in their language; and his German is considered virtually flawless. His Portuguese enabled him to fight alongside the Brazilians in Italy in 1944, and he has acted as interpreter for five presidents, participated in five wars, and been an awed witness to an atomic test in the Pacific. His father being English, but living in France, Walters spent five years at Stonyhurst, Britain's premier Jesuit public school. In 1941, after a brief period in a New York insurance company as a loss adjuster, he joined the US army as a private soldier and embarked upon an extraordinary career that, in 1972, gave him the rank of lieutenant-general, and his appointment by President Richard Nixon as Deputy Director of Central Intelligence. Within six weeks of his Senate confirmation in May 1972, Walters was embroiled in the Watergate scandal, and he remained at Langley until his retirement in July 1976, a period of unprecedented internal turmoil for the CIA, but one which he managed with much adroitness, being considered by some to have saved the embattled Agency.

Few men have had such breadth of experience, so it is not entirely surprising that he was selected by President Reagan to be his Ambassador at Large and given the task of cultivating the Pope. At their first meeting in the Vatican, he apologized for his inability to speak Polish and inquired whether the Holy Father would prefer to speak Italian or Russian? The Pope smiled and opted for Italian, remarking that 'although all Poles speak Russian, we don't voluntarily'.

Walters and the Pope developed a truly unusual relationship, based initially on the President's determination to have the Pontiff understand the American resolve to crush Soviet totalitarianism. Certainly Walters was entirely sympathetic to Reagan's views, often quoting a speech made by Reagan in 1962, before he was even governor of California, in which he advocated bankrupting Moscow by out-spending them. At their first encounter Walters was accompanied by a young US Navy lieutenant who carried a locked case containing satellite imagery of Soviet forces in the Ukraine. With practised skill, Walters explained that he had been authorized to share this highly secret data with His Holiness, but joked that he had been told not to bother going back to Washington DC if he mislaid it. The

KEYHOLE photos showed the distinctive thirteen inter-continental balistic missile (ICBM) silos and three protective perimeter fences surrounding them at Pervomiask, and Walters explained how each missile contained ten individually targeted warheads. That one facility could launch 230 nuclear weapons, and represented death to approximately 140 million Americans. The Pope was clearly impressed, and pinched the cheek of the lieutenant, sighing, 'so young, so young'. Years later, when Walters had made many more visits to the Vatican, he imparted the news that the same young man had left the navy to take up holy orders with the Dominicans: 'See what you have done, Holy Father!' Reportedly, the Pope was delighted.

For a period of four years Walters visited the Pope two or three times a year, on the authority of the secretary of state Judge Clark, to

> explain to him US policies in the fields of foreign affairs and defence. The administration was aware that there was a convergence of interests between the Catholic Church and the United States in seeking to contain communist expansion. According to my instructions, I was to present the facts based on the best intelligence available.[1]

Walters is characteristically reticent about discussing precisely what took place when he conferred with John Paul II, but he does admit that he discussed

> the threat we faced from missiles, from conventional ground forces, from the Soviet Air Force, and Navy. In addition, whenever appropriate I covered problems in Poland and I once touched on developments in the concentration camps in the Soviet Union that were then still operating. Sometimes he would tell me what subjects he would like next time.
>
> He always received me alone and whenever anyone attempted to interrupt the briefing he would wave them out of the room. The briefings were generally arranged through the Nuncio in Washington by Archbishop (now Cardinal) Laghi and our ambassador to the Vatican William Wilson. I tried to tailor the meetings so that they would not last more than forty minutes, including any questions the Pope might want to ask me. His questions were generally penetrating and insightful.[2]

President Reagan had a six-hour audience with the Pope in Rome on 7 June 1982, and simultaneously the secretary of state, William Clark, met with Vatican officials to discuss the exchange of intelligence. The precise nature of the discussion remains unknown, but it is now acknowledged that the Vatican acted as a conduit for financial support which was channelled from the United States to Solidarity. At the time Solidarity was involved in heavy expenditure, running offices in Frankfurt, London, Paris and Brussels. In order to insulate the organization from too obvious links with the CIA and local intelligence agencies, and to protect against hostile penetration by the SB, separate, compartmented offices were opened in London and Paris. In London the main office, already well established in Cheltenham Terrace, Chelsea, where *Voice of Solidarity* and other subversive leaflets were published, was headed by Marek Garztecki, and supported by a second representative bureau in Herne Hill in south London run by Tadeusz Jarski through Brussels, with Eugeniusz Smolar from Aneks, the Polish government in exile, and Professor Szczepanik, later to serve as a minister in the Polish government. There was a similar arrangement in the French capital where Miroslaw Chojecki liaised with the AFL-CIO.

Of Solidarity's overseas offices, it was the one in Brussels, headed by Jerzy Milewski and his deputy, Joanna Pilarska, that appears to have been targeted by the SB; certainly, General Wladyslaw Pozoga's boast that his men could read any Solidarity document within a matter of hours, seems to have been entirely justified. The Netherlands office, headed by Jan Minkiewicz, was also heavily penetrated, and suspicion fell on a Dutch truck driver, Frits Nieuwenhuizen, who was believed to have been a key source for the SB. Documents recovered from the SB's archive show that an agent codenamed REGINA was particularly effective at penetrating Solidarity's Swedish office in Lund, organized by Jozef Lebenbaum and Marian Kaleta in Malmo, which was responsible for smuggling much of the contraband into Poland. Similarly, the mysterious DIODOR was active in Germany, reporting on Fighting Solidarity, the more militant resistance group led by Konrad Morawiecki who returned to Warsaw despite having been arrested and deported.

Mirek Chojecki travelled to London frequently to add his contraband to consignments of humanitarian aid to Poland. In Frankfurt

Solidarity was helped by Dr Krystyna Graef who organized transports and financial support through the Internationale Gesellschaft für Menschen. In addition, equipment was sent to Poland from Cologne, Munich, Bremen, Wiesbaden and Hamburg. In Italy Nelly Norton, based in Turin, despatched aid, and in Sweden Jakub Swiecicki operated from Stockholm, with Jan Minkiewicz active in Holland. Chojecki coordinated their activities from London, and was responsible for more than half the total *matériel* delivered to Solidarity in Poland.

Although there is no evidence in any declassified documents to show that the KGB ever learned the full details of how Solidarity was funded by the CIA and other intelligence agencies, the Polish SB achieved considerable access to the highest levels of the movement and their reports, via the *rezidentura* in Warsaw, formed the basis of the KGB's conviction that the Vatican was responsible for fomenting subversion in Poland. The proof is to be found in a top-secret circular removed from the KGB's London *rezidentura* by Oleg Gordievsky in December 1984. Marked for distribution to all *rezidents*, and entitled 'Work on the Vatican', it was copied by Gordievsky, who was then a senior Line PR (political intelligence) officer who had been posted to England following a tour of duty in Copenhagen where he had been recruited as an SIS source in 1974. Dated 19 December 1984 and signed by Nikolai P. Gribin of the FCD's Third Department, the introductory message explained:

> In recent years the Head of the Catholic Church and right-wing circles in the Vatican have been stepping up subversive activity against the socialist countries. In view of this the heads of our Department attach great importance to more active efforts on the part of our organization abroad to penetrate, using agents and other operational means, into the leading Catholic centres of the West in order to obtain intelligence about hostile operations in preparation by the Vatican, and also to carry out large-scale active measures directed towards inciting prominent figures in the Catholic Church to protest in defence of peace and limitation of the arms race.[3]

Gribin claimed that the Vatican was planning 'an international alliance to combat communist ideology' and instructed *rezidents* to 'step up operational work with agents in the clerical circles of the country where you are stationed, in order to deal with the tasks set by the heads of our Department and Service for working against the Vatican'.

The attached five-page report, entitled 'Measures to counter the subversive activity of the Vatican', remains the most comprehensive insight into how the KGB viewed the developing crisis, referred to as the intensified 'ideological battle in the international arena' in which

> the Vatican has pursued a policy of more energetic subversive action by the Catholic Church in socialist countries, converting a religious movement into a political opposition force.
>
> The anti-socialist bias of the Vatican's activity has become particularly marked with the arrival on the papal throne of John Paul II, whose hostility towards the countries of the socialist community is conditioned both by his personal anti-communist and anti-Soviet convictions and by the influence exerted on him by the most conservative representatives of the Catholic clergy and reactionary political figures of the West, especially of the USA.[4]

The anonymous report identified the problem as the Pope's 'sharp pronouncements about the socialist countries' in which he was alleged to have asserted that 'Marxist doctrine is declared to be incompatible with the Christian faith'.

> The Pope and his entourage are endeavouring by every possible means to change the established relationship between church and state in the socialist countries. In the light of the 'Polish experience', they are trying in the first place to obtain actual complete independence of the church from the state, strengthen the position of reactionary clergy in the socialist countries and intensify anti-socialist feeling among the Catholic clergy and the faithful.
>
> The Vatican is at present putting the main emphasis in its so-called 'Eastern policy' on practical steps to revive the activity of Catholic and Uniate parishes, and on material and spiritual support for the most reactionary priesthood, inspiring and propagating negative attitudes among the faithful and setting up an organized 'religious opposition'

> to pursue the aim of strengthening the church's influence on the social and political processes in the socialist countries. Steps are being taken by the Vatican to pursue this strategic line using both legal and illegal forms of operation.

Having identified the Pope and his entourage as being responsible for the deteriorating situation, and for taking the initiative, the report turns to the Vatican's direct threat to destabilize the Soviet bloc:

> In leading circles in the Vatican, the Catholic Church is considered to be the sole, well-organized legal opposition institution capable of exerting an influence on the broad masses, including workers and young people, and they calculate that the tactics they have recently adopted may lead to destabilization of the political situation in certain states of the socialist community, or in some parts of the Soviet Union. The Vatican also assumes that the action of the Polish Church to strengthen its position in the state can be extended to other socialist countries.[5]

The author then turns to the Vatican's dangerous attempts to 'establish contacts' with other religious groups, such as the Russian and Georgian Orthodox churches, 'to combat communist ideology', and its concentration on Poland, Hungary and Yugoslavia, noting the Vatican's efforts to 'organize papal visits to Poland, Yugoslavia, Czechoslovakia and the Soviet Union'. Noting that

> Right-wing groups in the Vatican have recently considerably expanded their subversive activity against the national liberation movement, above all in Latin America', the analysis concluded that 'prominent reactionary Catholics, in active cooperation with the leaders of the chief NATO countries, are endeavouring, with the Pope's approval, to weaken the anti-war movement. John Paul II and his supporters in the Vatican are trying to prevent Catholics and Catholic organizations from being involved in this movement'.[6]

Thus, the Pope was undermining the Soviets at home by destabilizing the Eastern bloc, and further afield by putting an end to the Marxist liberation theology that had prevailed in Central America.

Having outlined the scale of the threat, the FCD demanded that 'the efforts of the intelligence service abroad must be directed to obtaining information' on a series of targets, among them:

> The plans, forms and methods of subversive activity on the part of the Vatican and churches and organizations under its control against the countries of the socialist community and national liberation and anti-war movements;
>
> Any action by the Roman Curia to strengthen the position of the Catholic Church in the states of the socialist community and turn it into a political force to oppose the socialist system;
>
> The attitude of the Pope and his immediate entourage in regard to the following grave, topical, international questions: East–West dialogue, political and military detente, the arms race, disarmament, etc.
>
> The Vatican's relations with the larger countries of the capitalist world and the People's Republic of China; co-ordination of policy and co-operation, especially with the United States and other NATO countries, in undermining the position of socialism and the national liberation and anti-war movements, including also co-operation with their special services.[7]

Thus the FCD set out the agenda for intelligence operations directed against the Vatican, making the Pope and his advisers a priority, together with obtaining details of the Vatican's relationship with the intelligence agencies of the chief NATO countries, meaning the United States and Britain. As for 'active measures', or operations of influence intended to impact on public and political opinion in the West, the FCD recommended:

> Discrediting specific manifestations of hostile activity on the part of the Vatican against socialist countries. Conveying to the leading groups of the Roman Curia and to John Paul II personally, the information that demands for expansion in the sphere of action of the Catholic Church within the social and state system in socialist countries is regarded by them as interference in their internal affairs and may in consequence lead to deterioration of relations between the

state and the church, and also between socialist countries and the Vatican;

Exploiting, in the interests of the socialist countries, the existence of any internal dissensions in the Vatican, any dissatisfaction ascertained on the part of influential cardinals with what is, in their opinion, the 'excessive enthusiasm' of Pope John Paul II for his 'Eastern policy', to the detriment of other sectors of the Vatican's activity.[8]

As well as advocating schemes to inhibit the Vatican's contact with 'Russian Orthodox, Georgian, Armenian-Gregorian and other Christian churches', the FCD suggested exposing 'plans to make use of the church as a weapon for ideological sabotage of the socialist system' and agitating among disaffected Italian members of the Roman Curia against 'the Pope's intention of strengthening his own position by promoting Poles, West Germans and other non-Italians in the Catholic hierarchy'.

Although in retrospect the FCD seems to have misunderstood or, perhaps for political motives, deliberately misinterpreted the Vatican's strategy, the reports leaked by Gordievsky shed remarkable light on the mindset in Dzerzhinsky Square, and the KGB's advice received by the politburo. There is, as one might expect, absolutely no discussion in the documents of the assassination plot three years earlier, but nevertheless the clear impression is given that John Paul II is held personally responsible for the Vatican's policy which was considered to be the cause of so many of the Kremlin's problems. That the Pope was behind so much of the unrest in Eastern Europe is acknowledged, and if this was an accurate reflection of opinions being expressed by the KGB leadership in 1984, it is not hard to imagine how high feelings must have run while Poland was slipping into what Moscow saw as turmoil.

Chapter XII

Cold War Crisis

The strategy adopted by the NSPG to destabilize the Soviet empire had been intended initially to be a low-risk policy with minimal 'blow-back' on NATO or the United States. However, there was a military dimension which was to prove highly controversial, not least because it amounted to psychological warfare, adding muscle to the political initiatives taken across the globe.

The 'psyops' aspect to the NSPG's scheme remains difficult to research, and there has been a suggestion, from Fred Ikle, the Rand Corporation strategist and former US undersecretary of defense for policy, that a deliberate decision was taken to ensure 'there would be no paper trail' once it had been authorized by President Reagan in March 1981. Accordingly, the evidence is hard to discern, but there can be little doubt that NATO and the US navy were encouraged to adopt a dramatically more aggressive stance, the principal manifestation being the change in the management of exercises. Whereas hitherto the Soviets had been given advance notification of major exercises, this policy was quietly dropped and replaced with what amounted to a return to pre-1970s Cold War tactics.

Prior to the introduction of reconnaissance satellites and a reliance on sophisticated, unmanned overhead intelligence collection platforms, NATO had deployed airborne 'ferrets' to test Warsaw Pact defences, and underwater had played dangerous cat-and-mouse games with Soviet submarines. These operations were highly classified and rarely reached public notice unless one of the flights ended in tragedy, as happened very occasionally when Soviet air defence forces shot down an intruder. The 'ferret flights' had been authorized originally by President Truman in late 1950, and his successor President Eisenhower had also given his approval for individual U-2 overflights which commenced six years later, in July 1956. Whereas the U-2 missions were intended to go undetected, and certainly at an altitude that was too high for Soviet fighters or SAM missiles, the 'ferrets' were deployed along the frontiers of Soviet airspace to detect hostile radar emissions, prompt signal traffic that could be monitored, and check reaction times for the scrambling and vectoring of interceptors. Similar, high-risk tactics had always been a feature of Western submariners who maintained a permanent roster of covert pickets outside Soviet naval bases to shadow transiting conventional and nuclear boats. Whereas it was hard to conceal the loss of an American spyplane that had come down on Soviet territory, the worst that happened at sea was the rare collision which, if reported at all, was usually described euphemistically as 'iceberg damage'. An unspoken convention emerged which prevented either side from registering formal complaints about these encounters, the other rule being that the use of active sonar, which effectively neutralizes a submarine, would be avoided. To 'ping' an adversary is exceptionally hazardous as everyone aboard the target is made fully aware that the enemy has made a successful identification. Such an episode can be the prelude to the live firing of weapons, thus creating a crisis that could be the prelude to a full-scale military engagement. Thus, for obvious reasons, while both sides constantly indulged in dangerous manoeuvres, they each drew the line at provoking a response that could easily escalate out of control.

'Ferret flights' were acknowledged to be provocative, and they were suspended in 1969, by which time two American planes had been shot down by missiles, eleven by fighters, and one lost without explanation, leaving fifteen aircrew dead, whereas the submarine missions continued for a further twenty years. However, the 'psyops' recommended by the NSPG were rather less subtle and required surface naval exercises to be conducted in waters that previously had been regarded as altogether too provocative. It was the NSPG's intention to take a far more aggressive position and keep the Soviets in a perpetual state of readiness, thereby creating an atmosphere of uncertainty and constructing a further potential drain on the already over-stretched Soviet military resources. Crudely put, the new administration committed itself to building a 600-ship navy, partly to restore the shattered morale of the armed services, still reeling from the horrendous failure of the mission to rescue the Iranian embassy hostages in April 1980, but also to tempt the Kremlin to compete, and thereby outspend it into bankruptcy. President Reagan's first defence budget totalled $258 billion, which was an increase of $43.7 billion, or a massive 13.2 per cent after inflation, of which rather more than half was devoted to conventional weaponry. In addition, Reagan announced that the controversial B-1 bomber project, mothballed by the Carter administration in 1977, was to be restored. Unexpectedly, the Soviets were facing massively more spending on infinitely more expensive ships, submarines, tanks, cruise missiles and enhanced Trident-II and MX ballistic missile programmes. As Bob Gates, then the CIA's national intelligence officer for the Soviet Union, observed: 'For the first time since the Soviets began their huge military build-up in the mid-1960s, an American military juggernaut was under way. And it scared the hell out of them.'

Instead of a resumption of the high-profile exercises that simply demonstrated NATO's naval strength, an entirely new approach was authorized. Rather than mounting well publicized, large-scale manoeuvres coordinated from Northwood, in August 1981 the carrier USS *Eisenhower* led a Second Fleet battle group, commanded by Vice Admiral Hank Mustin, right into the Norwegian Sea, an expanse of ocean that hitherto had been regarded as Soviet turf, in OCEAN VENTURE 81. The intention, as espoused in a military doctrine known as 'forward deployment', was to run a massive 'ferret' operation, taking more than eighty NATO vessels through the Greenland–Iceland–Faroes–Scotland gap, under strict combat conditions, including total radio silence and emission control, and occasionally taking advantage of the Norwegian fjiords. These four passages represented the sole access into the north Atlantic for the Red Banner's Northern Fleet, based in Murmansk, and were therefore arguably the most patrolled seas in the world. Underwater passive SOSUS sonar arrays, the size of double-decker buses, were laid on the ocean floor to monitor transiting Soviet submarines, and airborne surveillance flights operating from Bodo, Banak and Bardufoss in Norway, and Keflavic in Iceland, and RAF Kinloss in Scotland, regularly ran anti-submarine patrols to double-check on a suspected contact. Similarly, the Soviets operated a small flotilla of surface ships and

Okean, Balzam and *Primorye* class auxiliaries masquerading as trawlers to act as radar pickets.

OCEAN VENTURE involved all branches of the USA's armed forces, and drew on the navies of fourteen other countries, using seven aircraft carriers, 234 ships, twenty-nine national and international staffs and over 125,000 personnel. It was conducted in eight phases and run in parallel with various NATO exercises, including MAGIC SWORD NORTH, MAGIC SWORD SOUTH, OCEAN SAFARI and DISPLAY DETERMINATION, and became the largest exercise conducted by the US navy in twenty years.[1]

Officially, the exercise's objective was 'to provide an Atlantic-wide demonstration of command and control of national and international forces in a war-at-sea scenario' and the first three phases were run in the South Atlantic, Caribbean, and western Atlantic. Phase IV (20 August–1 September 1981) took the exercise to the North Sea and Phases V to VII (4–19 September) included MAGIC SWORD NORTH and SOUTH and a marine amphibious reinforcement group phase. Phase VIII, conducted in the Baltic, lasted from 29 September to 13 October.

At SACLANT, in Norfolk, Virginia, there were two schools of thought regarding the wisdom of taking a battle group north. While 'forward deployment' certainly had the advantage of suggesting to the opposition what NATO considered to be a likely war scenario, with a naval conflict right on the Soviet doorstep, there was also a view that such a strategy would inevitably lead to hideous losses in a real war. The Russians were estimated to have around 76 Tupolov-16 BADGER-G long-range jet bombers, of which one or two could reasonably be expected to get through a fighter screen. Armed with two AS-5 Kelt anti-ship missiles each, that meant contemplating very considerable loss of life in the Arctic where the endurance of a man in the water could be counted in seconds, not minutes or hours. Thus, realistically, NATO would be unlikely to choose the Norwegian Sea in which to engage the enemy, so was there any point in preparing for such an unlikely eventuality? On the other hand, the psychological and political implications of exercising in international waters so close to the bear's lair would be hard to exaggerate. To put it mildly, the Soviets were alarmed by the change in NATO's strategy.

What made the *Eisenhower*'s battle group so remarkable was that it remained undetected until a detachment of a cruiser and three escorts were discovered off the North Cape, apparently accidentally, by a Soviet long-range maritime reconnaissance aircraft on a routine mission from the Kola peninsula. When further flights were scrambled, NATO naval fighters harassed the refuelling planes at rendezvous points more than a thousand miles from their carriers, thereby confounding the Soviets. To add to their confusion, the cruiser practised evasion tactics in the Barents Sea for a further nine days, despite the launch from Plesetsk of a low-orbit nuclear-powered surveillance satellite, Cosmos 1299, on 24 August, and a heavy electronic intelligence platform, Cosmos 1300, from Tyuratam on the same day, while the battle group's final withdrawal was covered by a massive electronic jamming operation which left the defenders bemused about what had actually happened. Nevertheless, the message was clear: a large NATO force had penetrated close to the Soviet coastline, had engaged the air defences completely unexpectedly, and had prevented the Red Banner fleet from even shadowing the battle group or intercepting the cruiser's task force. Combined with the inability of Cosmos 1299 to find the intruders, and its operational failure after just thirteen days, the implications for the Soviet tactical warning systems were dire.

The *Eisenhower*'s extraordinary success had an unknown impact on the Kremlin but it proved to NATO's planners that it was perfectly possible to take the Soviets by surprise in their own backyard. To the admirals who had begun to suspect that the US navy's secure communications had been compromised, the imposition of radio silence and a total black-out on all references to the exercise in all signals strongly suggested that the Soviets had come to rely too heavily on wireless interception. This assessment, as it turned out, was wholly accurate, for John Walker had been selling the KGB the US navy's most classified ciphers since 1962, using another contact, Jerry Whitworth, to continue the supply after his retirement in 1975.

Despite the apparent advantage gained by Soviet espionage through the KGB's recruitment of the Walker family, it was clear that the Barents Sea episode had revealed a fundamental flaw in Russian satellite technology. There had been a routine launch on 4 August of Cosmos 1286 which had been intended to replace Cosmos

1220 (inserted in November 1980). However, a further launch, on 14 September, of Cosmos 1306, from Tyuratam, to replace Cosmos 1260 which had been put into orbit less than six months earlier, on 20 March, strongly suggested that the electronic ocean surveillance systems were malfunctioning; this was especially evident when the booster for Cosmos 1306 sent the satellite into the wrong orbit, a problem which it took eight days to correct.

NATO's new strategy of 'forward deployment' was quickly appreciated by the Kremlin and the KGB, and new measures were introduced in about May 1981 to give Moscow better advance warning of Western aggression, in the form of RYAN, the Russian acronym for *Raketno Yadernoye Napademie*, nuclear rocket attack. The fact that the Kremlin seriously anticipated a surprise nuclear strike by NATO demonstrates the mindset of Brezhnev's politburo and Andropov's KGB, but perhaps even more remarkable is the knowledge that several alerts were issued, particularly during NATO's massive ABLE ARCHER exercise held between 2 and 11 November 1983, and that the system was not dismantled until November 1991.

The basis of RYAN was the presumption that the deployment of modified Pershing II ICBMs in West Germany was a sinister development intended to give the West a distinct advantage in a nuclear exchange and undermine the well-established principle of mutually assured destruction, which had been the cornerstone of the Cold War's impasse, by giving one side the ability accurately to target and destroy enough of the Warsaw Pact's protected underground command bunkers to make the first-strike gamble worthwhile. Apparently, Soviet air defences had calculated that the anticipated twenty-minute warning of missiles launched in the continental United States would be cut to between an unacceptable four and six minutes. While in retrospect this may seem a trifle close to paranoia, the Kremlin clearly viewed the possibility of being caught off-guard extremely seriously, for instead of making RYAN one of a number of priorities for the KGB's 'Line PR' collectors of political intelligence, a complete, independent monitoring and communications infrastructure was developed to process information accumulated not just by overseas *rezidenturas*, but by other Warsaw Pact intelligence agencies, principally the East German HVA. A dedicated RYAN staff, equipped with a situation room manned twenty-four hours a day by fifty personnel was established to give an advance warning, code-named BONFIRE, of specific indicators of perceived aggression such as unusual military activity, mobilization, exercises and the deployment of troops and heavy equipment.[2]

The first RYAN directive was circulated to all Western *rezidents* in November 1981 and required regular, fortnightly reports on a list of threat indicators. These 'permanent operational assignments' remained in force for the next decade. They were first disclosed in the West by Oleg Gordievsky in early 1983 when, as the senior Line PR KGB officer in the London *rezidentura* since his arrival in June the previous year, he was indoctrinated into RYAN by his *rezident*, Arkadi V. Gouk. Dated 17 February 1983, the document set out seven objectives and a timetable for their completion. Information about the evacuation of government officials and their families was to be gathered, and suggestions made by the end of September about how such an evacuation could be monitored; underground shelters were to be located and checked periodically to see whether they had been brought into service; blood transfusion centres, likely to be of vital importance after a nuclear strike, were to be located and watched, as was the price paid to donors. Any significant change in the pattern of use of such centres was to be reported immediately to Moscow Centre. Civil defence installations were to be monitored, and the recreational venues visited by military and other personnel involved in planning nuclear attacks were to be kept under observation. Police and intelligence agencies were also to be watched for signs of preparation for a surprise attack. In addition, special emphasis was to be placed on the recruitment of sources with access to 'people associated with preparing and implementing the decision about RYAN'. The *rezidenturas* were instructed to concentrate on assessing 'the degree of likelihood that the heads of national churches and of international church organizations, and the leadership and institutions of the Vatican abroad would be aware of preparation for a nuclear attack and clarifying possibilities of obtaining information about RYAN from these circles'.

An attachment to the circular claimed that the demand for this information had 'acquired an especial degree of urgency' and was of 'particularly grave importance' because the US, NATO and China allegedly had 'stepped up the tempo and scale of military preparations'. Later in the year, as the first deadline for the various assignments approached, a further directive was circulated to the KGB *rezidents* in NATO countries, including Leonid Y. Nikitenko, who had taken over as acting *rezident* in London in the absence of Arkadi Gouk, who was to be expelled from Britain in April 1984. This second document focused on hostile counter-intelligence activity which, according to Vladimir Kryuchkov, had risen dramatically, and demanded greater vigilance for particular criteria, such as travel restrictions, limits on communications, stricter frontier controls, accumulation of emergency foodstocks, cancellation of leave and the introduction of censorship which were itemized as threat indicators.[3]

As international tension heightened, following the destruction of the Korean airliner flight KAL 007 on 1 September, Moscow Centre reduced the leadtime of a surprise missile launch to between seven and ten days, and on 5 November sent the London *rezidentura* a list of thirteen Ministry of Defence buildings where increased activity might be anticipated and should be watched for, as well as noting that unusual, unpublicized meetings could be expected at 10 Downing Street. A few days later an urgent *molniya* or flash signal was transmitted to all the GRU and KGB *rezidenturas* in Western Europe, warning them of an alert that had been sounded at American military bases. The implication of this, in the middle of ABLE ARCHER, was potentially very grave, for the Kremlin's military doctrine had long asserted that any NATO attack would be concealed behind ostensibly routine military manoeuvres. The *molniya* warning turned out to be false, but it is an indication of the confrontational atmosphere at the time that such a message could have been transmitted in earnest.

Even after the death of Andropov in February 1984 the Kremlin remained committed to RYAN, and on 10 July Kryuchkov reminded his *rezidents* to adhere to the 'permanent operational assignment' previously instituted, and chided those that appeared to believe that, with the succession of Konstantin Chernenko, the danger of a surprise attack had subsided. The codeword BONFIRE, he reminded them, remained valid, and was intended to bring every *rezidentura* to a heightened combat readiness.

These manifestations of Soviet jitteriness, especially during ABLE ARCHER, were not ignored by NATO, and in response the CIA circulated a special NIE *Implications of Recent Soviet Military–Political*

Activities, in October 1984. Not only was the West winning the Cold War, there was even an end in sight, as became clear when Mikhail Gorbachev was established in the Kremlin and discerned the parlous, even catastrophic state of the Soviet economy. Although not slow to grasp the need for *perestroika*, a reform programme of massive proportions, it would all prove much too late.

Postscript

John Paul II remains committed to his belief that his role in bringing about the end of Communism in Europe was his destiny, supervised and guided by the Virgin Mary. Curiously, he has achieved a convert to this belief, none other than his putative assassin, Mehmet Ali Agca. When the Pope celebrated Mass at Rebibbia prison on 27 December 1983 he visited Agca in his cell. During a brief conversation the Turk reportedly told the Pontiff that he had read that the failed attempt on his life had occurred on the anniversary of the apparition at Fatima, and he too had concluded that divine intervention had been responsible for saving the Pope and ensuring Agca's capture. Apparently the highly superstitious Agca had convinced himself that he was likely to become the target of some supernatural retribution, but was relieved to be told by his intended victim that he had received forgiveness.

The Pope, like his entourage, believes that the Soviets were ultimately behind Agca's assassination attempt, although His Holiness publicly will say only that 'the Devil shot the bullet and the Blessed Virgin stopped it'.

While speaking at a conference held at College Station, Texas, in November 1999 to mark the declassification and release of CIA documents relating to the end of the Cold War, former DCI James Woolsey remarked that the Pontiff should be included in any list of five people responsible for bringing about the Soviet collapse, which accurately reflects the view of the American intelligence community looking back on the momentous events a decade later.

The extent to which the final collapse was orchestrated, planned or predicted by anti-Soviet forces will be debated by historians for many years, but there is compelling evidence that a single-minded group of people worked unceasingly to undermine and then destroy the communist bloc for the sole purpose of freeing Eastern Europe from totalitarianism. That such an objective was really possible must have seemed unlikely in 1952, but General Donovan was convinced that freedom would prevail behind the Iron Curtain, and said so to anyone who would listen:

> One day the Iron Curtain will lift and the captive nations of the east will become part of a united Europe. Even Russia, purged by future events of its desire to bully and subdue its neighbours, will be a member, and given the innate genius of the Russian people, a highly respected and valued member. When Europe is truly unified, it will flourish, and Communism will be shown for what it is, not a wave of the future at all, but a dead ideology cut out of a cruel past which has been employed by cynical masters to control common mankind.[1]

Donovan's dedicated acolyte Bill Casey was equally certain that the Kremlin's house of cards would collapse once the key weak points had been identified and degraded.

Certainly the speed with which the edifice finally crumbled took everyone by surprise, with a border guard, a certain Harald Jager at the Bornholmerstrasse in Berlin, opening the gate to the crowd at precisely 9.12 p.m. on 9 November 1989. The chronology of momentous events leading up to that one moment, can be concertinaed into a few months beginning with the start of talks held between Solidarity and the Polish regime on 6 February. On 15 February the last Soviet troops left Afghanistan, in accordance with Gorbachev's commitment, and in retrospect these two events, while not obviously connected, marked a watershed. By the end of the month the Polish government had publicly acknowledged the unthinkable truth, that the NKVD had been responsible for the death in 1940 of 14,500 Polish officers in the Katyn forest, admitting for the first time that the atrocity had not been committed by the Nazis. The prisoners had been shot in the grounds of an NKVD dacha, just west of Smolensk, and when the massacre had been discovered by the Nazis in April 1943, the Kremlin had denigrated the announcement as mere propaganda. While the news that the Soviets had perpetrated the murders merely confirmed what was generally suspected, it was none the less an astonishing admission.

On 7 February 1989, Solidarity was legalized and allowed to contest elections which, on 22 August, resulted in a landslide victory, with the communists isolated as members of a coalition that formed the first non-communist government elected in Eastern Europe since 1948.

The momentous developments in Poland were quickly reflected elsewhere in the Soviet bloc. Red Army troops had already begun to withdraw, from Czechoslovakia on 3 February, and from Hungary on 25 April. It was the latter breakthrough that led a few days later to the Hungarian authorities starting to relax their frontier controls and allowing virtually anyone to enter Austria. As news spread that the Iron Curtain had been breached, thousands of East Germans made the journey to Hungary and the West.

That the Soviets, and in particular the triumvirate in control of the Kremlin in 1981, were willing to resort to murder and deception should not be a surprise, for quite apart from the assassination of Georgi Markov, there is considerable evidence that Brezhnev, Andropov and Kryuchkov regarded such tactics as entirely acceptable while formulating foreign policy. There are, for example, the extraordinary lies told repeatedly about the status of the huge Krasnoyarsk radar station in Siberia, which was built in 1983 and run in gross violation of Article 1 of the Anti-Ballistic Missile (ABM) Treaty which limited such early warning missile-tracking facilities to a total of eighteen, to be sited on the periphery of the Soviet Union. To conceal its true purpose, for six years Soviet negotiators persisted in claiming that the gigantic apparatus was intended to monitor spacecraft, despite the fact that photographs of the antennae orientation proved it could not fulfil such a role. It was not until 1989 that the Kremlin admitted the truth, and agreed to dismantle the huge structure.

Similarly, the Kremlin conspired for ten years to conceal the fact that the 'black box' flight data recorder of Korean Air Lines flight KAL 007 had been recovered successfully from the Sea of Okhotsk. Once news emerged in September 1983 that the airliner had been lost, the Kremlin quickly issued a denial that it had been shot down, only to admit soon afterwards that a Soviet fighter had indeed been responsible for firing a missile at the intruder. The cockpit voice and digital recorders were not surrendered to the International Civil Aviation Organization until January 1993, by which time the Soviet empire had ceased to exist. The final month of 1989 had ensured that the Warsaw Pact had disintegrated to a point well beyond recovery, with the resignation of the East German government on 3 December, followed the next day by a public condemnation by the Warsaw Pact of the 1968 invasion of Czechoslovakia. By the middle of the month a non-communist government had been installed in Prague, and on Christmas Day Nicolae Ceausescu and his hated wife Elena were given a brief trial, led straight into a courtyard, and shot.

By the end of the following year, as Vladimir Kryuchkov condemned the United States for having masterminded the destruction of the Soviet Union, it had really ceased to exist. The CPSU had abandoned its constitutional monopoly of power in March and German unification had become a fact in October. As for Mikhail Gorbachev, he had endured the humiliation of being jeered by the crowds during the traditional May Day parade in Red Square, had dodged bullets fired at him at the National Day celebrations on 7 November, and seen the constituent republics one after another declare their independence. The Kremlin's final, ultimately futile act of repression was to order the KGB's Alpha Group troops to seize Vilnius as Lithuania attempted to break away. The subsequent bloodshed, in which fifteen demonstrators were shot dead by OMON black berets outside the central television station, served only to enrage the population and ignite further protests in the other Baltic states, especially in Latvia where the black berets shot four demonstrators as they stormed the Ministry of the Interior in Riga. The result was a 90 per cent poll for Lithuanian independence in the referendum held early the following month, and in March, Estonians and Latvians produced a similar vote.

Officially the Warsaw Pact was not dissolved until 31 March 1991, by which time the Cold War had come to an end. The ailing Russian economy had become wholly dependent on external economic aid and the much vaunted military-industrial complex had reached a state of total collapse. President Reagan's 'focus of evil in the modern world', denounced by him so vehemently on 8 March 1983, had imploded, and a final attempt by Vladimir Kryuchkov in August to isolate Gorbachev in his villa at Foros on the Black Sea and restore Communism in Moscow ended in a humiliating defeat. The failure of the coup confirmed Boris Yeltsin's commitment to a democratic future for Russia, but what is less recognized is the role played behind the scenes by the CIA which had given President Bush four months' advance notice that a coup was to be mounted in Moscow, and had predicted that Boris Yeltsin would have to be assassinated for the plot to succeed.

The CIA had predicted 'a premeditated, organized attempt to restore a full-fledged dictatorship' and had disclosed that 'preparations for dictatorial rule have begun'. The Agency also criticized Gorbachev for virtually inviting a putsch by his unwise personnel appointments and increasing reliance on rule by decree.

The CIA stated that 'ominously, military, MVD and KGB leaders are making preparations for the broad use of force in the political process'. Surprisingly, the CIA accurately identified the ringleaders behind the plot, naming Vladimir Kryuchkov of the KGB, Marshal Akhromeyev, Defence Minister Dmitri Yazov and Marshal Varrenikov, commander of Soviet ground forces. The CIA also provided a detailed nine-page analysis of the background to the plot and described how 'democratically-inclined officers' had been forced to retire or had been quietly moved out of key positions. In addition, 'a sensitive source' had revealed that Yazov had arranged for 'particularly reliable' Soviet troops in Germany to be formed into special units to defend the future of the Soviet Union, and that 'a similar process was believed to be underway in the Soviet military districts'.

Most significantly, the CIA believed that just a month earlier, on 28 March, 50,000 loyal troops drawn from the army and the Ministry of the Interior, and backed by KGB elite units, had been deployed into Moscow in what had amounted to a full dress rehearsal. The operation had been conducted in complete secrecy, and the CIA concluded that it had gone off 'smoothly, indicating a command structure for such an operation has been set up'. The most chilling passage of *The Soviet Cauldron*, issued by the CIA's Office of Soviet Analysis, predicted that the plot's 'first target this time would be Boris Yeltsin': 'The attempt to restore full-fledged dictatorship would start in Moscow with the arrest or assassination of Yeltsin and other democratic leaders such as Mayor Popov and Deputy Mayor Stankevich.'[2]

In an entirely accurate forecast, the CIA said that 'a committee of national salvation – probably under a less sullied name – would be set up and proclaim its intent to save the fatherland through tough but temporary measures that would pave the way for democracy and economic reform'. The CIA also predicted that, despite 'an intimidating display of force', the coup would fail because not enough troops could be relied upon to enforce repression: 'The long-term prospects of such an enterprise are poor, and even short-term success is far from assured.'

Remarkably, an element within the CIA has hinted that Gorbachev might himself be part of the plot, which some allege may explain why President Bush failed to alert the Kremlin to the imminent crisis. The element within the CIA did not spell out or substantiate Gorbachev's involvement, which remains a matter of considerable controversy to this day. However, the element did refer to the arguments the new regime would use, mentioning that 'Gorbachev, or whoever was in charge, really had no choice but to restore order'. Thus this element at least believed that there was a chance that Gorbachev would survive as leader following a successful coup.

Exactly what happened to Mikhail and Raisa Gorbachev, isolated by a disloyal KGB security section at their holiday retreat in the Crimea as the drama played out in Moscow, has never been fully explained, and some historians have gone so far as to suggest that Gorbachev encouraged the coup leaders and even stayed at his holiday retreat of his own volition until he realized the scheme would fail, and then seized the opportunity to make a triumphant return to the Kremlin to denounce the plotters.[3]

Gorbachev himself later admitted that 'to a certain extent, I did foresee that something of the kind might take place'[4] and acknowledged that there was a 'rumour being put about suggesting that Gorbachev's communications were not cut off, but that he kept out of the way so as to sit it out and then arrive "ready to serve". A "no-lose" situation, so to speak'.[5] What really happened at Foros remains unresolved.

A subsequent CIA analysis asserts that the 1991 coup was sparked off by a summit held by Gorbachev at Nova-Orarevo with Boris

Yeltsin and leaders of nine of the Soviet republics. During the secret conference the reformers had demanded the sacking of the politburo's hardliners, among them Kryuchkov, but the discussion had been taped by the KGB officer who had headed Gorbachev's personal bodyguard, and handed straight to Kryuchkov. His role as leader of the coup has always been considered strange because, as the CIA has now confirmed, he was particularly close to Gorbachev, and it may be that he has acted to protect his president from being implicated as a central figure orchestrating the coup behind a screen of frontmen. Curiously, Kryuchkov has been freed from a prison sentence for his part in the coup, and now lives in quiet seclusion in Moscow, doubtless reflecting on one date in particular, 31 December 1991, the day the Soviet Union officially ceased to exist under international law.

For John Paul II the collapse of the Soviet bloc was the ultimate victory, and one that he had been preordained to orchestrate. He remains totally committed to his belief that his destiny has been charted by the Virgin Mary, and has pledged himself to the beatification of Sister Lucia's two young companions at Fatima. Indeed, on the anniversary in May 2000 he attended the celebrations which marked the process of sainthood, almost unprecedented for a candidate who is a child to whom no miracles have been attributed, and gave holy communion to the elderly nun who doubtless will herself be proposed for sainthood in due course. It was on that occasion at Fatima that the Vatican announced that the decision had been taken to publish the full text of the third secret, and confirmed that His Holiness had interpreted one passage within the document as a prediction of the assassination attempt on 13 May 1981.

Whether supernatural intervention is truly the explanation for the astonishing events that day is a matter for personal, religious belief, but there can be no doubt that the world's first Slavic pontiff was utterly convinced that he had been entrusted with a sacred duty, and his vision of a Europe freed of Soviet totalitarianism was shared by a small group of other 'true believers' who shared the faith, among them Bill Casey, Vernon Walters, Alexander Haig, William Clark and some of their subordinates, including Milton Beaden and Jack Devine. It is equally clear that Yuri Andropov and Vladimir Kryuchkov were alive to the threat and were determined to take ruthless counter-measures.

In astrological terms, such celestial events are thought to occur when the planets are in alignment, but there is no equivalent in the intelligence world where scepticism rules out coincidence. Whatever the explanation, the conjunction of John Paul II, Bill Casey and Lech Walesa set the scene for an end of the Cold War, the collapse of the Warsaw Pact, the defeat of Soviet troops in Afghanistan and the restoration of democracy across Eastern Europe.

Notes

I. *St Peter's Square, 13 May 1981*

1. See Henze, *The Plot to Kill the Pope.*
2. Martella, *Indictment.*

II. *The Bulgarian Connection*

1. See Fein, *The Murder of Aldo Moro.*
2. See Sejna, *We Will Bury You.*
3. Sterling, *The Terror Network.*
4. Claire Sterling identifies the date of the warning from the Comte de Marenches as April 1981 (*The Time of the Assassins*, p. 275), whereas de Marenches refers to it as January 1980 (Marenches and Ockrent, *The Evil Empire*, p. 153)
5. Andrew and Mitrokhin, *The Mitrokhin Archive*, p. 381.

III. *Soviet Assassins*

1. See Doyle, *Inside Espionage.*
2. Michael Burke in *Outrageous Good Fortune*, p. 164.
3. Khokhlov, *In the Name of Conscience.*
4. See Sudoplatov, *Special Tasks*, p. 246.
5. Khokhlov, *In the Name of Conscience*, p. 201.
6. See Deacon, *Spy!*
7. Frantisek August in August and Rees, *Red Star Over Prague*, p. 83.
8. Andrew and Mitrokhin, *The Mitrokhin Archive*, p. 381.
9. Vladimir Kostov in *The Bulgarian Umbrella*, p. 147.
10. Ibid., p. 155.
11. Kalugin, *SpyMaster*, p. 180.
12. Bereanu and Todorov, *The Umbrella Murder.*
13. Ibid.
14. See Kalugin, *SpyMaster*, p. 181.
15. Pacepa, *The Tail that Wagged the Dog.*
16. Ibid., p. 331.
17. Ibid., p. 334.
18. Ibid., p. 338.
19. Ibid., p. 342.
20. Marcus Wolf, *Man Without a Face*, p. 275. Voight was sentenced to four years' imprisonment in 1994 for complicity in terrorism.

IV. *The Target*

1. Andrew and Mitrokhin, *The Mitrokhin Archive*, p. 250.
2. Ibid., p. 664.
3. Ibid., p. 665.

4. Ibid., p. 667.
5. Ibid., p. 669.
6. Ibid., p. 670.
7. Gates, *From the Shadows*, p. 217.
8. Kramer (ed.) *Cold War History Project*, Bulletin 3.
9. Gates, *From the Shadows*, p. 321.
10. Ibid.
11. *Agca's Attempt to Kill the Pope: The Case for Soviet Involvement* (unpublished CIA DI document).
12. Gates, *From the Shadows*, p. 315.
13. *Agca's Attempt to Kill the Pope: The Case for Soviet Involvement.*
14. Kay Oliver's rebuttal.
15. Ibid.
16. Ibid.
17. Assessment by John Hibbits (unpublished CIA document).
18. Kay Oliver's rebuttal.
19. US Congress: The Nomination of Robert Gates. Select Committee on Intelligence, 19 September 1991.
20. Ibid.
21. *The Times*, 4 November 1999.

V. ***Kuklinski: the Hidden Asset***

1. Biographical data from *Reader's Digest*; *Kultura*, April 1987, interviews with Benjamin Weiser, *Washington Post*, September 1992.
2. Boguslaw Kuklinski, who experienced many difficulties after he had been resettled in the USA, disappeared while sailing in the Gulf of Mexico in January 1994. His older brother, Waldemar, died in a car accident on 4 July the same year.
3. Dubicki was sentenced to four to five years' imprisonment *in absentia*, which was increased to twelve years. The conviction was quashed in 1991, and he won a libel action against General Czeslaw Kiszczak who described him as 'crazy' in his memoirs. Dubicki returned to Warsaw in 1996 and was diagnosed as having a tumour on his kidney. He returned to Germany for treatment but was hospitalized in Nurnberg following a car accident. Aged eighty-two, General Leon Dubicki was found dead in Spandau, Berlin, in March 1998, having been tied to his bed, killed with a knife and hammer. His second wife, Wieslawa, was declared mentally unstable and convicted of his murder.
4. The Teufelsberg intercept station remained active until it was decommissioned in 1995. The efficiency of the NSA's collection effort there is believed to have been severely handicapped by information supplied to the East German HVA by two American technicians based at the facility. Warrant Officer James Hall and his Turkish intermediary, Yildrim Husein, are now known to have compromised much of the site's operations.

They were arrested in December 1988 and sentenced to forty years' imprisonment in the following July. Hall had worked at the NSA's intercept facility at Schneeberg in 1977 and had been transferred to Teufelsberg in March 1981. According to his confession, he had volunteered to spy for the Soviets in the autumn of 1982.

5. Texts of Kuklinski's messages in Kramer (ed.), *Cold War History Project*, Bulletin 11, pp. 50–6.
6. Ibid.
7. Interview, Zbigniew Brzezinski, Washington, October 1999.
8. MacEachin, *Martial Law in Poland*.
9. Ibid.
10. *Scouting the Future*, p. 95.
11. *National Intelligence Daily* quoted in MacEachin, *Martial Law in Poland*.
12. Ibid.
13. Ibid.
14. Kramer (ed.), *Cold War History Project*, Bulletin 11.
15. MacEachin, *Martial Law in Poland*.
16. Kramer (ed.), *Cold War History Project*, Bulletin 11.
17. MacEachin, *Martial Law in Poland*.
18. Colonel Kuklinski was convicted of treason and sentenced to death *in absentia* in May 1984. The sentence was commuted to twenty-five years' imprisonment in March 1990, and then quashed by the Supreme Court in March 1995. He returned to Warsaw briefly in April 1998, and now lives under a new identity in Florida.

VI. *Martial Law*

1. MacEachin, *Martial Law in Poland*.
2. Gates, *From the Shadows*, p. 319.
3. Ibid.
4. Persico, *Casey* p. 265.

VII. *William J. Casey*

1. Karlow, *The OSS War Report* Vol. II, p. 285.
2. Admiral Robert Inman, quoted in Gates, *From the Shadows*, p. 321.
3. Ibid., p. 325.
4. The BND's relationship with the Chinese meant that fifty Chinese intelligence officers were at Pullach during the Tiananman Square massacre. As well as supplying training, the BND also provided information on Chinese dissidents resident in Germany, and sophisticated electronic surveillance equipment for use in Beijing. See Schmidt-Eenboom, *The BND, German Military Forces and Sigint in the Cold War*.

VIII. *The Kremlin's Vietnam*

1. Connor, *Ghost Force*, p. 278.
2. Ibid.
3. Bearden, *The Black Tulip*.
4. Andrzej Skrzypkowiak was later murdered in Afghanistan while on an assignment for

BBC Television in the Kantiwa. See Sikorski, *Dust of the Saints*, p. 253.
5. Interview, Washington DC, October 1999.
6. Felix, *A Short Course in the Secret War*.

IX. *The Crusader*

1. See Clarridge, *A Spy for All Seasons*.
2. *The Tower Commission Report* (New York Times, 1985).
3. See Woodward, *Veil*.
4. Pacepa, *Red Horizons*.

X. *Solidarity*

1. Interview with Oleg Kalugin, Washington DC, August 1998.
2. Gates, *From the Shadows*, p. 216.
3. Ibid.

XI. *The Vatican Pipeline*

1. Walters, *The Wall Came Tumbling Down*, p. 112.
2. Ibid.
3. Kramer (ed.), *Cold War History Project*, Bulletin No. 11.
4. Gordievsky and Andrew, *More Instructions from the Centre*, p. 48.
5. Ibid., p. 49.
6. Ibid.
7. Ibid., p. 51.
8. Ibid.

XII. *Cold War Crisis*

1. SACLANT History Staff, Norfolk.
2. Andrew and Mitrokhin, *The Mitrokhin Archive*, p. 565.
3. Gordievsky and Andrew, *Instructions From the Centre*, p. 71.

POSTSCRIPT

1. Dunlop, *Donovan: America's Master Spy*, p. 499.
2. CIA Assessment: *The Soviet Cauldron*, in *At Cold War's End*, p. 113.
3. See Amy Knight in *Spies Without Cloaks*, p. 18.
4. Gorbachev, *The August Coup*, p. 28.
5. Ibid.

Bibliography

Adams, James, *Sell Out* (Michael Joseph, 1995)
Andrew, Christopher and Vasili Mitrokhin, *The Mitrokhin Archive* (Penguin, 1999)
Arnold, Anthony, *The Fateful Pebble* (Presidio, 1993)
August, Frantisek, and David Rees, *Red Star Over Prague* (Sherwood Press, 1984)
Baker, G.L., *The Finger of God is Here* (St Paul Publications, 1961)
Bearden, Milton, *The Black Tulip* (Random House, 1998)
Bereanu, Vladimir and Kalin Todorov, *The Umbrella Murder* (TEL Books, 1994)
Brother Michael of the Holy Trinity, *The Third Secret of Fatima* (Tan Books, 1991)
Brzezinski, Zbigniew, *Power and Principle* (Farrar, Straus, 1985)
Burke, Michael, *Outrageous Good Fortune* (Little, Brown, 1984)
Cimbala, Stephen, *Mysteries of the Cold War* (Ashgate Publishing, 1999)
Clarridge, Duane, *A Spy for All Seasons* (Scribner's, 1997)
Cline, Ray S., and Yonah Alexander, *Terrorism: The Soviet Connection* (Crane Russak, 1984)
Cockburn, Andrew, *The Threat: Inside the Soviet Military Machine* (Random House, 1983)
Collit, Leslie, *Spy Master* (Addison-Wesley, 1995)
Connor, Ken, *Ghost Force* (Weidenfeld and Nicolson, 1998)
Cruz, Arturo, *Memoirs of a Counter-Revolutionary* (Doubleday, 1989)
Deacon, Richard, *Spy!* (BBC Publications, 1980)
Doyle, David, *Inside Espionage* (St Ermin's, 2000)
Dunlop, Richard, *Donovan: America's Master Spy* (Rand McNally, 1982)
Earley, Pete, *Confessions of a Spy* (Hodder and Stoughton, 1997)
Fein, John, *The Murder of Aldo Moro* (Doubleday, 1989)

Felix, Christopher, *A Short Course in the Secret War* (E.P. Dutton, 1963)
Fischer, Benjamin B., *A Cold War Conundrum* (CIA Center for the Study Intelligence, 1997)
——, *At Cold War's End* (CIA Historical Staff, 1999)
Follain, John, *Jackal* (Weidenfeld & Nicolson, 1998)
Gates, Robert, *From the Shadows* (Simon and Schuster, 1996)
Gorbachev, Mikhail, *The August Coup* (HarperCollins, 1991)
Gordievsky, Oleg and Christopher Andrew, *KGB: Inside Story* (Hodder and Stoughton, 1990)
——, *Instructions from the Centre* (Hodder & Stoughton, 1991)
——, *More Instructions From the Centre* (Frank Cass, 1992)
Goren, Roberta, *The Soviet Union and Terrorism* (Allen and Unwin, 1984)
Henze, Paul B., *The Plot to Kill the Pope* (Scribner's, 1983)
Hoffman, Bruce, *Inside Terrorism* (Columbia University Press, 1988)
Hunter, Gaz, *The Shooting Gallery* (Victor Gollancz, 1998)
Kalugin, Oleg, *SpyMaster* (Smith Gryphon, 1994)
Karlow, Peter, *The OSS War Report* (Walker & Co, 1976)
Khokhlov, Nikolai, *In The Name of Conscience* (McKay, 1959)
Knight, Amy, *Spies Without Cloaks* (Princeton University Press, 1996)
Koehler, John, *Stasi* (Westview Press, 1999)
Kostov, Vladimir, *The Bulgarian Umbrella* (St Martin's Press, 1988)
Kramer, Mark (ed.), *Cold War International History Project*, Bulletin 5 and 11 (Woodrow Wilson International Center for Scholars 1995, 1998)
Lundberg, Kirsten, *The Politics of a Covert Action* (Kennedy School of Government, Harvard, 1999)
Luxmoore, Jonathan and Jolanta Babiuch, *The Vatican and the Red Flag* (Geoffrey Chapman, 1999)
MacEachin, Douglas, *Martial Law in Poland* (Kennedy School of Government, 2000)
Marenches, Alexander de and Christine Ockrent, *The Evil Empire* (Sidgwick and Jackson, 1988)
Meyer, Herbert E. (Ed.), *Scouting the Future* (Regnery Gateway, 1989)
Morgan, Ted, *A Covert Life* (Random House, 1999)
Nelson, Michael, *War of the Black Heavens* (Brassey's, 1997)
Pacepa, Ion, *Red Horizons* (Regnery, 1987)
——, *The Tail that Wagged the Dog* (unpublished)
Pavlov, Vitali, *I Was Rezident in Poland: Who Really Ruled Poland* (Warsaw, 1998)

Persico, Joseph, *Casey* (Viking, 1990)
Richelson, Jeffrey, *America's Space Sentinels* (University Press of Kansas, 1999)
Riste, Olaf, *The Norwegian Intelligence Service, 1945–1970* (Frank Cass, 1999)
Rubinstein, Richard E., *Alchemists of Revolution* (Basic Books, 1987)
Schmidt-Eenboom, Erich, *The BND, German Military Forces and Sigint in the Cold War* (unpublished)
Schweizer, Peter, *Victory* (Atlantic Monthly Press, 1994)
Sejna, Jan, *We Will Bury You* (Sidgwick & Jackson, 1982)
Semelin, Jacques, *La Liberté, au Botu des Ondes* (Belfond, Paris, 1997)
Seth, Ronald, *The Executioners* (Hawthorn, 1967)
Sikorski, Radek, *Dust of the Saints* (Chatto and Windus, 1989)
Solovyov, Vladimir, and Klepikova, Elena, *Yuri Andropov* (Macmillan, 1983)
——, *Behind The High Kremlin Walls* (Berkeley Books, 1987)
Sontag, Sherr and Drew, Christopher, *Blind Man's Bluff* (Public Affairs, 1998)
Sterling, Claire, *The Terror Network* (Holt, Rinehart and Winston, 1981)
——*The Time of the Assassins* (Holt, Rinehart and Winston, 1983)
Sudoplatov, Pavel, *Special Tasks* (Little, Brown, 1994)
Sweetman, Bill, *Soviet Military Aircraft* (Hamlyn, 1981)
Thomas, Gordon, and Max Morgan-Witts, *Pontiff* (Granada, 1983)
Turner, Stansfield, *Secrecy and Democracy: The CIA in Transition* (Houghton Mifflin, 1985)
——*Terrorism and Democracy* (Houghton Mifflin, 1991)
Urban, George R., *Radio Free Europe and the Pursuit of Democracy* (Yale University Press, 1997)
Walters, Vernon, *The Wall Came Tumbling Down* (privately printed, 1998)
Weigel, George, *Witness to Hope* (Cliff Street Books, 1999)
Wolf, Marcus, *Man Without a Face* (Jonathan Cape, 1997)
Weiner, Tim, *Betrayal* (Richard Cohen Books, 1996)
Woodward, Bob, *Veil* (Simon and Schuster, 1987)
Yousaf, Mohammad and Mark Adkin, *The Bear Trap* (Leo Cooper, 1992)

INDEX

Index

INDEX